Seaworthy

ESSENTIAL LESSONS
from BoatU.S.'s 20-Year Case File of
THINGS GONE WRONG

ROBERT A. ADRIANCE JR.

INTERNATIONAL MARINE / McGRAW-HILL

Camden, Maine • New York • Chicago • San Francisco • Lisbon •
London • Madrid • Mexico City • Milan • New Delhi •
San Juan • Seoul • Singapore • Sydney • Toronto

FOR MY PARENTS

The McGraw·Hill Companies

Visit us at: www.internationalmarine.com

2 3 4 5 6 7 8 9 DOC DOC 0 9 8 7 6

Library of Congress Cataloging-in-Publication Data
Adriance, Robert A., Jr.
  Seaworthy : essential lessons from BoatU.S.'s case file of things gone wrong / Robert A. Adriance.
     p.   cm.
  Includes bibliographical references and index.
  ISBN 0-07-145327-X (hardcover)
  1. Boats and boating—Safety measures. 2. Navigation—Safety measures.
  3. Boating accidents—Prevention. I. BoatU.S. Foundation for Boating Safety & Clean Water. II. Title.
  VK200.A37 2006
  623.88—dc22   2005019343

Questions regarding the content of this book should be addressed to
International Marine
P.O. Box 220
Camden, ME 04848
www.internationalmarine.com

Questions regarding the ordering of this book should be addressed to
The McGraw-Hill Companies
Customer Service Department
P.O. Box 547
Blacklick, OH 43004
Retail customers: 1-800-262-4729
Bookstores: 1-800-722-4726

Illustrations by Jim Sollers.
Photos courtesy BoatU.S. unless otherwise noted.
Page 11, Bolling Douglas; page 34, John Bailey; page 45, Petroleum Association of Japan; page 55, bottom (2), Bill Novak; page 84, Doug Fenton; page 88, Tim Rosenwald and Deborah Dido; page 122, from *The Elements of Boat Strength* by Dave Gerr, page 332; page 155, Dolores Derrington and Jon Hartwell; page 156, Thomas June; page 158, Greg Group; page 159 (3), Jason Arnold; page 166, Paul Messick; page 184, Dolores Derrington and Jon Hartwell; page 190, Peter Graves; page 194, Jack Hornor; page 200, John Myran; page 221, Rob Goldwitz; page 227 (2), Jack Hornor; page 252, Bob Gibble.

Contents

Foreword [

THOUGH FEW OF US LIKE TO ADMIT IT, there's something compelling about other people's disasters. Part of the attraction surely comes under the heading "there but for the grace of God . . ." Part of it is certainly the desire to learn how to avoid similar situations. And part, let's face it, is simply morbid curiosity, the all-too-human emotion that sustains tabloid newspapers and TV "reality" programs.

The more closely we can identify with a debacle, the more fascinating it is to read about, which is why thousands of boatowners look forward eagerly to each issue of *Seaworthy* magazine. Published by BoatU.S., *Seaworthy* bills itself as "The Insurance and Damage Avoidance Report," which is accurate as far as it goes. In a wider sense, however, the publication is a chronicle of all the things that can happen to boaters who are unlucky, thoughtless, foolish, or all of the foregoing at once. The magazine's longtime editor, Bob Adriance, could certainly be forgiven if his unparalleled access to waterborne catastrophe had turned him into a mere connoisseur. But it hasn't: He clearly cares about the problems and catastrophes he writes about. At the same time, experience hasn't robbed him of his sense of humor, and probably few journalists need it more.

Until now, if you wanted to benefit from the wisdom contained in a particular *Seaworthy* article, you had to find it first—and that's assuming you'd kept all your copies of the magazine. Now, the literally hundreds of often vital pieces of information have been reorganized and placed between two covers. The result is a boaters' guide as important and practical as any I've read. And if you can ignore the occasional frisson of guilty pleasure, one that's as engrossing to read as *The Perfect Storm*.

Much of the data contained here is statistical: Did you know, for instance, that four boats sink in their slips for every one that sinks underway? By itself that's just an intriguing factoid, but what makes this kind of information deeply useful to the boater is Bob's analysis of why it's true. And what makes this book hard to put down are the specific stories that back up the author's points. Technically, Bob's reports are case studies, but they read as smoothly as any good magazine piece—and they're far more reliable than most, having been composed by a writer who knows what he's talking about. The combination of Bob's access and his perspective have made this book a unique volume in boating literature.

Many of the cases deal with life-or-death situations, and for me perhaps the single most gripping segment of the book is the extended report on the loss of

Morning Dew, the cruising sloop that came to grief with its entire four-person crew in late December 1998 (see Chapter 4). You may remember that the 34-foot boat was making a passage south from Myrtle Beach, South Carolina, to Florida on the Intracoastal Waterway when it was seen heading out to sea at Winyah Bay, north of Charleston.

A few hours later, in the middle of the night, *Morning Dew* ran up on a jetty at the entrance to Charleston harbor, with the loss of her experienced owner and all three members of his teenaged crew—his two sons and a nephew. Two fragmentary distress calls were ignored by the local Coast Guard station's watchstander, who heard only part of one of them and was unable to replay the tape recording of it.

The tragedy excited national headlines, with commentators (and some government investigators) laying blame in all directions. Bob Adriance's meticulous recounting will probably convince you, as it did me, that there was plenty of guilt to go around, but the initial, probably irreversible, cause was the skipper's poor judgment, for which he and his family paid the ultimate price.

It's not possible now to reconstruct with absolute assurance what made *Morning Dew*'s owner leave the safe ICW for the open sea in an inadequately equipped, 20-year-old boat manned by teenagers. Nor is it possible to see what the ill-equipped, overstretched Charleston Coast Guard could have accomplished—as opposed to what they might have attempted. A book full of speculation could be written on the case, and probably will be, but the essential facts are here, and the lesson is clear.

But *Seaworthy*'s strength is not based on any single incident. Rather, it comes from the author's deeply knowledgeable analysis of the general causes of boating accidents. Not long ago I bought an elderly trawler that had been for several years a liveaboard. The previous owner, who had no intention of ever putting to sea, had created a home afloat for himself. The problem, as I discovered, was that he'd wired the boat like a house, since that was the way he thought of it. Also, since he'd run out of unused circuit breakers on the original board, he'd simply wired his new appliances in on top of other connections—but there were no labels indicating what was what. (Anytime you want a stimulating—literally—day, try crawling around in a damp bilge tracing mystery wiring.)

To shorten this story, if you examine the Problems in the DC Electrical System section at the beginning of Chapter 2, you'll have a tolerably complete picture of the cat's cradle I inherited.

With the help of trained people, I eventually found and corrected all the problems, but the real point is that if I'd had a copy of *Seaworthy* in hand, my task and theirs would have been a great deal easier.

That's one reason the boating community at large should vote Bob Adriance a vote of thanks. There are plenty more.

To go back to the matter of boat sinkings, a long series of reports reveals that fully half of boats that go down do so because of leaking hull fittings—and almost 10% of those fittings are above the nominal waterline. Armed with solid information about the bad things that have happened to other mariners, you'll be better able to examine your own situation and correct problems before they get out of hand.

Or consider the newest worry boaters have been asked to consider—carbon monoxide. No book I've seen, until this one, has dealt with the prevention of this kind of fatality, and boating courses are just beginning to address the question.

In so many of the basic areas of boating knowledge, from collision avoidance to maintenance, this book provides not just what my mother used to call a lick-and-a-promise approach, but a considered, thoughtful summary of what's known to work.

So read the good advice contained herein and take it to heart. But don't be ashamed to find yourself enjoying it. I did.

—Tony Gibbs
Editor (retired) of *The New Yorker*,
Yachting, and *Islands*

Preface

THIS BOOK IS BASED ON MATERIAL from *Seaworthy*, the BoatU.S. damage-avoidance magazine. For over 20 years, the latter has been mailed quarterly to the 250,000 or so boatowners who are insured with BoatU.S. The idea behind *Seaworthy* is simple: take actual claims and let readers know what went wrong and how the claim (the accident) could have been avoided. The book *isn't* based on sensationalized—"how could someone be that stupid"—claims. Quite the contrary; the thrust has always been to try and identify accidents that involved otherwise responsible skippers (with some notable exceptions) whose claims could be traced to a simple lack of knowledge and experience.

Note that nowhere in the following pages is there a single account of a claim that doesn't include a detailed explanation of how the accident could have been avoided. That's the key to this book: Other skippers made mistakes that, but for dumb luck, could have been made by you or me. And it's a wise man or woman who learns from someone else's mistakes.

⋏ page 11

⋏ page 21

⋏ page 20

What happened here? To learn more about any of these photos, turn to the given page.

Λ page 84

Λ page 57

➢ page 83

◄ page 25

∨ page 135

⋀ page 105

⋀ page 159

∧ page 170

➢page 171

⋏ page 198

⋏ page 198

≺ page 192

≺ page 206

➢page 235

➢page 190

Avoiding Collisions

OF THE MANY TYPES OF ACCIDENTS in the BoatU.S. claim files—including fires, explosions, and sinkings—those involving a collision are the most common. Boatowners collide with docks, buoys, bridges, and each other. The latter should not be a surprise to anyone who spends much time on the water. The National Marine Manufacturers Association (NMMA) reports over 17 million registered boats in the United States, a number that includes everything from small, open boats and personal watercraft (PWC) to giant offshore sportfishermen, sailboats, and motoryachts. That's maybe twice as many boats as only a few decades ago.

Impressed? Not likely. Numbers, however large, are only numbers. To put them in perspective, consider a beautiful fall weekend on the Chesapeake Bay near Annapolis, Maryland. A small sailboat is anchored in a quiet cove off Rhode River with perhaps a dozen other boats. One by one, the boats pull up their anchors and head out toward the Chesapeake Bay.

These boats join a larger procession of boats leaving marinas and anchorages in West River. As the river widens, streams of other boats can be seen entering the Chesapeake from South River, Annapolis, Severn River, Whitehall Bay, Kent Narrows, Eastern Bay, and, farther to the south, from Deal, Fairhaven, and the Choptank River. Just north of the Chesapeake Bay Bridge, they come from Baltimore, the Magothy River, Middle River, and Chester Rivers to join the other boats moving out onto the Bay. Each of these tributaries has many smaller tributaries with dozens of marinas and thousands of homes and boats. Just how many boats are out on the Chesapeake is difficult to estimate, but it is, after all, a beautiful day.

Shortly after the small sailboat clears Curtis Point at the mouth of West River and heads north for Whitehall Bay, its home port some 15 miles away, it encounters a fleet of over thirty identical racing sailboats, Mumm 30s, that are competing in a national championship. Whatever the crossing situation, it's a good idea and a sensible courtesy not to sail through a racing fleet. Not more than a half-mile away, the Naval Academy 44s are also racing, flying downwind with their blue and gold spinnakers set like giant balloons. Better give them room, too. The same with the Melges National Championship fleets (24s and 30s), which are

Rules of the Road

IN 1972, THE U.S. COAST GUARD adopted the International Regulations for Prevention of Collisions at Sea (72 COLREGS), which apply to all vessels operating in international water. Included in the COLREGS is a proviso, Rule 1(b), that national rules conform as closely as possible to the International Rules. In 1980, the Inland Navigation Rules Act of 1980 was subsequently adopted to replace a confusing patchwork of various inland rules, some of which dated back to the 19th century.

Together, the Inland Rules and COLREGS make up the Navigation Rules, often referred to as the Rules of the Road, which contain the steering and sailing rules, sound signals, and requirements for navigation lights and day shapes. Despite a considerable effort to bring the International and Inland rules into harmony, some differences remain and two versions are presented side by side.

being held. Also visible are *Weatherly* and *American Eagle*, two restored, wooden 12-meter sailboats that are reliving their glory days. Altogether, there are perhaps a dozen sailboat races, both Performance Handicap Racing Fleet (PHRF) and one-design, being hosted by local clubs on this autumn day. Each race includes committee boats, buoys, and, occasionally, a fleet of spectator boats.

Fall is also a good time for catching rockfish and bluefish in the Chesapeake Bay, and every few minutes the small sailboat encounters a boat with lines trolling astern. There are tiny open boats, gigantic sportfishermen with outriggers and fly-bridges, small cruisers, and even a houseboat, all trailing lines. Just about anything that floats can be used as a fishing boat. The U.S. Coast Guard Navigation Rules, International–Inland, say that these recreational fishing boats should give way to a sailboat under sail, but lures are expensive and you don't want to snag one on your keel by passing too close astern. As with the fleets of racing sailboats, it's a courtesy—an "unwritten rule"—to give anglers plenty of room too.

The little sailboat picks its way gingerly through the various boats and fleets. Each maneuver has to be anticipated carefully, with special attention given to any subsequent maneuvers that might be necessary; no use sailing into a situation that puts you in harm's way. Also to be reckoned with are a submarine and three giant tankers anchored in the bay. Best not to pass to leeward, where the wind might be blocked and steerage lost.

Several times during the afternoon, the small sailboat passes near, but not too near, tugs towing barges up and down the bay. Other boats that pass by include a small fleet of mini-warships, probably being used to train midshipmen from the Naval Academy; several "performance boats" flying by at maybe 60 mph; an excursion boat filled with sightseers (all busy waving at anyone who looks like they'll wave back) headed for St. Michaels; assorted PWC; and a beautiful old schooner that has been on the cover of several local magazines. In addition to the boats, there are thousands of crab pot markers to be reckoned with.

Several hours and many, many tacks later, the small boat is back at its slip in Whitehall Marina. In truth, it has been a quiet, relaxing sail, especially when compared with the crowds that are out there on the Bay over Fourth of July weekend.

IMAGINE PUTTING SEVERAL THOUSAND AUTOMOBILES on the Nevada Salt Flats. Some are small sports cars; others are as large as skyscrapers. Each is going a different direction, some making zigzag patterns, while others engage in odd maneuvers like towing people on roller blades. This one is going 60 mph; that one is barely moving. When a few pass too close, those nearby are rocked violently. There are no lines, signs, or traffic lights.

It's no wonder that a large part of boating education is devoted to teaching boaters how to avoid collisions with other boats. Education starts with the Navigation Rules, also known as the Rules of the Road, Nav Rules, or just Rules, but that's only a bare-bones start. Avoiding collisions takes experience. Even if the Rules say it's OK, you don't sail into a fleet of tightly packed Mumm 30s or cut directly behind a small fishing boat that has lines trailing astern. If you own a large sportfisherman, you don't blast by a small boat full of fishermen or, for that matter, any boat in a narrow channel. Do all boaters follow the Rules of the Road? Of course not. Some boaters have probably never laid eyes on them. And many more seem to regard unwritten rules as no rules at all.

Comparing the number of collision claims filed at BoatU.S. Marine Insurance over the past ten years with the number of boats insured, we can estimate the probability of a specific type of boat being involved in a collision during any one year. For example, in any given year, the chances of a trawler being involved in a collision are 7 in 1,000 or 0.7%. The numbers include collisions with other boats, collisions with the dock, and collisions with fixed objects.

Collision Frequency

Sailboats		Powerboats	
TYPE	FREQUENCY PERCENTAGE	TYPE	FREQUENCY PERCENTAGE
racing	0.19%	houseboats	0.8%
cruising	0.7%	trawlers	0.7%
multihull	0.6%	cruisers	0.5%
		runabouts	0.3%

But the frequency of collision for any given type of boat does not necessarily reflect the severity of the collision. Severity, as used here, refers to the percentage of the boat's overall value. For example, the average cost of repairing a trawler after a collision represents 5% of its value.

Collision Severity

Sailboats		Powerboats	
TYPE	PERCENTAGE OF VALUE	TYPE	PERCENTAGE OF VALUE
racing	11%	houseboats	2%
cruising	5%	trawlers	5%
multihull	11%	cruisers	6%
		runabouts	14%

Collisions Between Boats Underway

Rule 5—Looking Out

Want to avoid collisions? It all starts with Rule 5 of the Navigation Rules: "Every vessel shall at all times maintain a proper lookout by sight and hearing as well as by all available means appropriate in the prevailing circumstances and conditions so as to make a full appraisal of the situation and of the risk of collision."

At first glance, this rule seems simple enough—you or someone else on board watches for other boats. But defining a "proper" lookout isn't always easy. Everybody knows what a proper lookout *used* to be: it was the guy who, in fair weather or foul, dutifully sat in the crow's nest saying things like "Land ho!" "Iceberg dead ahead!" and occasionally "Zzzzzz." But even on large merchant ships, the practice of posting a dedicated lookout day after day has long since passed. When the Coast Guard added "in the prevailing circumstances and conditions" to Rule 5, the lookout climbed down from the crow's nest, to return only when the conditions warranted it.

On recreational boats, the same rule applies. The lookout is typically the helmsman, unless the circumstances and conditions warrant another set of eyes. Just what those circumstances and conditions are isn't spelled out by the Rules of the Road but is instead left to the skipper's judgment.

There may be times when the skipper is the only one aboard. Jim Mercante, a maritime attorney in New York, says courts have found that Congress did not intend that any person who operates a small boat alone should be in violation of Rule 5. If another person is available, however, that person, depending on the circumstances and conditions, may be expected to act as lookout.

What at first seemed obvious is starting to get complicated. So when is another set of eyes—assuming a set is available—warranted? Primarily, it has to do with visibility. Let's begin with the obvious.

Whenever visibility is restricted by darkness or weather, skippers should post a dedicated watch and proceed slowly. At night, this lookout should be away from sources of spilled light, which would impede his or her ability to see in the darkness. He or she should not have been drinking alcohol, as alcohol affects a per-

Errant Autopilot

THIS HANDSOME WOODEN TRAWLER smashed into an abandoned concrete pier at 8 knots when the autopilot mysteriously meandered off course. Conditions were clear, and the seas were calm. The impact knocked several gaping holes in the planking and shoved the engine off its mounts.

The surveyor who investigated the accident found that the autopilot's erratic behavior was caused by a steel aerosol can that was located in a drawer a scant 2 inches from the remotely mounted fluxgate compass.

A can rolling around in a drawer may explain why the autopilot went bonkers, but when the boat took an unexpected detour toward the pilings, where was the skipper?

son's peripheral vision and ability to see primary colors (like red and green running lights) in the darkness.

It's also a good idea for the watch to be situated well away from the engine to minimize interference from engine noise. Aside from looking for other boats and markers, the watch should be listening for engines, bells, and whistles, all of which could indicate other boats or buoys. Listening is especially effective in fog, which projects sound more readily. The sound of waves breaking, either against the shore, another boat, or a breakwater, indicates trouble.

In one claim, a 27-foot powerboat in Southern California was wrecked in a pea-soup fog when it was caught in breaking surf. The skipper, who had been trying to find his way back to the harbor entrance by hugging the coast, was preoccupied with listening to his VHF and talking with guests.

Skippers should also post a dedicated watch and proceed slowly whenever visibility is restricted by the boat itself or by wandering guests or crew members. According to the recreational boat standards of the American Boat and Yacht Council (ABYC), an organization that writes voluntary standards for boatbuilders, boatbuilders that comply must minimize obstructions in the helmsman's field of vision. This is true whether the helmsman is standing or seated. If, for whatever reason, the boat does have a blind spot, the ABYC requires a placard at the helm: "Warning: Visibility from this helm station is limited . . ."

A more common problem is crew crowding onto a foredeck or sitting along

An Autopilot Is Not a Lookout

AS WITH MOST COLLISIONS, especially ones involving a fatality, there were two versions of what happened in this case: The owner of a 60-foot motoryacht said that he and his wife were both looking ahead and must not have seen the smaller boat because of the glare that was on the water. The sole survivor in the boat that was struck, however, said that he and his three companions had tried frantically, by waving their arms and yelling, to warn off the rapidly approaching boat. Even seconds before the collision, the survivor said there was no one visible at the helm.

The collision occurred 2 to 3 miles off the New Jersey coast. The motoryacht had been on autopilot, and the men in the second boat were drift-fishing. The motoryacht's owner, who prior to the accident had an unblemished boating record, immediately stopped his boat and rescued the sole survivor. The owner had not been drinking.

The jury who tried the case, a criminal case, could not reach a verdict, and the judge ordered a new trial. The 64-year-old owner said he couldn't put his wife through another trial, and after a plea bargain was sent to jail for six months. In sentencing the owner, the judge said, "It is an extraordinary plea bargain for extraordinary circumstances." At the time of writing, the civil suit was still pending.

the cabin in front of the helm. A 32-foot boat in Texas had been anchored with several hundred other boats to watch a hydroplane race. Shortly before the races ended, the skipper decided to leave and began to move through the fleet of anchored boats at about 8 knots. There were eleven people on his boat, including six people on the bow. Unfortunately, all the guests were still watching the races; no one had been asked to look out for other boats. Given the boat's excessive speed, the large number of spectator boats, the lack of visibility, and the lack of a designated lookout, it shouldn't be too surprising that the boat collided with another spectator boat.

Not all "crew members" have eyes and ears. Autopilots are becoming more and more common on boats and for good reason: they steer a reasonably straight course and, unlike other crew members, they don't whine or complain. What they can't do is see or hear; therefore, they make lousy lookouts.

Several years ago, an enthusiastic promotion in a well-known periodical touted the convenience of switching on an autopilot and going below to make lunch. What the ad didn't say was who would be watching out for other boats, which in the real world tend to appear quickly out of nowhere. In one typical case, a 34-foot powerboat on autopilot on Lake Michigan, collided with a smaller boat 18 miles offshore on a clear sunny day. The larger boat's owner was sunbathing and had asked a guest to "watch out for things."

In another well-publicized collision, a large motoryacht cruising 3 miles off the New Jersey coast on a weekday collided with a small fishing boat. Again, the weather was clear and the seas were calm. Three men in the smaller boat were killed and one was injured. The owner of the motoryacht had engaged the autopilot so he could study his charts.

Radar is another convenience that is finding its way on to many boats. But using radar to avoid collisions or find your way when visibility is restricted takes considerable expertise and should not be trusted to just anyone. Distortion, clutter, and multiple echoes can affect the accuracy of the image on the screen. And situations that are readily apparent in clear weather may be ambiguous on a radar screen; the position of the targets must be manually recorded over time to determine true location and progress relative to your boat. Then too, the radar may not be aligned to the boat's heading, which caused one skipper in our case files to go hard aground and damage his keel. The radar's improper alignment meant that targets on the screen were skewed.

The solution is to practice using radar on a clear, calm day. With an experienced crew member at the helm, concentrate solely on the radar screen and try navigating from buoy to buoy using just the bearings and distances your set is providing. This exercise will help you and your crew understand what the radar is seeing as well as alert you to any problems with the set's alignment.

Probably the most perplexing collisions are those that occur in daylight when conditions are clear and visibility is excellent. Two boats, a 22-foot powerboat and a 36-foot sailboat, for example, collided a half-mile off the entrance to San Diego harbor in 15-foot swells and 30-knot winds. Both skippers had their faces glued to their compasses, and their boats were periodically hidden from each other by the large swells. One skipper said he had seen the other boat briefly, but he lost sight of it until seconds before they collided. Similar accidents have occurred when skippers of sailboats failed to designate someone to watch behind the sails (and the skippers also failed to do so themselves). Powerboat skippers may become distracted when they're fishing or pulling water-skiers. With regard to the latter, many states have laws that require a spotter to watch a skier, which leaves the skipper free to watch for other boats.

Finally, even the relatively simple job of standing watch requires at least a basic understanding of how boats behave. Able hands are in short supply on many boats, and it behooves the skipper to spend a few minutes explaining what is expected of less-experienced crew. For example, a senior underwriter at BoatU.S. was sailing with his family and sent his young son forward to keep an eye out for any boats that might be hidden by the jib. A few minutes later his son said something like, "Hey Dad, look, there's a catamaran!" What the son didn't say was that the catamaran was only a few yards away and closing quickly. The two boats collided.

Guests who lack experience should also be monitored constantly whenever they are at the helm. This means that you—the boat's owner—must remain on deck to act as lookout. Accounts of boats that slam into other boats, jetties, and shoals at the hands of an inexperienced guest who has been left alone at the

Plotting Radar Positions

THE DIMINISHING SIZE AND AMPERAGE DRAIN of radar systems has made their operation fairly common on boats as small as 25 feet. Unlike larger commercial ships, however, radar operators on recreational boats are not required to obtain a certificate of proficiency. The danger of using sophisticated equipment without prior training or experience is that a skipper might install a radar system on a boat, turn it on, and go speeding off in a pea-soup fog thinking he'll see targets on the screen as clearly as he can see approaching boats on a sunny day. He won't.

As with visual sightings, bearings that remain constant while the range is decreasing indicate targets on a radar screen that may be on a collision course. Plotting these targets, which is required by the USCG Navigation Rules, also indicates dangerous course changes being made by approaching boats that would instantly be apparent in clear weather, but are otherwise slow to become apparent on a radar screen.

On older models, plotting involved transferring information from the screen onto a plotting sheet (and, ideally, marking the time of each observation) to better estimate closing speed. Plotting at least two positions was necessary to estimate the target's course and speed. Three or more observations were necessary to note a change in relative position.

The next generation of radar, which had television-type screens that didn't require hoods during the day, meant that a grease pen could be used to mark the positions of other boats directly on the glass screen. This reduced the time that was required for a navigator to observe changes in the relative position of other boats. Again, at least three observations had to be made for the operator to ascertain any changes. The newest sets leave a target trail on the screen to indicate an approaching boat's course. Some new sets also allow you to click on a target to get its speed and closest point of approach.

Even with the best set, however, experience is essential to make adjustments for sea conditions and range as well as to interpret information on the screen. Rule 7 requires that radar, "if fitted and operational," shall be used properly to determine if a risk of collision exists. Proper use includes "radar plotting or equivalent systematic observation of detected objects." This leaves open the possibility that in a courtroom battle over liability, radar could be the basis for finding fault against you if it was available and not used properly. To date, there have been no BoatU.S. claims that wound up in court because of the improper use of radar.

helm are common. One of the more unusual BoatU.S. Marine Insurance claims involved a guest who took the helm one night on a lake in New York. Before the skipper went below, he told the guest to "head for the red light," referring to a light marking a channel some distance away. Instead, the guest headed for a red light that, as it turned out, was on the back of a train. The boat bounced off a rock jetty and wound up high and dry on the railroad tracks. A few minutes later a second train came tearing down the tracks and slammed into the boat. Miraculously, both men escaped unharmed.

Navigation Rules That Apply to the Use of Radar

Rule 6—Safe Speed

In determining safe speed on vessels with operational radar, the following factors shall be among those taken into account:

(i) the characteristics, efficiency and limitations of the radar equipment;

(ii) any constraints imposed by the radar range scale in use;

(iii) the effect on radar detection of the sea state, weather and other sources of interference;

(iv) the possibility that small vessels, ice and other floating objects may not be detected by radar at an adequate range;

(v) the number, location and movement of vessels detected by radar;

(vi) the more exact assessment of the visibility that may be possible when radar is used to determine the range of vessels or other objects in the vicinity.

Rule 7—Risk of Collision

(b) Proper use shall be made of radar equipment if fitted and operational, including long-range scanning to obtain early warning of risk of collision and radar plotting or equivalent systematic observation of detached objects.

(c) Assumptions shall not be made on the basis of scanty information, especially scanty radar information.

Rule 8—Action to Avoid Collision

(b) Any alteration of course and/or speed to avoid collision shall, if the circumstances of the case admit, be large enough to be readily apparent to another vessel observing visually or by radar; a succession of small alterations of course and/or speed should be avoided.

Rule 19—Conduct of Vessels in Restricted Visibility

(d) A vessel which detects by radar alone the presence of another vessel shall determine if a close-quarters situation is developing and/or risk of collision exists. If so, she shall take avoiding action in ample time, provided that when such action consists of an alteration of course, so far as possible the following shall be avoided:

(i) an alteration of course to port for a vessel forward of the beam, other than for a vessel being overtaken;

(ii) an alteration of course toward a vessel abeam or abaft the beam.

Such are the pitfalls of Rule 5; the definition of what constitutes a "proper" lookout tends to become clear only *after* a collision.

The Question of Liability

For many years, the Rules made a distinction between "privileged" vessels and "burdened" vessels in meeting, overtaking, and crossing situations. Eventually, the two terms were abandoned because they were misleading. The Nav Rules were never intended to establish liability in the event of a collision, as these older terms seemed to suggest. The reason is that *both vessels have a responsibility to avoid a collision.* The terms used today, "stand-on" and "give-way," indicate the course of action that each boat is supposed to follow. If the skipper of the give-way vessel doesn't appear to be following the Rules or isn't keeping a proper lookout, it's up to the skipper of the stand-on vessel to take the necessary steps to prevent a collision. This is also in the Rules under Rule 17(b): "When, from any cause, the vessel required to keep her course and speed finds herself so close that collision cannot be avoided by the action of the give-way vessel alone, she shall take such action as will best aid to avoid collision." Rule 17(b) is the ultimate rule, the last rule to be applied before an impending collision.

How do you establish liability? In some collisions the fault is obvious, such as when the skipper of a 45-foot powerboat in Florida ran over a 31-foot boat late one night in a narrow waterway. The skipper of the larger boat had been drinking heavily, and his boat was traveling at almost 50 mph, over twice the posted speed limit.

But with many, perhaps most, collisions, assessing liability isn't so easy. For example, a small fishing boat and a trawler collided on a clear day on Chesapeake Bay after having each other in sight for almost 10 minutes. Seas were calm, and the open stretch of water near the mouth of the Potomac River was remarkably free of other boat traffic. The first boat, a 26-foot center console, was heading north off Smith Point Light, and its skipper said later that he thought his boat was moving faster and would pass in front of the trawler. He admitted that his attention was focused elsewhere.

The second boat, the trawler, was headed northwest toward the Potomac River. The trawler's skipper said that he was well aware of the smaller boat, but his boat had the right-of-way and he held his course until a few seconds before the collision—too late to turn out of harm's way.

Sooner or later, every skipper will approach another boat whose skipper either doesn't know the Rules of the Road or isn't keeping a proper lookout. When the two boats collided on Chesapeake Bay, the skipper of the center console—the give-way vessel—didn't give way because he wasn't keeping a proper lookout (Rule 5). That *does not* make him solely liable for the collision, however.

Farwell's Rules of the Road, the classic mariner's reference to the Rules of the

Road, states, "It [Rule 5] is not meant to imply that whenever two vessels collide, that mere proof of improper lookout on either vessel, in the technical sense, will *ipso facto* condemn that vessel for the collision. On the contrary, it has been held by the Supreme Court that the absence of a lookout is unimportant where the approaching vessel was seen long before the collision occurred."

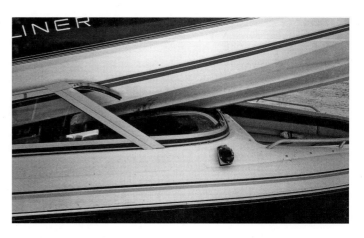

Besides turning to avoid the collision, the skipper of the stand-on vessel could easily have slowed down or stopped, which would have allowed the give-way vessel time to pass safely in front of his boat.

One of the more serious collisions in the BoatU.S. claim files involves a runabout that was cruising on the left side (the wrong side) of a waterway heading north and met a boat heading south at a sharp bend. Both boats made a quick series of offsetting maneuvers before finally colliding head-on. Although the investigating officer noted that the northbound boat was cruising on the wrong side of the channel, both skippers were cited for failure to slow their boats before the collision.

There are situations where liability is less likely to be shared. An overtaking vessel (more than 22.5° abaft the other vessel's beam) that runs into the stern of a boat, according to *Farwell's*, "is *solely* [emphasis added] liable as long as the vessel being overtaken maintains her course and speed as required under the Rules."

If a vessel passes relatively close to another vessel from any direction more than 22.5° abaft the latter's starboard beam, draws ahead, and subsequently turns to port to come onto a crossing course, *Farwell's* says that the overtaking vessel is not relieved of her duty to keep clear and notes that the courts have found that this applies not only in restricted waters, but wherever an attempt to pass might mean risk of collision.

A Practical Approach

The following is an excerpt from a surveyor's report: "Officer Figular related that the initial cause of the accident was [the other skipper's] failure to give way. He said she turned to port and the [skipper of the stand-on vessel] responded at the same instant by turning to starboard. Officer Figular said both boats were cited because neither vessel backed off the throttle in an attempt to avoid the collision."

In any crossing situation, the best way for the skipper of the give-way vessel to avoid frantic last-minute maneuvering, which creates confusion and increases the likelihood of a collision, is to make course changes early—the sooner the better

A seagoing tailgater. It's hard to believe, but alcohol wasn't involved in this accident. Drugs weren't either. What was involved was inattention—lots of it—on a boat that was going too fast and following another boat too closely through a narrow, crowded channel.

The helmsman on the trailing boat didn't notice the skipper of the lead boat throttle back. In a split second, his boat crashed over the lead boat's transom and came to rest in the position you see here. Although there were five kids and two adults aboard, the collision, somewhat miraculously, resulted in only one serious injury.

The next time you're the stand-on vessel in a crossing situation and the other boat's skipper doesn't seem to be awake, it may be that he isn't even there. The owner of this mangled boat was alone on a sunny afternoon and went aft to secure the swim platform. The boat, meanwhile, continued zipping along at cruising speed. While he was fiddling with the swim ladder, he was bounced over the transom by a passing wake and somersaulted into the water. He was rescued unharmed, but the boat eventually smashed into a seawall.

in fact. At 1 to 2 miles, a slight change of course will usually suffice, but the closer the two boats approach, the more important it becomes to make a course change that will be immediately obvious to the other skipper. One tactic is to head for the other boat's wake until you're certain it is going to pass safely in front of your boat.

What if you're the stand-on vessel and the other skipper either isn't following the Rules or doesn't see you? Five or more short blasts, signaling danger, should get his or her attention. (This tends to convey the intended message, even if the other skipper doesn't understand whistle signals, which is likely.) If not, slow your boat immediately and turn away from the collision. DON'T wait until the boats are a few yards apart to take evasive action. The longer you wait, the more radical your maneuver will have to be, and the more likely the other skipper will become confused.

When one boat approaches another head on, *both* boats are supposed to turn to starboard—Rule 14a—to avoid a collision. The turn must be obvious, so that the other skipper clearly sees your boat's port side. In a crowded channel or fairway, boats should keep to the right side of the channel, just as when driving a car on a highway.

Besides crossing and approaching, the other situation addressed by the Navigation Rules is overtaking. When you're approaching another boat from astern, sound one short blast if you'll be leaving the other vessel on your port side and two blasts if you'll be leaving the vessel on your starboard side. (Memory aid: port and left have fewer letters than starboard and right.) While you can't be sure your signals have been understood, signaling has the advantage in any situation of getting the other skipper's attention. (If you *respond* to another vessel's signal, respond with the same signal or the danger signal—*never respond with a contradictory signal*.) You can also try contacting the boat's skipper on your VHF. As the overtaking boat, you will be the give-way vessel, even if you pass to the right and move into the other boat's danger zone. Finally, to save aggravation and possible injury, both boats should slow way down to reduce the size of their wakes until the overtaking boat is safely clear.

Are You on a Collision Course?

The skipper of a 27-foot sailboat that was motorsailing across Lake Michigan flipped on his autopilot and went below to check his charts. After a few minutes, the sailboat's skipper poked his head out of the hatch and saw a large fishing trawler several miles away that seemed to be moving very slowly. He watched for several minutes and then—a big mistake—went back to his chart, convinced the trawler would pass well astern of his boat. It didn't. In what the sailboat skipper described as "a very short amount of time," he heard a series of loud whistles, but it was too late to avoid a violent collision with the trawler.

It's easy to misjudge the speed of another boat at great distances. Depending on its height, a trawler or large ship that is a mere speck on the horizon can be on top of you in 20 minutes. The time from first sighting to imminent collision also can be reduced considerably if the vessel is initially hidden by large seas or foul weather. Rather than wait until the last minute, use a hand-bearing compass (or the boat's compass) to assess the risk of collision:

- If your boat's speed and heading are constant and the compass bearings are moving forward, the other boat should pass ahead.

- If the bearings are moving aft, the other boat should pass astern.

- The more the bearings move, the farther apart the two boats should be when they cross.

- *A series of bearings that remain constant over time indicate that the two boats are converging on a collision course—you must take the appropriate action to avoid a collision!*

You can also take relative bearings by lining up an object on your own boat—a stanchion, for example—with the vessel in question. If you continue to steer a

This 30-foot cruiser was traveling at 20 knots in poor visibility when a marker suddenly loomed up. The skipper tried to steer away at the last minute, but the stern struck the piling, tearing open a hole and sinking the boat. Fortunately no one was seriously injured. The lesson is obvious but well worth repeating: *When visibility is limited, either from weather or darkness, slow down!*

steady course and the other vessel remains in line with the reference object, the two vessels are on a collision course.

Lining up the approaching vessel with an object on land is another way to assess the risk of collision. For example, if there is a water tower on land that appears to be moving astern of the other boat, the boat should safely cross your bow. If the water tower appears to be moving ahead of the approaching boat, your boat is moving faster, and you should cross ahead of the other boat. If the water tower remains in the same position relative to the other boat, you are likely on a collision course, and you must take the appropriate action to avoid a collision. The exception would be two boats heading in the same direction abeam of each other and slowly converging.

Collisions at Night

While collisions during the day often involve boats that saw each other long before they collided and failed to take appropriate action, collisions at night frequently involve boats that did not see each other until a split second before impact. There could be several reasons for this: one or both boats didn't have their running lights on, the skippers were not paying attention, or the boats were speeding. But often—too often—collisions occur at night between boats that had their running lights shining brightly and skippers who had throttled back to a prudent speed and were looking ahead. Here's an example:

Lady Duck: "As we started to leave the harbor, I turned on the spotlight for approximately 10 seconds. I know that my running lights were on because that's the only way my instrument panel will light up.

"I continued to idle about 400 to 500 yards into the bay, looking from port to starboard and back and did not see any sign of red, green, or white. I had just started to accelerate slightly when the other boat plowed into me."

Low Commotion: "About 9 P.M. I was following a course in toward the harbor entrance. Because it was after dark, of course, I had my running lights on. My wife and nephew were with me. From a distance, the channel lights became clearer. The accident occurred near the mouth of the channel.

"I was preparing to enter the channel when I saw the other vessel bearing down on us. The bow of the other vessel was high out of the water, obviously not on plane. The other vessel didn't have his running lights on and this sighting was just a split second before the accident occurred."

Despite their own contradictory statements, both boats almost certainly had their navigation lights on. This was confirmed by investigators who interviewed witnesses. Both skippers were also sober, which is especially important because at night drinking not only inhibits an operator's judgment—drink-

ing does that day or night—it also affects a person's ability to recover from glare as well as to perceive basic colors. (Drinking is involved in many collisions at night. It's a dangerous problem discussed further in the Collisions at Night and Alcohol section below.)

But if the two skippers had not been drinking and were both watching ahead, why didn't they see each other?

There are several possible explanations. First, the skipper of *Low Commotion* may not have seen *Lady Duck*'s lights because they were "camouflaged" against the lights onshore. Certainly when you are headed into port and the background lights are becoming brighter and brighter, it's time to slow down and give yourself more time to react to boats and/or markers that suddenly appear. In Rule 6, the Coast Guard cites the presence of background light, such as from a building onshore or from backscatter of a boat's own lights, as reasons a skipper must reduce speed.

Backscatter: Spilling Your Own Lights When the skipper of *Lady Duck* turned on the boat's powerful spotlight, he may have created a glare, which, according to experts, can affect a person's vision for several minutes. (The older a person is, the longer it takes for his or her eyes to adjust to darkness.) If you use a spotlight, you should:

1. Avoid shining the light directly at another boat, which will temporarily blind its operator(s).

2. Keep the beam shining well out from the boat, where it won't bounce off the white deck, a chrome railing, or a deck fitting.

3. Slow down until your eyes recover from the glare.

A spotlight, however, is only one source of spilled light. Another source, less obvious perhaps but potentially more debilitating, is your boat's own navigation lights, especially an all-round light or masthead light. Either of these can spill light and create glare that will seriously affect the helmsman's ability to see other boats in the darkness.

Navigation Lights and Glare According to the Navigation Rules, a power-driven vessel that is less than 12 meters (39 feet 4 inches) in length and is underway must exhibit a masthead light, sidelights, and either a steering stern light or an all-round white light and sidelights.

Be aware that these lighting requirements may present a problem with glare. Namely, the lower the mast is in relation to the helm, the greater the area of the deck that will be illuminated, and depending on the mast height and where the light is mounted, the more likely the light will shine directly into the helmsman's eyes.

Annex 1 in the International Regulations for the Prevention of Collision at Sea (COLREGS) states that the masthead, or the all-round light, on power-driven vessels less than 12 meters in length and built after July 31, 1983, "shall be screened to prevent direct illumination of the vessel forward of the operator's position." Similar wording is used for boats over 20 meters.

It should be noted that boatowners, and not manufacturers, are ultimately responsible for running lights. As early as 1975, the Coast Guard's Office of Boating Safety tried to address the issue of glare by enacting a regulation that would have put the onus on the *manufacturer* to make each of their models comply. The idea certainly had merit, but it was shelved because instruments sensitive enough to measure minute amounts of light, which participants reported were interfering with their nocturnal vision, didn't exist.

Manufacturers could have reduced the glare voluntarily, of course, but with a very few exceptions, most didn't. On some boats, the 360° light could either have been split—one 225° light on the bow and one 135° light on the transom—or the light could have been placed on a tall pole with a shield beneath it that would cast a shadow over the boat. There were no other options. A spokesman for the NMMA at the time said that putting a light on a tall pole with a shield to eliminate glare was ugly, expensive, and would vibrate underway. Splitting the lights, he said, added to the boat's cost.

The quest to reduce glare extended beyond the Coast Guard to the ABYC. Its A-16 Navigation Lights Standard (A-16.5.2) states: "Navigation lights shall be mounted, or means shall be used, to minimize the effect on the operator's vision of both light reflected from the vessel structure and direct light . . ."

Despite writing "voluntary" standards, the ABYC has considerable clout with manufacturers. But while most ABYC standards are adhered to by manufacturers, A-16.5.2 was all but ignored. Tom Hale, a former ABYC Technical Director, said there was a concerted effort by both boat and navigation light manufacturers to find a solution to the glare problem. First, in 1995, the ABYC's Navigation Lights Committee updated the standard to be more specific (16.5.3): "The all-round

Many collisions could have been avoided by using a little more common sense. A case in point: The skipper of this boat got lost one night and was trying to find his way home by "following the shoreline." Unfortunately, the shoreline wasn't straight (most aren't), and his boat plowed into a cliff at 15 knots. One man was badly injured and had to be airlifted to a hospital.

Even the best skipper can get disoriented on the water, especially at night. It's not uncommon to have trouble finding a marker or to become confused by lights that don't seem to line up or are hidden by lights onshore. But considering the severity of the injuries that can occur, until you're sure—very sure—where you are, the rule should always be to slow down.

light shall not be directly visible from the helm station." Unlike the earlier version, which dealt only with minimizing spilled light, the newer standard goes at the problem more directly. The older 16.5.2 was revised to state: "Navigation lights shall be mounted or means shall be used to prevent direct illumination of, or reflection off, a vessel structure within the operator's vertical and horizontal range of visibility."

This newer standard has led to the development of navigation lights that tend to cast light out but not down, thereby reducing glare at the helm. Some are available on telescoping poles, which can extend the light further away from the helmsman's eyes. These newer lights aren't foolproof. Depending on how they're mounted, the newer lights can still create some glare, but they are a vast improvement over the older lights. Many builders now use them, while others, including some houseboat and pontoon boat builders, also use a shield beneath the light that creates a shadow effect to reduce glare. (The newer all-round lights and clamp-on shields are available at West Marine.) On older boats, the problem remains, and it's still up to boatowners to achieve compliance.

Collisions at Night and Alcohol

While glare may sometimes be a contributing factor in nighttime collisions, the deadliest collisions at night almost always involve alcohol. A collision on the St. Croix River in Minnesota between two boats sometime in the dark and early morning hours of July 3, 1999, is typical. One boat was estimated to have been traveling between 50 and 60 mph, and the other at about 30 mph. All of the occupants of the two boats, a total of five people, died in the collision. All five had been drinking heavily.

Boating accidents, even some of the worst accidents, tend to make headlines for a few days and are then forgotten. But the St. Croix collision captured national attention when the National Transportation Safety Board (NTSB), the organization that is best known for analyzing the causes of major airline accidents, announced that it would begin an investigation. Unlike the wreck of *Morning Dew* (page 139), there were no unanswered questions that prompted the NTSB to investigate the St. Croix River collision. Quite the contrary; NTSB was well aware that boating accidents involving alcohol occur frequently on the nation's waterways, especially at night. And while the St. Croix accident involved more fatalities (one short of being considered a Major Marine Accident), the NTSB was interested in becoming more involved in recreational boat safety. The St. Croix collision—a nighttime collision involving alcohol—seemed like a good place to start.

The St. Croix Collision According to accounts given to NTSB investigators, on July 2 the owner of one of the boats, a 27-foot Advantage, had spent most of the afternoon and evening drinking with friends at a bar adjacent to his marina. Witnesses also confirmed that the owner of the second boat, a 22-foot Bayliner, had also been drinking. After the accident, autopsies found that both owners had blood alcohol concentration (BAC) levels over 0.2%. The other victims had BAC levels ranging from 0.127% to 0.197%. *A BAC of 0.10% is considered legally intoxicated in Minnesota;* in many other states the legal limit has been lowered to 0.08%.

Both owners were experienced boaters. The Advantage owner had been employed as an Advantage salesman and had received factory training in various high-speed Advantage models. The Bayliner owner had also been boating for several years and was described as "friendly and calm" by the marina manager. One finding, however, was especially telling: his driver's license had once been revoked for driving under the influence of alcohol, although it had since been reinstated.

In summarizing their report of the accident, NTSB concluded that the probable cause was ". . . alcohol impairment, which led the two boat operators to indulge in high speed operations at night, and which impaired their ability to determine the movements of other vessels and to take appropriate action to avoid a collision."

While neither of the boats on the St. Croix collision was insured by BoatU.S., there are many similar accidents involving alcohol in the BoatU.S. claim files:

- A man in Tennessee was injured when his boat left the channel at a sharp turn and crashed into a seawall.

- A man at the helm of a small cruiser was killed when his boat was struck amidships by another boat in the channel leading into a Virginia marina.

- Seven people were injured and one killed when a boat slammed into an anchored barge late at night on the Potomac River.

While Coast Guard statistics indicate a reduction in boating fatalities—the result of ongoing efforts by boating safety groups—the occurrence of even one fatal accident that could easily have been avoided is disturbing.

Protecting Yourself at Night No one should be surprised when a skipper who has been drinking heavily is involved in a boating accident. It's common knowledge that people who are clearly intoxicated—slurring their words and stumbling—are much more likely to hurt themselves, as well as anyone else unlucky enough to cross their path. The question then for a responsible skipper is how do you protect yourself out on the water at night from boats whose owners have been drinking heavily and are liable to be driving recklessly? It's an important question. Consider this startling statistic: a study by the BoatU.S. Foundation for Boating Safety found that boaters faced a 280% greater risk of involvement in an accident at night and a staggering 433% greater risk of being killed (based on the assumption that boating activity at night represented 5% of the total boating activity).

The sooner you see another boat, the sooner you can take evasive action, regardless of who has the right-of-way. And if the other skipper has been drinking heavily, it will almost certainly be up to you to take evasive action. Here are four ways to avoid nighttime collisions:

1. **Avoid drinking *any* alcohol.** The NTSB report notes that even small amounts of alcohol can inhibit a person's ability to operate a boat safely at night. According to studies quoted in the report, BACs ranging from as low as 0.04% (roughly the equivalent of two beers) can degrade a person's ability to discern faint lights or other objects; notice objects just outside the direct line of sight (peripheral vision); respond to a constantly changing stimulus; and select a response based on the nature of the stimulus. It takes longer for a person who has had one or two beers to process information, such as recognizing whether a potentially dangerous situation is developing and then deciding how to avoid an accident.

   A BoatU.S. Marine Insurance claim several years ago shows clearly how a person's night vision can be affected by small amounts of alcohol. The skipper of the claimant boat had been diligently following a series of markers back to his marina when the boat was struck by another boat just forward of amidships. One passenger was killed. The skipper had been drinking but was not found to be legally drunk.

   Asked sometime later why the collision occurred, the skipper recounted how the boat appeared suddenly: "I can't figure out how it got as close to us as it did without me seeing it. I don't understand to this day . . . how the devil this thing can come from nowhere. It is more than I will ever understand."

   Why didn't he see the other boat? Seas were calm that night, and the moon was full. One study cited in the NTSB report found that glare—from a

Boats Shouldn't Climb Trees

A BOATU.S. INSURANCE CLAIM: "On June 11, at approximately 7:45 P.M., [the owner of the boat in the photo] was operating the vessel on the Middle River [in Chesapeake Bay]. He reports that another vessel was operating at high speed and he decided to race them. He accelerated rapidly, pushing his vessel to what he estimated was in excess of 55 mph. Apparently during the pursuit, his vessel hit a wake and he was thrown overboard. His vessel continued to run at full throttle.

"At the same time, a 1967, 37-foot Viking was operating in the same area at idle speed. The Viking's owner saw the operator get ejected and then watched as the unattended vessel came directly toward his boat. He attempted to avoid the oncoming boat and was able to avoid a head-on collision. The unattended vessel made a glancing blow high up on the port side, ripping out approximately 15 feet of planking.

"The unattended vessel continued to cross Middle River with the throttle still in full position. The vessel then struck a dock and became airborne, apparently gaining an altitude of 30 [feet]. It traveled 56 feet through the air, flying over the seawall and a small tree before slamming into a 200-year-old oak tree. The vessel's engines continued to run. The owner of the house came outside and shut off the engines.

"Meanwhile, the operator was rescued by a third vessel. The police were called, and he was later arrested and charged with driving while intoxicated. The exact level of intoxication has not been determined at this time."

boat or from a full moon—can significantly affect nocturnal vision, even with low BAC levels. Greater amounts of alcohol will result in even more impairment. Studies have also found that a person who has consumed small amounts of alcohol has less ability to notice stimuli outside his or her immediate field of view. The studies found that alcohol doesn't narrow a person's field of vision, it only narrows their focus of attention (the skipper had been diligently following a series of buoys). In fact one study found that alcohol might enhance a person's ability to concentrate on a task (in this case, steering toward a buoy) in the presence of a "peripheral stressor." So while a skipper who has had moderate amounts of alcohol may do a better job of watching a specific buoy, he or she would be much less likely to notice an

Even small amounts of alcohol can affect a person's ability to operate a boat at night. The skipper of this boat had been diligently following a series of markers and failed to notice a boat approaching. One person was killed. While the skipper was not found to be legally intoxicated, he had been drinking alcohol. Studies have shown that a person who has been drinking moderate amounts of alcohol has a significantly impaired ability to see lights, notice stimuli outside his or her immediate field of view, and make the appropriate response based on the nature of the stimulus.

approaching boat, especially when it is on the periphery of his immediate field of view.

Finally, blood alcohol concentrations as low as 0.04% can significantly affect a person's ability to select and execute one or more alternative responses, such as deciding whether to turn to port or starboard, pull back on the throttle, etc. The more complex the task, the greater the effect of alcohol on reaction time. In this case, the skipper first reported that he had turned to starboard. He was surprised to learn later that his boat had been struck on the starboard side, which meant that he had turned to port.

While someone who has been drinking heavily is more likely to take foolish risks that cause an accident, someone who has been drinking moderately may find that he or she is less competent to prevent an accident.

2. **Post a dedicated lookout.** Whenever darkness (or weather) restricts visibility, skippers should post a dedicated watch when one is available. This is called for by Rule 5 of the COLREGS, and it's also common sense. It's best for the lookout to be away from sources of spilled light, which will impede his or her ability to see in the darkness. It's also a good idea for the watch to be as far from the engine as practical, where engine noise is minimal. Aside from watching for other boats, he or she will be better able to hear the engines of approaching boats.

3. **Reduce speed.** This is also called for by the COLREGS, Rule 6: "Every vessel shall at all times proceed at a safe speed so that she can take proper and effective action to avoid collision and be stopped within a distance appropriate to the prevailing circumstances and conditions." At night, when other boats (as well as markers, cans, buoys, etc.) can come up quickly, this means slow down—way down.

4. **Keep night vision sharp.** The sooner you see another boat, the sooner you

can take evasion action should it be necessary. Aside from keeping vision sharp by eliminating sources of glare from lights on board, it is also prudent to protect your eyes during the day. According to optometrists who study the effects of glare, bright sunlight bouncing off the water at low angles can "bleach" photoreceptors, which fatigues the eyes and temporarily impairs vision. Anyone who has walked from bright sunlight into a dark building has experienced bleached eyes, but what most people don't realize is that the lingering effects of bleaching can affect the eyes for up to 8 hours. In the meantime, night vision may be reduced by as much as 50%. As a practical matter, you can't totally eliminate glare on the water, but experts say that you can increase your ability to tolerate glare, avoid eye fatigue, and keep your night vision sharper by always wearing a hat and an effective (wraparound) pair of sunglasses during the day.

Appointing Designated Skippers Given some of the horrific boating collisions that have involved alcohol, the campaign to appoint a designated skipper would seem like welcome advice. Nobody would argue that a skipper needs to be sober—day or night—to safely operate a boat. After all, a similar designated driver campaign has been credited with reducing alcohol-related accidents in automobiles. Others are free to drink, although maybe too much, because a designated—*sober*—driver will deliver them safely home.

Boats, however, are not automobiles. The designated skipper can't help everyone climb aboard and then fasten his or her seatbelts. On a boat, passengers may be free to roam about and have another drink or two. An examination of ten BoatU.S. Marine Insurance claims involving serious accidents and alcohol found that only two involved collisions. Of the remaining eight, one involved a woman who was injured when she tumbled backward out of her chair, and another involved a woman who stumbled off a flybridge onto the deck below. There was one death at a dock, where the guest fell overboard and drowned while trying to step onto the pier. The remaining five claims involved people who fell or jumped overboard while the boat was underway.

Several years ago, the *Journal of the American Medical Association (JAMA)* published an article questioning the wisdom of the designated skipper campaign. The article said public education efforts that imply (by omission) that intoxicated boat passengers are safe represent a "clear and present danger to the public's health." The article included both statistical and medical evidence to support its conclusions. Only 18% of the boating fatalities in the year of the study involved collisions. Almost half—46%—involved boats that were not underway. The Coast Guard data, according to the doctors who authored the *JAMA* article, suggest that drinking passengers are at risk regardless of the drinking behavior of the boat's operator.

The conclusion: on a boat, appointing a designated skipper shouldn't be a green light for everyone else aboard to overindulge.

Collisions at Marinas: So Many Boats, So Little Room

Aside from alcohol and maybe darkness, the single biggest factor in collisions is crowds. As waterways have become more congested, the likelihood of colliding with another boat has increased. While searching the BoatU.S. Marine Insurance claim files, it became apparent that a significant number of collisions occurred in the crowded, narrow confines of marina *fairways* (the channels or inlets leading to open water).

It makes sense: marinas are beehives of activity on weekends, and with so many boats passing so close in the restricted confines of the marina fairway, there is bound to be an increased risk of a collision. It should be noted that these weren't collisions with docks or pilings, although there are plenty of those, too. Collisions while docking typically involve boat-handling skills or lack thereof. To be fair, winds can be fluky and currents can swirl through pilings so that even the best skipper can sometimes be caught off guard. A single misstep can mean a collision. Collisions in fairways, however, tend to occur because of a combination of three factors: inattention, blind spots, and too much speed. Here are a few suggestions:

1. Give the helm your undivided attention. Make sure the crew has their gear stowed *before* lines are cast off. A sailboat in Hampton, Virginia, ran into the stern of another sailboat because the skipper was leaning over the wheel telling the crew where to stow sleeping bags, food, etc. Even routine jobs like stowing fenders and docklines can be a distraction and are best put off until the boat is in open water and clear of marina traffic.

2. Beware of moored boats—a fairway may be much narrower than it first appears. Anchors, dinghies, outriggers, etc., often protrude beyond the line of other moored boats. A 39-foot powerboat in Seattle, for example, snagged an inflatable dinghy on davits because the dinghy stuck out far—perhaps too far—beyond the other boats in the fairway. The powerboat was OK, but the encounter ripped one of the inflatable's pontoons. Another common accident involves sailboats that snag various parts of other boats—anchors, dinghies, etc.—on their shrouds.

3. Reduce blind spots on your boat as much as possible. When returning to the marina, for example, sailboats should have their sails secured so that visibility isn't restricted, either by the sails themselves or by crew furling the sails. As a general rule, too many people up front, either on the foredeck or cabin top, is a bad idea.

Approach Another Boat Port to Port, Not Bow to Bow

THIS BOAT was in the middle of a busy channel when it turned to the right to avoid an incoming boat and met a third boat bow-on. This type of claim isn't unusual. In reviewing the BoatU.S. claim files, there are many collisions in *fairways* (the well-marked channels that lead into and out of marinas and moorings).

The solution to this type of collision is very simple: stay to the right! You'd think that staying to the right would be obvious in a country where automobiles drive on the right, but once you get rid of the yellow and white lines, it seems that some skippers have trouble knowing where they are. In an otherwise orderly procession of incoming and outgoing boats, all it takes is one boat on the wrong side of a channel to create chaos.

Imagine an automobile coming at you on the wrong side of a busy highway. Sooner or later somebody gets bumped. The solution: *Stay to the right!*

4. Maintain only as much speed as you need to maneuver the boat and be prepared to back down. Many marinas are like crowded parking lots: boats back out of slips unexpectedly, appear suddenly at corners, and come scooting out of nowhere, such as the small inflatable full of kids that almost got run down by a trawler in Tennessee. The trawler missed the kids but plowed into a pontoon boat.

5. Above all, drive defensively—you never know what you're going to encounter. A skipper in Marina del Rey, California, for example, was rammed by a boat that backed into his boat at close to full throttle. The boat had been backing out of its slip when its skipper shoved the accelerator forward while the gears were still in reverse. The boat shot backward, surprising the skippers of both boats. Another marina collision involved a small sailboat that "sailed" into an outbound boat—literally—at about 4 knots because the sail got hung up on a spreader. I mention these two incidents because you might someday encounter skippers like these at your marina. Be prepared.

6. Remember to slow down and stay to the right when you leave the marina and are in the fairway. According to the BoatU.S. claim files, these narrow fairways leading in and out of busy harbors are one of the likeliest places for

a collision. All it takes is one boat to stray to the left of a crowded channel or into the middle to create mayhem and possibly cause a collision. The rule is that vessels should pass one another port to port.

Collisions Between Racing Sailboats

Another of the more likely places for collisions to occur is on a sailboat race course. To nonracing sailors, this may be difficult to understand. At a distance, a racing sailboat rounding a mark seems graceful, almost poetic, as the boat spins, the spinnaker bursts open in an explosion of color, and the boat glides silently

These three photos show a collision between two sailboats racing off Annapolis, Maryland. The boat sailing away from the camera, *Enduro*, tries to duck *Eroica*'s stern but the rudder can't compensate for the overtrimmed mainsail. (Note *Enduro*'s skewed wake in the first photo.) Both boats were badly damaged, and there was one injury.

toward the next mark. But on the deck of a racing sailboat, it's a different story. In a matter of seconds, the crew has to get the spinnaker on deck; raise the spinnaker pole; attach the spinnaker sheet, halyard, and guy; trim the genoa; raise the spinnaker; trim the spinnaker sheet and guy; remember to duck when the boom comes over; and wrestle the flailing genoa onto the foredeck. The harried scene must be directed by the skipper, who is also responsible for steering the boat through a fleet of equally distracted skippers.

BoatU.S. examined fifty racing sailboat collision claims to learn where they occurred on the course and, more important, how they could have been avoided.

Racing Sailboat Collision Frequency

Location on the Course	Frequency Percentage
at the start	26%
on the course	52%
rounding a mark	22%

At the Start

Let's look at a fairly typical claim:

Like most of the other boats, *Sea Stooges* was at the favored end of the starting line when the gun went off. Struggling for clear air amid the logjam of boats, the skipper failed to see another boat to leeward, which was hidden behind the genoa. *Stooges* struck the other boat on its transom, doing considerable damage to both boats. A genoa was torn, a backstay parted (fortunately, the boat wasn't dismasted), and the bow and stern pulpits on the respective boats were bent.

Slightly more than a quarter of all racing collisions occur in the hectic first few minutes of the start. Aggressiveness at the start is typical. A bad start usually dooms the skipper to wind shadows—bad air—from other boats throughout the remainder of the race. The strong emphasis on a good start, unfortunately, often comes at the expense of prudent seamanship. Even though he was surrounded by other boats, *Stooges*' skipper and the rest of the crew were perched on the windward rail to keep the boat flat and improve boat speed. But this violated Rule 5 of the International–Inland Rules—"Every vessel shall at all times maintain a proper lookout"—which is one of the basic tenets of good seamanship.

According to the claim files, collisions like that of the *Stooges* are likely to occur at a crowded start, but they can, and do, occur anywhere on the course. Someone—and not the someone who is also in charge of packing the spinnaker and making sandwiches—must be appointed lookout. This person's job can be made a lot easier if the genoa and mainsail have collision windows (transparent squares sewn into the sail) to improve visibility to leeward. In the highly competitive J24 Nationals off Annapolis, Maryland, several years ago, almost half of the eighty-five-boat fleet had collision windows. "The reason," quipped one partici-pant, "was that collisions definitely lose races." Unfortunately, the practice of using collision windows, for whatever reason, seems to be declining.

On the Course

About half of all racing collisions are on the relatively open stretches of water between the start and the various marks. Aside from blindly plowing into other boats, one of the most common causes of racing collisions has to do with boat design. Mike Kaufman, a naval architect who has designed both racing and cruis-ing sailboats, says that the control surfaces of a racing sailboat—the keel and especially the rudder—are typically cut down as much as possible to reduce the wetted surface area. Masts, meanwhile, have tended to get taller and taller, which has given racing sailboats more power. You don't need to be a naval architect to know that more power and less control means trouble on a sailboat, especially on a blustery day.

Consider, for example, a claim involving the racer *Magic*. About 20 seconds prior to the collision, the crew of *Magic* was told by the skipper that they would be ducking the stern of *Good Cookin'*. *Good Cookin'* was on a starboard tack; *Magic* was on a port tack. Both boats were approaching the windward mark at about 6½ knots.

About the same time, *Magic's* skipper began bearing off, a gust of wind hit (according to the skipper), and the mainsheet jammed. (This account was later disputed by *Good Cookin's* skipper, who said the other boat's mainsheet was never touched.) The tiller did not respond, and *Magic* rammed *Good Cookin'* squarely amidships, putting a 12-inch gash in the side of its hull. About 10 seconds before the collision, one of the crew on *Good Cookin'* yelled "No way!," but *Good Cookin'* made no attempt to avoid the collision.

The remedy for avoiding this type of collision is relatively simple: Whenever a crossing situation exists, the mainsheet should be taken out of the cam cleat before attempting to duck another boat's stern. If the sheet is jammed in the cam, tack immediately. Don't attempt to duck another boat's stern without easing the mainsheet.

One other important note: according to the International Racing Rules, both skippers must make a reasonable attempt to avoid a collision. In this case, the only thing *Good Cookin's* crew did to avoid the collision was yell "No way!" then stare blankly as *Magic's* skipper struggled to control his boat. Even if the collision couldn't have been avoided completely, *Good Cookin's* skipper could have less-ened the impact by steering away from the blow.

In a similar claim, a boat passing close by another boat became entangled in the second boat's rigging when it rounded up suddenly in a gust of wind. Round-ing up is one of the more common thrills of sailboat racing. Downwind, the

Notable Quotes from the BoatU.S. Claim Files

"The collision was unavoidable, as neither boat saw each other."

"I had the lookout check for other boats regularly—about every 5 minutes."

"The reason I am so upset over this is because he was wrong in every way except possibly that he was on starboard tack."

"I thought we were the last boat in the pack so I wasn't concerned about watching for boats on starboard tack."

"He was somewhat surprised when I told him there were also rules governing right-of-way when boats are not engaged in a race." (Said regarding a collision before the start of a race.)

spinnaker can create horrendous control problems when the afterguy, which controls the fore-and-aft trim of the spinnaker pole, is eased when the boat starts to broach. Always ease the spinnaker sheet!

While a windward vessel must keep clear of a leeward vessel, it should also be noted that the International Racing Rules state a yacht that establishes an overlap to leeward from clear astern (normally the burdened vessel) shall allow the windward vessel ample room to keep clear. How much room is "ample"? The rules aren't specific. But on a blustery day, it would be wise to leave more than just a few yards when passing.

Rounding a Mark

While approaching a mark, *Stinger* was clearly ahead of *Frenzy*. Both boats were on port tack with no overlap. This was still the case when the boats came within two boat lengths of the mark, which, according to the International Racing Rules, meant that *Frenzy* had to give way to *Stinger* at the mark. *Stinger* hailed *Frenzy* to warn that there was no overlap. But instead of maneuvering outside, *Frenzy* continued hugging the mark, hoping to intimidate *Stinger's* skipper into giving him room to round inside.

But *Stinger* held its course, and *Frenzy* was pinned between *Stinger* and the mark. Seconds later *Frenzy* plowed into *Stinger*, putting a 2-inch hole in its side. The skipper of *Frenzy* was aware that he was at fault (he admitted later that he had been "bullheaded") and immediately withdrew from the race.

The skipper of *Frenzy* should have begun maneuvering to get outside *Stinger* as soon as it became apparent that he might not have an overlap. All too often racers throw caution to the wind to gain a few feet or seconds of advantage. Lack of experience may also have been a factor, although an inexperienced skipper should be more, not less, cautious.

Again, according to the Racing Rules, *Stinger's* skipper should have made a reasonable attempt to avoid a collision and then raised a protest flag when it became apparent that *Frenzy* was not sailing by the rules. But, like the skipper of *Frenzy*, *Stinger*'s skipper chose to race all out and ignore the rules.

Drinking and Sailboat Racing

It's no secret that alcohol inhibits a skipper's ability to operate a boat properly. Even small amounts of alcohol, according to tests conducted by the Coast Guard, may be too much. Called Visual Alertness Stressor Tests (VAST), the tests measured the effects of the elements—wind, sun, waves—on a boat operator's reaction time, visual acuity, and psychomotor coordination. The tests found that a skipper who has had two beers and 4 hours of exposure to the elements can be expected to demonstrate the equivalent performance of a rested operator who has had six beers.

While BoatU.S.'s racing collision claim files contain plenty of accusations and counteraccusations about who was at fault, who should have done what, and so forth, none of the files mention alcohol. Captain John Bonds, the former director of US Sailing and a member of the BoatU.S. National Advisory Council, says that alcohol used to be common among racing sailors but is now almost nonexistent.

Bonds says that the few skippers who do allow crew to consume alcohol during a race tend to be casual racers who finish back in the fleet, out of everyone's way. Bonds has even noticed that parties ashore tend to be breaking up much earlier when a race is being held the next day. "Competitive racers don't drink during a race, period."

Collisions Involving Personal Watercraft

Whether you "love 'em" or "hate 'em," personal watercraft (PWCs) are everywhere these days and difficult to ignore. As a practical matter, if you're on a boat that is approaching a PWC, the same Rules of the Road are applicable: PWCs are boats too. Many PWC owners also own larger boats and are well aware of the Rules. However, according to a study of the BoatU.S. Marine Insurance claim files, most collisions involve someone other than the PWC's owner; a majority of accidents occur when a PWC is being operated by a friend or by one of the insured owner's children.

Perhaps because of a PWC's relatively small size—about 8 feet—people who would never consider letting someone use the family cruiser have no qualms about loaning a PWC to an inexperienced friend or even a child. The following claim is typical:

According to this PWC's owner, he was watching from his living room window as his 15-year-old son and two of the son's friends motored quietly out of the creek. His son was driving his father's PWC, and the other two boys—both inexperienced boaters—were on a PWC they had borrowed from friends. The boys' boating behavior, according to the father, had been exemplary. He was surprised

This PWC was damaged when it collided with a 17-foot runabout. Its driver, a 51-year-old man who had borrowed the PWC, was seriously injured. According to the BoatU.S. Marine Insurance claim files, a majority of PWC accidents involve borrowed PWCs.

when he found out a short time later that the boys had been involved in a serious collision (although luckily no one was injured).

A local game warden, on the other hand, was not surprised. The warden had seen the boys operating their PWCs recklessly earlier that day and had issued them a verbal warning. When the warden got a call reporting a collision between two PWCs, he said he knew immediately who was involved. He charged the two drivers with reckless driving, which would go on their driving record once they started driving cars.

As can be seen from the following table, the majority of PWC accidents occur when someone other than the owner is operating the PWC.

PWC Accidents

Person at Helm	Accident Percentage
owner	18%
friend of owner	53%
owner's child	29%

BoatU.S. Marine Insurance isn't alone in noting the correlation between a lack of experience and PWC accidents. A study in Florida of PWCs involved in accidents found that 68% of the operators had either rented or borrowed the PWCs, and 47% of the accidents involved drivers with less than 10 hours' experience.

Back in the early 1990s, states began passing laws restricting the use of PWCs after a series of much-publicized accidents involving small children. Florida was one of the first states to place restrictions on the age of a PWC operator, passing its law after a 5-year-old boy was killed when the PWC he was operating collided with a ski boat. Similar laws have now been passed in most states, with the average age being in the mid-teens.

Loaning Your PWC: Some Suggestions

Many states now have laws that require a potential operator to take a boating education course before operating a PWC. Most of these courses, however, don't require hands-on operation of a PWC but focus instead on teaching things like the Rules of the Road.

If you own a PWC, don't loan it (or any other boat) to anyone who doesn't have basic boating skills. The waterways are too crowded, and a PWC is too speedy and erratic. Insist that the person take a boating course even if it isn't mandatory in your state, and encourage him or her to gain experience by crewing on larger boats before you introduce him to the quirky handling characteristics of your PWC. This *can't* be done in a few minutes by showing someone how to work

PWC Inexperience and "Operator Error"

IN ONE OF THE MORE PUBLICIZED PWC accidents, a college student on a rented PWC was killed when he fell into the propeller of a large powerboat in Miami's Biscayne Bay. The news made headlines nationwide, not because PWC accidents are unusual—far from it—but because the powerboat was owned by Gloria Estefan, a popular singer. Tucked away in the copy about the accident was a telling fact: the man who was killed, according to his father, had never operated a PWC before the accident.

As the man approached Estefan's boat, he slowed down and abruptly lost control of the PWC. (Unlike larger boats, PWCs can't be steered at slow speeds.) According to eyewitness accounts of the accident, the PWC began heading toward the larger boat's stern. Eyewitnesses said he moved the handlebars back and forth, but the PWC didn't respond. At the last moment, the man accelerated, apparently attempting to regain control, but it was too late. The PWC struck the boat's transom, and the driver was thrown into the props. He was one of twelve people who died in Florida that year while operating a PWC.

Captain Michael Lamphear of the Florida Marine Patrol, who investigated the man's death in Biscayne Bay, says that while PWCs make up a small fraction of the registered boats in Florida, they are involved in over a third of the accidents. Captain Lamphear attributes the high number of accidents to operator error. He says that anyone who doesn't have operating experience on a PWC, even if they have a lot of experience operating more conventional boats, won't realize that it can't be controlled at slow speeds, that it will come off a plane quickly, and that it turns much faster than an average runabout.

His view is supported by the BoatU.S. Marine Insurance claim files. In one claim, a 27-year old Florida woman on a PWC turned slightly to avoid an oncoming boat, lost control, and slammed into a concrete bridge abutment. Miraculously, she wasn't hurt. In another case, a skipper in Virginia ran into his own anchored boat because he failed to realize that he couldn't steer at slow speeds. Two other men were injured on PWCs when one turned abruptly (without looking) and hit the other, who had been following too closely. An investigator concluded that both were at fault.

the accelerator, make turns, etc. The BoatU.S. Foundation for Boating Safety has an online PWC course available at www.boatus.com. Many dealers also have printed materials on PWC operation and safety videos they will loan to customers or potential customers. And both the U.S. Power Squadrons and the U.S. Coast Guard Auxiliary offer excellent courses that address the safe operation of PWCs.

There is no substitute for hands-on experience. Spend time instructing a beginner until you are both comfortable that he or she knows how to safely operate a PWC. *Finally, make sure beginners stay well away from other boat traffic!* Even with proper instruction, their driving at first is likely to be erratic.

Avoiding Tugs and Barges

It's easy to understand why someone might fail to notice a PWC, which can zip around other boats like a tiny water bug, but how could a sober and otherwise competent skipper collide with a tug and barge? The massive bulk of most barges should attract the attention of even the most distracted skipper. And tugs, with their broad beams and deep displacement hulls, plod through the water like giant seagoing turtles, giving a skipper plenty of time to get out of their way.

But tugs and barges aren't like other boats. Offshore, a tug and its barge may be separated by as much as one-half mile, with the massive steel towing cable hidden beneath the water. And in narrow waterways, a tug's deep draft, wide beam, and powerful engine can create tremendous suction around the hull. When you consider that tugs and barges must wind their way through narrow rivers and canals that were never intended for anything more than tiny canal boats, it becomes easier to understand why collisions occur.

Tugs and Barges Offshore

"A most unusual sensation," was how the skipper of a 32-foot sailboat in one claim described how it felt to tack behind a tug and then stop abruptly in 48 feet of water. There was a "scraping sound" coming from somewhere down by the keel, and his first reaction was that he had hit a submarine. But as the boat was spun around he glanced over his shoulder and saw a barge off in the distance heading directly toward him. Scary? You bet. In a matter of seconds he would be run down by a barge—unless his keel wasn't cut in half first by the steel cable.

In this case, the skipper was lucky. A deckhand on the tug had seen what was happening and immediately alerted the bridge. By putting the tug's engines in neutral, the tug's operator slackened the cable and freed the sailboat in time to avoid a collision with the barge. A damage survey later indicated that the 1½-inch cable had been well on its way—within millimeters—of sawing completely through the fiberglass surrounding the keel.

Bruce Law, one of the owners of Allied Towing in Norfolk, Virginia, says that crossing over tow cables is the number-one cause of serious collisions between recreational boats and tugs. Law says that a skipper involved in a collision typically never realizes that the "big ugly box" is connected to the tug via a thick steel cable. These cables can be up to 3 inches in diameter and are capable of sawing boats in half in a matter of seconds.

Don't be deceived by the smooth water behind a tug; tow cables are almost always underwater. On inland waters, where the tug and barge may be relatively close, the cable may be only a few feet beneath the waves. At sea, where the distance between the tug and barge may be as much as a half mile, a cable could be 100 feet underwater or close to the surface, since the cable acts like a shock absorber in heavy seas and is constantly rising and dropping. Skippers of small boats should never attempt to cross a tug's wake without first checking to make sure that there is not a barge somewhere off in the distance.

Narrow Waterways and Canals

In another claim, the skipper of a 36-foot sailboat inched his boat farther to port to see beyond the series of barges pulled by a towboat he had been following in a narrow canal. Not caring much for the smell of diesel fumes or the sight of the nearest barge's rust-streaked stern, he decided to pass.

Before passing, the skipper tried to raise the towboat's captain on VHF Channel 16, but got no answer. He then switched to Channel 68, but again, his call raised only silence. He tried signaling, but the steady drone of the towboat's massive diesels drowned out his feeble air horn.

So the skipper threw the helm over, kicked the throttle forward, and began inching past the line of elephantine barges. When he was abeam of one of the barges, his boat and the barge began mysteriously edging toward each other. He maneuvered to give it more room and abruptly grounded. The larger vessel scraped the side of the sailboat's hull, doing considerable damage.

When his VHF and whistle signals went unanswered, the impatient skipper should have waited for open water before attempting to pass. Engineers who never anticipated today's mammoth towboats and barges designed most canals centuries ago. The sailboat and barges began "mysteriously" edging toward each other because of the inevitable suction created by the deep-draft towboat and barges moving through the shallow, narrow canal. One former tugboat captain said he had seen the water level drop as much as a foot in a narrow canal as water was pulled into the tug's prop. But while this phenomenon is a fact of life for towboat captains, it can be an unpleasant surprise to skippers of smaller boats.

Towboat captains are familiar with maneuvering in restricted waters, and the sailboat skipper was correct to have tried to raise him on his VHF before passing.

A deep-draft tug and barge moving through a shallow canal create enormous suction as water is pulled into the props. This suction can temporarily reduce a canal's depth by as much as a foot. The message for skippers of small boats? Stay clear!

His mistake was trying to raise the skipper on Channel 16; towboat and most other commercial captains communicate on Channel 13.

Rivers and Currents

At least one claim in BoatU.S.'s files involved a bass boat in a fishing tournament. As usual, the local fishing tournament had attracted hordes of small boats to the river. Trophies don't go to the timid, so the skipper and his partner anchored their bass boat in a favored spot that was close to the channel near a sharp bend in the river.

After only a few minutes of fishing, the skipper spotted an empty barge poking its gigantic bow around the bend. At first he thought the barge was heading toward the beach, but a few seconds later it began swinging toward his anchored boat. The two men stared briefly at the towering wall of steel moving ominously toward them before frantically trying to start the engine. It coughed a few times, sputtered, and quit. The skipper and his fishing buddy then dove overboard shortly before their boat was run down. Both men had no trouble reaching shore.

The tug's captain had been using the current and the wind, which was blowing 20 to 35 knots that day, to "flank" his barge through the tight bend in the river. It appeared to the men on the smaller boat that the wind had caught the barge's bow and swung it too far toward the middle of the river. The tug's captain, however, claimed he was right where he wanted to be, and the small fishing boat had left him no room to maneuver.

The sheer size and number of barges that must be maneuvered through currents and narrow bends by a tug's pilot boggles the mind. Course changes as well as starting and stopping take time and require planning. Rule 9b of the Navigation Rules states that "A vessel of less than 20 meters in length or a sailing vessel shall not impede the passage of a vessel which can safely navigate only within a narrow channel or fairway." Certainly recreational boats are much more maneuverable and should give the tugs and barges ample room.

This sailboat collided with a coal barge at night in Chesapeake Bay. Although conditions were clear and the seas were calm, the sailboat's skipper didn't spot the barge's lights until seconds before the collision, most likely because they were hidden among the lights onshore.

Avoiding Inland Towboats:
A View From the Bridge

IN *LIFE ON THE MISSISSIPPI*, Mark Twain bitterly lamented the passing of the steamboats, upon whose decks he had studied to be a pilot—"a profession I have loved better than any I have followed since." Despite its prominence in American folklore, the golden era of steamboats lasted less than a generation—"a twinkling of an eye"—from the 1820s to the Civil War. Railroads intruded everywhere, carrying passengers from Mississippi, Kentucky, and Tennessee to the thriving cities up north. And freight, which had been the economic lifeblood of steamboats, was increasingly carried by "vulgar little tugs" that Twain said could tow the equivalent of a dozen steamer cargoes.

Standing on the deck of the *Christopher M. Parsonage* near its home port in St. Louis, it's difficult to think of a towboat as vulgar—the low, sweeping design and towering superstructure of this one are reminiscent of Twain's steamboats. And it certainly isn't small; at 180 feet and with 8,000 horsepower, the five-year-old *Parsonage* is large and tremendously powerful, with state-of-the-art electronics on the bridge as well as fax machines, computers, and telephones.

The *Parsonage* is headed downriver to New Orleans with a load of grain and coke. It begins the 1,200-mile trip with only fifteen barges, but after making several brief stops downriver, it will soon be pushing thirty-five 200-by-35-foot barges, a cargo that is the equivalent of 665 railroad cars or 1,820 tractor trailers. The first question that is likely to pop into anyone's head is, How do you steer

5 acres of barges down the Mississippi's swift current, over its constantly shifting shoals, and around its notoriously tight bends? In Twain's day, a pilot had to spend many years learning boats and the river, and that's still the case today. The *Parsonage*'s captain, David Hogancamp, and pilot, Henry Kelly —the only crew aboard who ever touch the helm—have over seventy-five years' experience on towboats between them. Both started on deck and worked their way up to the pilothouse; there is no other way. Several years ago, Hogancamp said that a school tried to speed up the process by turning out towboat "pilots" in eighteen months. It didn't work; the graduates were woefully unprepared for the job, and the idea was soon abandoned.

One reason piloting can't be taught in a classroom becomes clear as we approach the lock above St. Louis. The tow at this point in is "only" 105 feet wide and 1,000 feet long. Standing in the wheelhouse, four stories above the deck, the bow of the tow is almost ⅕ mile away. The lock is 110 feet wide, which means that Kelly has 2½ feet on either side to somehow coax the barges in through the narrow opening. Slowly, even though the boat is in current and the bow is in calm water, the tow glides into the lock. It never touches, not even once, a feat that seems impossible. Is Kelly some sort of magician? "Naw," he says in his thick Tennessee drawl. "If you do something long enough, sooner or later you get the hang of it."

Judging from the dark scrapes at the lock's

Avoiding Inland Towboats (continued)

entrance and along the sides, not all pilots have gotten the hang of it. Hogancamp says later that there is a wide range of competence among the various pilots and captains (both are equally qualified to operate towboats; captains have the added responsibility of managing the crews). MEMCO Barge Line, which operates the *Parsonage*, is the industry's third or fourth largest towboat company and has a reputation for paying excellent wages and benefits. The crews live in air-conditioned quarters and have luxuries such as satellite television, movies, and good food. Some of the smaller companies operate on a shoestring with much older boats (quite a few go back to the forties and fifties) and lower pay, which tends to attract less qualified crews. Hogancamp cites as an example the infamous towboat that collided with a railroad bridge in Alabama one night in a thick fog. Sometime later that same night a train plunged off the bridge, and the case received national attention. An investigation found that the towboat's captain had mistakenly entered the wrong canal. Hogancamp noted that this captain had taken the licensing exam seven times before passing. He also notes that it is accepted practice among towboat captains not to operate in fog, at least not when a boat is headed downriver with the current. Despite the two impressively large radar screens on the bridge, the *Parsonage* will be nudged into the riverbank twice on the trip to wait out early morning fogs.

Twain described the river between St. Louis and Cairo as varied and beautiful. The woods, flat plains, and farms are still there, but the river itself has been changed slightly by the Army Corps of Engineers. There are dikes—piles of rocks perpendicular to the shore—that reach out into the river to control silting and promote a single, deeper channel. Like most attempts to tame nature, the dikes are only partially successful. The channel for much of the river changes constantly, and the Coast Guard is hard pressed to keep buoys in place. It's worth noting that the charts used by the *Parsonage* don't indicate buoys or depths. Several times on the trip, buoys appear to have shifted, prompting Hogancamp and Kelly to "read" the water and find the channel. Towboat skippers talk to each other frequently, and the information about shifting channels is passed along to the companies and the Coast Guard. Groundings are not uncommon and can sometimes result in tows coming apart and barges going adrift. One night when the *Parsonage* encounters an especially shallow area, Kelly notifies the office at MEMCO. A smaller boat is dispatched to take soundings, which are then shared with other towboat operators and the Coast Guard.

Flanking is a technique that is used several times on the trip to turn the tow, either when a buoy appears to have shifted or to negotiate a sharp bend in the river. The tow's bow is edged toward the bend, almost touching the shore, while the engines are backed to keep the towboat's stern out in the river. The current, and not the boat's engines, then slowly pushes the tow around the bend. The entire process can sometimes take a half-hour or more. It's a technique that can be confusing to skippers of small boats.

When asked about their own encounters with small boats, both Hogancamp and Kelly immediately mention licenses (neither has been personally involved in a collision). Perhaps because they

A view from the bridge of the *Christopher M. Parsonage* (taken with a telephoto lens). The *Parsonage* is pushing the equivalent of 665 railroad cars or 1,820 tractor trailers of grain and coke down the Mississippi River. Don't plan on it turning or stopping quickly.

David Hogancamp (shown) and Henry Kelly, the only two aboard who touch the *Christopher M. Parsonage*'s helm, have over 75 years' experience operating towboats between them. In *Life on the Mississippi*, Mark Twain noted, "The true pilot cares nothing about anything on earth but the river, and his pride in his occupation surpasses the pride of kings." His words still ring true today.

themselves had to put in so many years of work and study to become licensed, both note that anyone can buy a small boat and go out on the water. No license is needed, which means that the skippers aren't required to know fundamentals like horn signals or how to use a VHF radio, both of which are used routinely by towboat skippers to avoid collisions. Several times on the trip down river, skippers of small boats call the *Parsonage* on VHF Channel 13 to ask how they should pass. The answer typically is a terse "one toot" (to port) or "two toots" (to starboard), depending on the situation. Hogancamp always thanks them. He says that the owners of larger recreational boats traveling up or down the river during the week—he calls them transients—typically know and follow the Rules. Problems are most likely to occur on weekends near cities—Cincinnati, St. Louis, Louisville, Pittsburgh, Madison—when the waters become crowded with hundreds of small boats.

By late Friday afternoon, the *Parsonage* has picked up all its barges, and the tow now measures an astounding 245 feet by 1,000 feet. The weekend is getting underway, at least for the owners of small boats that have begun buzzing around the tow. At one point, Hogancamp points to a small boat crossing under *Parsonage*'s bow and wonders aloud why it doesn't pass astern. "What happens if his engine stalls or he hits a log?" Hogancamp seems agitated. One well-documented accident occurred last year when a small boat's engine broke down, and it drifted into a towboat. The anchor rode didn't hold against the river's strong current. It takes at least a mile to stop the *Parsonage* when it's moving downriver, and a sudden sharp turn is out of the question on weekends—a fact that seems lost on the smaller boats' skippers. Hogancamp says he's seen parents pulling their children on water skis and inflatable tubes directly in front of giant towboats. As a parent himself, it's a practice that makes him especially angry.

At dusk, *Parsonage* passes five or six small boats that are beached on one of the many stretches of sand along the river. It's a pleasant

Avoiding Inland Towboats (continued)

scene with people stretched out on lawn chairs surrounded by charcoal grills and coolers. Both Hogancamp and Kelly mention that alcohol can sometimes be a problem on the river. The *Parsonage*'s tow is lighted on both port and starboard with an amber light blinking amidships at the bow. Most tows aren't lighted abaft the bow, which means there can be a stretch of 1,000 feet that is unlighted. Accidents on the river often happen at night, because small-boat operators drive their boats toward the dark area between the bow lights and the lights on the towboat. Most of the accidents they mention involve alcohol.

The trip passes slowly and without incident; the "noble science of piloting," that Twain feared was passing 150 years ago, is still very much in evidence on the *Parsonage*. The boat and even the crew ("rough and hardy men . . . yet faithful to promises and duty") are remarkably the same. The river itself is little changed. Thanks to its periodic floods, there are no con-

dos or amusement parks crowding its banks. The few cities and towns that are in evidence are safely behind levees, a respectable distance from the river's powerful flow.

While the Mississippi remains a working river dominated by the giant towboats, the one thing that has changed is the small boats that are now so prevalent. Whether these smaller boats can share the river in anything approaching harmony with the towboats would seem to be completely up to the skippers of the smaller boats.

Avoiding Collisions with Tugs and Barges: A Few Suggestions

1. Remember Rule 9b of the Navigation Rules: "A vessel of less than 20 meters in length or a sailing vessel shall not impede the passage of a vessel which can safely navigate only within a narrow channel or fairway."

Recognizing Lights on Tugs and Barges

The importance of running lights is demonstrated in this claim. As the skipper recalled, "I was heading for Cobb Island [on the Potomac River] when I saw this tug coming. I thought I was on a safe course to pass when I lost his green running light. I realized he was getting close and swung to starboard, which turned out to be the wrong direction. I went across his bow and got hit right in the middle of my boat."

With all there is to remember these days, it isn't easy to learn the various light configurations for tugs and barges. The masthead, stern, and yellow towing lights are configured differently to indicate towing distance, the size of the tug and/or barge, and whether it is behind, ahead of, or beside the tug. (And if you're on the Mississippi River, the rules for lights are different on either side of the Huey P. Long Bridge.)

But throwing up your hands and not bothering to learn the light configura-

2. In narrow waterways and canals, passing a towboat can be especially difficult as water—and occasionally small boats—is pulled against the hull by the giant props. Don't pass until you can give the bigger boat a lot of room.

3. When passing, use your VHF radio (Channel 13) to contact the towboat's operator for instructions. Know the whistle signals. These are much more likely to be given over the VHF. The signals you are most likely to hear on an inland river are one or two short blasts. One whistle means "I intend to leave you on my port side." Two whistles means "I intend to keep you on my starboard side." Three short blasts means the vessel is backing. And—an important one—four or more short blasts means danger. The latter won't be given on the VHF.

4. Engines break down, and any boat that operates on a body of water with large boats and a current needs a longer rode than a boat that spends its time put-

putting around a shallow lake. Some rivers can be surprisingly deep with strong currents, especially in the early spring and summer. Carrying at least 150 feet of rode with 10 feet of chain would not be overkill.

5. Know the various configurations for navigation lights. The masthead, stern, and yellow towing lights are configured differently to indicate whether a tow is being pushed or pulled; the towing distance; the size of the tug and/or barge; and whether it's behind, ahead of, or beside the tug. On the Mississippi, the rules for lights are different on either side of the Huey P. Long Bridge.

6. Avoid sharing locks with large towboats. There have been many instances where a smaller boat was shoved into the lock walls by prop wash. If you're going to share a lock with a large towboat, talk to the captain and lock operator before selecting a spot, well away from the props, to secure your boat.

tions for tugs and barges is a dangerous mistake. In the claim above, the skipper recognized just one of the lights—the starboard light—amid all of the other lights on the tug. Although he could see the lights, he had no idea what they meant. Had the skipper been able to recognize the lights, he would have known where the tug was headed and that it was pushing a barge. Since he couldn't discern the light configurations, he should have steered well away from the tug.

Avoiding Big Ships

The Rules take into account the lack of maneuverability of large ships. You can't expect to cruise down the middle of a shipping channel and get off lightly in court using some David and Goliath "I'm just a little boat" defense if there's a collision (and if you survive). Quite the contrary. Rule 9b is very specific: "A vessel of less than 20 meters [66 feet] in length or a sailing vessel shall not impede the passage of a vessel which can safely navigate only within a narrow channel or fairway."

Avoiding Big Ships: A View From the Bridge

NOT TOO LONG AGO, *Sea-Land Performance* was the largest containership in the world—almost 1,000 feet long and over 100 feet wide—so you might think the first thing you would notice about the ship would be its enormous size. But as it is eased by the tugs into its berth in Charleston, South Carolina, the stacks of containers piled high up on its decks obscure *Performance*'s towering hull and massive superstructure. Eight hundred of the 2,300 containers are about to be off-loaded by the two gangs of longshoremen—sixty-two men—who are standing by at a cost of over $2,000 an hour. It's almost dusk on a steamy July evening, and the longshoremen are scheduled to work most of the night.

Seconds after the docklines are secured, two giant cranes swing out over the foredeck, and the longshoremen swarm up the gangplank. Shipping is an intense business. Unlike a few decades ago, when the job of unloading a ship could take days or even weeks, *Performance*'s breakneck schedule means the ship will be in port for only a few hours. The Charleston terminal is miles from downtown and the crew, the ones who go ashore, barely have time for a quick meal. Ship's officers remain aboard, taking care of dozens of small details: paying crew who are leaving and completing paperwork on their replacements; arranging to have a refrigerator container repaired; and answering questions about which of the other containers must be reloaded.

Captain Russell Woodill finally sits down at 11 P.M. to talk for a few minutes about shipping schedules, small boats, and the problems of operating a giant ship with a crew of only twenty-one. He begins by saying that fierce competition in the shipping business means a U.S.-registered ship must operate at "razor-thin" profit margins, and once he commits to an arrival time—and to having the crew of longshoremen standing by—he is under tremendous pressure to get the ship alongside the dock. That doesn't mean *Performance* is going to run down small boats, of course, but he says it would certainly make his job easier if small boats didn't cruise in the shipping lanes. Captain Woodill notes that in Rotterdam and Bremerhaven, two of the European ports visited regularly by *Performance*, the movements of shipping and small boats are strictly controlled by vessel traffic systems. In the United States, there are no comparable systems, and it's up to the skippers of small boats to stay clear of large ships.

The next morning, two of the mates are on the bridge plotting the course on a chart in preparation for the ship's 6 A.M. departure. As the last of the containers is off-loaded, Steve Swann Jr., the pilot who will direct *Performance* through the harbor to the open ocean, comes aboard. The engines have already been started, and everyone seems eager to get underway, if for no other reason than to escape the swarms of mosquitoes on the bridge. Commands are given via handheld radio, the tugs roar to life, and the ship moves slowly away from the dock.

Once clear, *Performance* begins inching slowly forward. Looking toward the bow, way off in the distance, it seems impossible that anything as large as an office building could be maneuvered gingerly through a twisting, narrow channel. *Performance*'s visibility forward was reduced during the night, according to one of the mates,

Looking forward from the bridge of *Sea-Land Performance* as it enters Port Everglades, Florida, on a "quiet" weekday morning. To put the size of the ship into perspective, this shot of the ship's bow and beyond was taken with a telephoto lens.

when the containers were off-loaded. The ship is now sitting higher out of the water, giving *Performance* a "blind spot" at the helm of 1,000 feet—almost a quarter of a mile—ahead.

An able-bodied seaman (AB) at the masthead acts as lookout while *Performance* is leaving the harbor, and another AB steers the ship with a small wheel that looks like something taken off a car. Rudder adjustments are done electronically, like playing a video game. Swann begins ordering course changes—"Come right ten degrees"—and each order is repeated by the AB at the helm. Two large signs, placed in front of the helm by law, indicate RIGHT RUDDER and LEFT RUDDER, with arrows to assist the helmsman; any lapse in attention could be catastrophic.

As the ship approaches the open ocean, Pilot Swann begins talking about his experience with small boats, interrupting himself occasionally to make a course correction. Sometimes, he says, a small boat will come straight at the ship's bow, as if the boat's driver is trying to scare his girlfriend. Other times, skippers either don't know or don't care that a ship is there. While he is talking, two small center-console fishing boats,

one following the other, disappear beneath the bow. Swann walks over to the bridge until he sees them come zipping out the other side of the blind spot. If one of their engines had stalled, he says, there wouldn't have been time to stop the ship.

That's an understatement. Even at slow speeds, with the engine at full astern, it would take almost a mile to stop *Performance*. The ship can't be turned sharply either, even if there were ample room in the channel, which there isn't. Making a sharp turn would over-torque the engine, shut it down, and leave the ship out of control in a crowded harbor with no power and no steerage.

As we approach the ocean, *Performance* approaches a sportfisherman cruising on the outside of the channel. Swann looks over and nods his head approvingly. That's how it's done. He deplores the lack of experience shown by many other boaters, and wonders what Charleston Harbor will be like when the new container facility and 460-slip marina are completed. The harbor itself can't be made any larger, and he worries that Charleston will become as jammed with ships and smaller

Avoiding Big Ships (continued)

boats as Port Everglades, the harbor in Florida where *Performance* is headed.

Once we clear the sea buoy, the pilot departs, and the ship takes on an air of businesslike efficiency with only two crew—one officer and one AB—remaining on the bridge. The lookout is brought down from the masthead. Under routine conditions, the job of looking out is handled by the watch officer.

The ship is put on autopilot, and the wheel won't be touched again until we arrive at Port Everglades. To a small-boat skipper, the use of an autopilot and lack of a dedicated lookout on an oceangoing ship is daunting, but after an hour or two, it becomes clear that the ship is not cruising down the coast blindly. The AB does odd jobs on the bridge and glances around frequently for traffic. The mate also keeps an eye open for small boats and does the navigating. In bad weather, at night, and near the coast, the AB and mate say they devote most of their time to watching for other boats.

While the size of the ship is intimidating, much of the electronics on *Performance*'s bridge are comfortably familiar to a small-boat navigator. There are charts and dividers, the same ones you see in boating catalogs. Position is indicated on an ordinary-looking Trimble GPS (with built-in differential). A Standard Horizon VHF near the nav station is left on at all times. There are two backup Trimble GPS units, an old Northstar loran, two backup VHFs, and three pairs of Swift binoculars.

The two radar units on *Performance*, however, aren't your usual small-boat models. One has a wide 10 cm wave to pick up large targets sooner, and the other has a narrow 3 cm band

to pick up smaller targets more clearly. (The latter is so sensitive, one of the mates said it has picked up schools of tuna feeding on the surface.) Both sets plot targets automatically and give the closest point of approach (CPA), a number that a mate refers to constantly when approaching another vessel. One comment, made by several of the mates, is that they are frequently surprised when a large approaching blip on the radar screen turns out to be a small boat with a radar reflector. In rough weather, when the smaller boats look like whitecaps to the naked eye and sea clutter obscures weaker blips on the screen, a good radar reflector is invaluable.

While the technology may be continually upgraded, life at sea seems remarkably the same as it has been for decades. The ship has miles of wires and pipes, mysterious-looking valves, rust, splattered paint, coils of incredibly large docklines, and bare lightbulbs in protective cages. On deck, there is the smell of salt air and diesel fuel—*Performance* burns 75 *tons* of fuel a day—and the sound of water hissing by the hull. And from everywhere on the ship, you hear the hum of the giant, 28,000 hp diesel.

One thing that has changed is the size of the crew. Thirty years ago, Captain Woodill says the typical ship carried 10,200 tons of cargo and had a crew of forty. *Performance*, by contrast, carries 42,000 tons of cargo with a crew of twenty-one. Of the twenty-one, three are cooks or stewards, seven work in the engine room, one is a radio operator, and one is the captain. This leaves nine men to stand the watches, navigate, chip paint, troubleshoot containers, etc. And while ships in the future will be larger—

much larger—Captain Woodill says, the size of the crews will shrink further.

A European study sanctioned by the International Maritime Organization (IMO) on modern, specially equipped ships, found that a mate does a 54% better job of looking out on the bridge by himself than a mate and an AB. This result is being used by the companies conducting the study as a rationale for eliminating the requirement to have an AB on the bridge. If successful, one man would have to stand watch, navigate, and look out for boat traffic.

Captain Woodill says he strongly opposes the loss of the AB, even though he suspects the change is inevitable. He points to Don, the AB standing outside on the bridge, and says Don can *hear* trouble—small-boat horns, running water, whistles, buoys, stowaways, and strange noises that are often the first hint of mechanical problems. Electronic sensors, Woodill says, aren't good listeners.

Don, a veteran AB, also has uncanny vision. The first night at sea after leaving Charleston, he stands outside on the bridge staring ahead into a stiff southerly breeze. A line of thunderstorms is moving across the horizon. Keith, the third mate, moves quietly among the glowing red and green lights on the darkened bridge checking the radar, GPS, charts, and gauges. Seven times in 3 hours, Don sticks his head in the door to warn of running lights up ahead—"Lights two points off the port bow, mate." In each case, Keith walks over to the radar and adjusts the Gain until he locates and marks the target. The thunderstorms are creating clutter on the screen, and Don, the AB whose job is threatened by the European study, consistently spots targets *before* they are picked up clearly by radar.

Collisions at sea aren't always with other boats. Several years ago, *Performance* was struck by a gigantic wave one night in a North Atlantic gale. No one aboard could see the wave, much less measure its size, but on the foredeck, 50 feet above the water, the crew found that the ½-inch steel breakwater was twisted, steel stringers were bent, the foremast had been shoved aft, and a section of the deck was peeled up. *Performance* looked like it had been hit by a mortar.

One of the containers at the top of a stack was crushed and turned 45°, but the crew, despite the fierce weather, somehow managed to get it back aboard and secured. Captain Woodill notes that *Performance* has never lost a container, a record he attributes more to the ship's size than to luck or skill. Had that same monstrous wave struck a smaller ship's bow, one that was only 25 feet above the water, a dozen or so containers could easily have been swept overboard.

No one knows how many containers are drifting around the world's oceans, but Capt. Woodill says that some ships have lost thirty or forty containers in a single voyage. Lost containers aren't lighted or marked on charts, and collisions with drifting containers have sunk boats. They're one reason small boats must maintain more than a casual lookout at sea.

The following morning, *Performance* approaches Port Everglades, a surprisingly snug harbor despite its reputation, with a narrow entrance framed on two sides by rock jetties that jut several hundred yards out into the sea. The harbor itself is lined on its western shore with docks and piers that routinely accommodate large container ships and cruise ships. Numerous other smaller commercial vessels—

Avoiding Big Ships (continued)

charter fishing boats, dive boats, sightseeing boats, tugs, and barges—also visit Port Everglades. There are 40,000 recreational boats registered in the surrounding county, and many more that migrate down the Inland Waterway, which runs smack through the middle of the busy harbor.

The pilot, Brian Hanley, comes aboard near the sea buoy and quietly takes his place on the bridge. It's midweek in August, not an especially busy day on the water by South Florida standards, and there are only about a dozen boats moving between the two rock jetties. Hanley is concerned about some dark clouds a few miles to the southwest that are moving quickly out over the water with lightning flashes and two scary-looking waterspouts. He mumbles something about microbursts, and the captain nods his head. Both men seem relaxed, but their eyes don't stray from the water up ahead, not even for an instant.

As *Performance* approaches the jetties, two PWCs come zipping out from the beach to jump its wake; a large yawl stops in the middle of the channel while the crew raises the sails; and another sailboat glides serenely toward the harbor. Several boats near the sea buoy appear to be drift-fishing. Hanley seems to hold the ship back, most likely to give the small-boat skippers time to realize we are approaching. The pilot-boat that brought Hanley out to the ship, meanwhile, goes over to the inbound sailboat, and someone on the pilotboat points back toward *Performance*. The sailboat quickly moves outside the channel.

Performance continues inching slowly forward, and one by one the small boats move to the side. Once the ship reaches the harbor, it is turned and backed toward the container pier by three tugs. Hanley runs from one side of the bridge to the other, talking on his handheld radio, checking boat traffic, and calculating distances from shore and the tug's angle of pull. To an outsider, it seems like an impossible job. At least the black clouds, lightning, and waterspouts have moved safely out to sea.

After docking the ship, Hanley takes a few minutes to talk about small boats and the problems he encounters piloting large ships through a crowded harbor. Not surprisingly, he begins by saying that collisions are his number-one concern. Boats have been hit in Port Everglades and, if they were lucky, he says they just bounced along the side of the ship. He doesn't say what happened to the ones that weren't lucky. Ships have also been damaged by close encounters with small boats, like the container ship that ran aground rather than hit a sailboat, or the cruise ship that dinged a prop near the jetty trying to avoid a large yacht. Thanks to quick work by the pilot, the cruise ship missed the yacht, but the ship's owners had to refund the cost of an entire cruise because of the time it took to repair the prop. "Damned if you do, damned if you don't," Hanley says.

His advice, like Captain Woodill's and the Charleston pilot's, is for small-boat skippers to stay out of the shipping channel. As he talks, Hanley becomes much more animated, and the calmness he displayed while piloting the ship vanishes. "Boats sail in the channel, fish in the channel, cruise down the center of the channel . . . boats have even anchored in the ship channel at night!" he says. Hanley owns both a sailboat and a powerboat and says he doesn't know whether other skippers are rude or just don't know what they're doing.

After talking for a while longer about boat wakes, speed limits, and Rules of the Road, the pilot turns to leave. *Performance*'s crew has left the bridge and cranes are already unloading the first of several hundred containers. There is no time to waste; the ship is scheduled to sail again that night.

Avoiding Collisions with Large Ships: A Few Suggestions

It seems odd that men who spend half of their lives at sea would return from a long voyage only to head back to the water in a small boat, but many do. Several of *Performance*'s twenty-one-man crew and both of the harbor pilots own recreational boats. Here are their suggestions for avoiding collisions with large ships:

1. Small boats *don't* have to honor the buoys marking a big ship channel. Whenever possible, cruise to the side of the channel. *Never anchor or fish in a shipping channel.*

2. A sailboat crossing a ship channel should keep its engine running. Even if it isn't on a collision course, a large ship can blanket the wind, and the sailboat could then be drawn toward the ship's prop.

3. Big ships can be deceptively fast, even at "slow" speeds. Get out of their way early.

4. If you break down in the channel, make your condition known to an approaching ship on Channel 16. If nothing else, wave your arms. As one pilot said, "We're watching."

5. Know your whistle signals—five or more is a danger signal. (Pilots do not usually use the whistle signals before making turns because the signals could be misunderstood.)

6. When you're crossing the shipping lanes at night or in inclement weather, use a radar reflector—a good one—high in the rigging to make your boat more visible on radar. The mates on *Performance* said they had been impressed by the size of a blip on the radar screen that proved to be a small boat with a radar reflector.

7. Know your light configurations. The

Avoiding Big Ships (continued)

distance between *Performance's* lights on the bow and its lights aft is almost ¼ mile. The crew has heard stories of small boats running between the forward and aft lights on large ships thinking they were steering between two smaller ships.

When You See a Ship Approaching

One point made by Captain Woodill and the two pilots is that American-registered ships like *Sea-Land Performance* have the highest standards in the world. The crews, the ships themselves, and the equipment are second to none. The standards vary for other countries, and there can be significant differences in the training and professionalism of the crews. Once when *Performance* was in Galveston, Texas, to cite one example, Captain Woodill overheard a foreign ship that was approaching a sea buoy trying to raise the local harbor pilot. The pilot responded, but the ship was nowhere to be seen. Sometime later, they learned the ship had arrived at the wrong harbor. Captain Woodill wasn't sure what flag the ship was flying.

It's a rule that the Coast Guard takes seriously. In one case, a ship's pilot was preparing to pass a large tug and barge at night in Delaware Bay's shipping channel when a sailboat ahead failed to tack and instead maintained its course across the ship's bow. The pilot sounded five horn blasts (danger), which only seemed to confuse the sailboat's skipper, who held his course. The pilot was forced to turn the ship, which collided with the tug, inflicting a total of $377,000 worth of damage to the two vessels. The Coast Guard located the sailboat's skipper later that night and held him completely liable for the damage. It is worth noting that the sailboat's skipper only had $100,000 worth of liability coverage, which meant that he was *personally* responsible for the remaining $277,000!

Passing Under Drawbridges

Why is it that the skipper of a boat tends to be slightly nervous, if only for a moment or two, when passing beneath a drawbridge? A horn is sounded, the bridge tender responds, and the bridge opens. Boats proceed *slowly* through, like cars at an intersection when a traffic light changes. The course is certainly well defined and there are lights, port and starboard, to mark the course at night. What could go wrong?

According to the claim files, a lot. For one thing, skippers become impatient waiting for the span to open and shove the throttle forward—way forward—no doubt hoping to make up for lost time. One type of accident, perhaps the most common, involves boats that get slammed into the bridges and abutments by the wakes of other boats. The skipper of a boat that was going under a bridge in Florida, for example, was confronted by the wake of a larger boat blasting through in the other direction. He reported later, "The wake caught us as we were passing under the bridge and threw us into the roadbed superstructure." As with other incidents involving wakes and bridges, the skipper was eager (an understatement) to get the name of the other boat, but had to spend over 30 minutes dislodging his radar arch from the bridge.

The current beneath bridges can be surprisingly tricky and is another cause of accidents. A normally docile tidal flow can become a swiftly flowing torrent as the water is squeezed between the bridge abutments. A skipper may have to increase speed in order to maintain steerage, but not so much that it results in a huge wake. As a practical matter, boats that are traveling with the current that might be having trouble maintaining steerage should be given the right-of-way. Another consideration includes the size and maneuverability of larger vessels, especially tugs and barges, which should also be allowed to pass through before you proceed. For example, a 13-foot Boston Whaler tried to zip under a bridge in Massachusetts and was thrown into an abutment by the wake of a large ferry. The smaller boat was almost swamped.

Bridge Tenders and Mast Benders

There are a few bridge tender horror stories, like the inexperienced tender in Florida, on his first day of work, who neglected to close the gates and stop traffic

After a bridge is opened, proceed *slowly* through the opened span. Any current increases significantly as it is squeezed beneath the pilings. Boats traveling with the current, which may be having trouble maintaining steerage, should be allowed to pass through first.

before raising the span. According to newspaper accounts, one of the cars crossing the bridge couldn't stop and jumped across 8 feet of open water before landing safely on the other side. The newspaper reported that the bridge tender, a 16-year-old who had lied about his age to get the job, fled on his bicycle.

Fortunately, there are no accounts in the BoatU.S. Marine Insurance claim files about cars landing on boats. Unfortunately, there are several accounts of other bridge tender indiscretions, such as bridges that weren't opened sufficiently or were closed prematurely while boats were still passing underneath. A bridge tender in Massachusetts, for example, flashed on a green light to coax the skipper of a 32-foot sailboat through the bridge before the span was completely opened. As he approached the bridge, the sailboat's skipper became apprehensive about the clearance, but it was too late: "The forestay struck the bridge, and we could feel the boat bounce back." The bridge tender later admitted his error.

Clearance at mean high water is indicated on a navigation chart. A bridge should also have markings beneath its tallest span to indicate clearance. Boats can often get under many bridges by lowering antennas, outriggers, etc. If a bridge is opened, skippers of sailboats and larger powerboats should be careful to stay directly in the center as they pass through. In one example of the consequences of not following this guideline, the skipper of a sailboat in New Jersey strayed too far to the right, struck the lower portion of the opened span, and lost his mast.

There have been instances when skippers disagreed with bridge tenders about the clearance of a bridge. A BoatU.S. member in New Jersey wrote that a bridge tender argued with him after he had requested that the bridge be opened. The bridge marker was indicating 39 feet of clearance, and the skipper's boat had a 42-foot mast. The tender was eventually persuaded to open the bridge, but the member asked whether his BoatU.S. yacht policy would have covered the damage to his mast if he had obeyed the bridge tender (it would have) and wondered what can be done if a bridge tender is negligent.

Bridges come under the authority of various county, state, and other agencies, and tenders are typically very well trained. All, however, operate under the authority of Title 33 of the Code of Federal Regulations. Unreasonable bridge operators, or disagreements over clearance, should be brought to the attention of the authority that has jurisdiction. (Call the state highway department; if they don't have jurisdiction, they will know who does.)

Passing Through a Drawbridge: The Basics

The sound signal to request an opening is *one long and one short blast*. This signal must be used even if the bridge is already open, and even if the signal has already been given by another boat. The bridge tender will respond to each signal separately: one long and one short blast if the bridge will be opened; five short blasts if the bridge can't be opened immediately. (If you have to wait, stay clear; currents near a bridge can be tricky.) A bridge that has restricted hours should be indicated on your chart.

An alternative to all this tooting of horns is to contact the bridge tender on your VHF, on either Channels 13, 16, or maybe 9. Transmissions must be made on 1 watt and the caller (you) should specify the name of the bridge you need raised. If there is another bridge directly beside the bridge you're trying to raise, each must be notified separately (by sound signal or by VHF) before either span is opened. Some bridges have red and green signal lights (other than the lights marking the channel) to stop and start boats.

If, for whatever reason, a bridge that is open needs to be closed immediately, the bridge tender will sound five short blasts. You should acknowledge the signal by also sounding five short blasts—and quickly getting out of the way.

What Should You Do If Your Boat Is in a Collision?

Let's say that despite your best efforts, you are involved in a collision. It may or may not be your fault. You're at the wheel, staring at a twisted, banged-up mess. Nobody was hurt, but your kids are crying, your spouse is looking at you accusingly, and it's hot. What should you do?

Above all, stay calm, and don't lose your temper. According to one account in the claim files, the skipper of a 42-foot ketch who was worried about his mast's clearance admitted that he might not have been paying attention to boats coming through the other side of the bridge. His boat banged hard against a 34-foot trawler, doing considerable damage to both boats. The trawler's skipper responded by yelling a string of obscenities, and then perhaps feeling embarrassed at his outburst, or maybe remembering his own liability, he pushed the throttle forward and left. The sailboat's skipper wasn't too eager to swap names either, considering, he said later, that the other skipper was "berserk." BoatU.S insured both boats.

It's true a collision at sea can ruin your whole day, but losing your temper after the collision could ruin the next few months. In this case, the skippers shared the same insurance company, and the issue was resolved quickly. But there have been incidents where temperamental outbursts led to lawsuits that took months, even years, to resolve.

Should you ever be involved in a collision, stay calm. Your first duty is to render assistance. This is required by tradition as well as the Federal Boat Safety Act of 1971. Serious injuries should be reported immediately to the Coast Guard or Marine Police on VHF Channels 16 or 22. The same is true of boats that are in danger of sinking. Only when crews and boats are out of danger should your attention turn to swapping names, addresses, phone numbers, state registry (or documentation) numbers, and hull identification numbers (HINs) with the other skipper.

Witnesses' names, addresses, phone numbers, and vantage points should also be collected, but don't try to get statements from witnesses. If someone was injured, you'll need to note his or her age, occupation, marital status, the nature of the injury, as well as the treatment received (including the name of the doctor). The names of any Coast Guard personnel involved could also be helpful later.

If possible, take photos of the damage to both boats, make sketches, or both. *Don't trust your memory!* Make notes on the position of the two boats, which parts of the boats were damaged, weather conditions, and events leading up to the accident. Write a more complete narrative as soon as possible after the accident.

Don't admit fault in the accident. The question of fault is usually complex, and any decision on liability will come later. Maritime law, unlike the civil law in many states, provides for an analysis of comparative or proportionate fault among the participants in a boating accident. Parties must often share fault. Remember that Rule 17(b), which requires that both boats must take action to avoid a collision, leaves open the possibility of shared fault.

Reporting Accidents

The liability question as well as any other questions, including the repair of your boat, is best resolved by contacting your insurance company's claims adjuster as soon as possible.

When you call, have your policy number ready as well as the information you collected at the scene. The claims agent can direct an investigation, assign an attorney (if necessary), and decide what, if anything, should be done to compensate injured parties. The sooner a collision claim is reported, the more likely the settlement will be fair and reasonable.

Collisions and other accidents involving injury or damage of $500 or more must also be reported to the state, usually through the state police or the state department of natural resources. These reports are forwarded to the Coast Guard. (The one exception is Alaska, where reports must be filed directly with the Coast Guard.) According to Coast Guard guidelines, the penalty for not reporting ranges from $25 to $100.

State laws vary slightly, but the Coast Guard requires that the operator of a vessel file a report within 48 hours if a person was injured and required medical treatment, a person disappeared from the vessel, or a person died within 24 hours after the accident. Otherwise, if there was damage to property or to the vessel exceeding $500, a report must be submitted within ten days.

If the operator is injured or missing, the responsibility for filing rests with the owner. And if the owner or operator can't complete the report, the obligation passes to any other person on board at the time of the accident.

When Small Accidents Cast Giant Shadows

What about "small" accidents—the ones you would rather forget and not involve your insurance company? Accidents involving other parties, even if you don't plan to file a claim, should be reported anyway. The reason has to do with liability, or the potential for liability.

In one example, several years ago, Vance Naumann was anchored on a quiet lake watching the sunset when a small sailboat appeared out of nowhere and crashed into the side of his boat. After listening to an unpleasant tirade by the boat's skipper, Naumann untangled the rigging and the other boat departed. Sometime later he repaired the damage to his boat himself without notifying BoatU.S. Marine Insurance, and the experience was soon forgotten.

Two years to the day after the incident, Naumann was working in his office when he was approached by a sheriff, gun on hip, who handed him some papers with a woman's name on them. Needless to say, he was stunned. What had he done?

He'd never heard of the woman, but it seems she owned the boat that had plowed into his boat two years before, and she was suing Naumann for the cost to repair its hull and rigging. He quickly called BoatU.S., admitting later that he felt awkward filing a claim for an incident he could barely remember.

Almost immediately, the case began taking unexpected turns. The man who was at the helm of the claimant's boat that day had only borrowed the boat, and shortly after the collision, he had moved out of the country. The boat's owner was a paralegal who waited until the day the statute of limitations would have expired to file the papers herself. A clever tactic, Naumann thought. The initial suit claimed that Naumann's boat had been anchored illegally, but this was quickly dismissed by a judge. An amended lawsuit was then filed accusing Naumann of jumping aboard the boat and tearing its sails and rigging apart. The accusations got more and more ludicrous, but they had to be defended, and witnesses who would have supported his case were long gone.

BoatU.S. provided an attorney, but the lawsuit dragged on through many months of legal maneuvering. Naumann, who had been eager to fight the suit, became increasingly discouraged. In the end the suit was settled for half the sum the plaintiff had demanded. Naumann felt as though an enormous weight had been lifted from his shoulders.

The Naumann case isn't unusual. He never imagined that he would (or could) be sued by someone who had run into his boat in broad daylight while it was anchored. For various reasons, a suit may not be filed for months or even years after an accident. In the meantime, what may have been a relatively minor incident can escalate into something altogether different.

In another case, a woman aboard a boat in Texas was injured by a pan of spilled grease. She made one trip to the doctor, and the boat's owner paid her medical bill without notifying BoatU.S. Sometime later, the owner ended his relationship with the woman, and her injury from the spilled grease suddenly took a turn for the worse. A suit was filed accusing the skipper of negligence. He finally called BoatU.S.

Whenever there is an accident that involves another party and your boat, you should report it to your insurance company *immediately*. Even if you don't file a claim, an adjuster will be able to give you professional assistance and may contact the other party on your behalf and pay any medical bills up to the limit on the policy. By contacting the other party quickly, potential problems can usually be averted, but once an attorney is hired, reaching an agreement becomes much more expensive and complicated.

Subrogation: Another Reason to Report Claims Quickly Another reason to report claims quickly involves something called *subrogation*, which means that whoever is at fault in an accident should pay for repairs. This doesn't happen automatically. In some cases, your insurance company may be able to negotiate with the other party to recover some or all of the repair costs. A man whose boat was bashed against the dock by a collision with a tug assumed that the tug company would do the honorable thing and pay for the damage. After all, several people had witnessed the incident. What other choice did the tug company have?

As it turned out, the company did have another choice: it didn't pay. Months later, when the skipper finally realized he was being ignored by the tug company, he filed an insurance claim. Repairs were soon made to his boat, but the chances of recovering the repair cost from the tug company had diminished considerably.

Prompt Reporting: A Form of Damage Control There are also situations where reporting a minor accident can prevent further damage. A Seattle man, for example, arrived at his boat and found water sloshing over the floorboards. Soon after turning on the pumps, he discovered the source of the leak (the stuffing box) and corrected the problem. Next, he flushed the engines and ran them briefly before concluding that everything was OK.

Had the owner contacted his insurance company—in this case BoatU.S.—a qualified marine surveyor could have been dispatched to inspect the boat. Instead, the owner never realized that salt water was in the transmissions until sometime later, after they had been ruined. Incidentally, even if someone doesn't pursue a claim after an accident, the insurance company can opt to send a surveyor—a professional—to inspect for related damage.

Preventing Fires

12

OF ALL THE SITUATIONS A SKIPPER could face on a boat, fire is probably the most frightening. Should a fire get started aboard, one expert estimates that it would have to be extinguished in 25 to 30 seconds before the skipper and crew will be forced by heat and smoke to abandon ship. Sound like an exaggeration? The BoatU.S. claim files suggest otherwise.

Consider the cook aboard a trawler yacht in Texas who was startled when grease splattered from a pan. She jumped back, knocking the pan over and spilling burning grease down the side of the stove. "Fire was everywhere . . . all over the floor, a roll of paper towels, the bunk, the curtains behind the stove . . . I panicked . . . John grabbed me and yelled 'Get the hell off the boat.' " There were five extinguishers aboard, but none was used. The boat burned to the waterline.

Could quick action have saved the boat? Maybe. At least there was someone present when the fire started. All too often the skipper and crew are elsewhere. And sometimes the first indication of trouble isn't smoke or even flames, it's an explosion. There isn't much need to fumble around with a fire extinguisher when the back of the boat has been blown open.

Of all the dangerous situations that can occur on a boat, fire is probably the scariest. Knowing how and why fires get started is the key to prevention.

How Boat Fires Start

Fires don't just happen. To combust, fires need oxygen, fuel, and a source of ignition. Oxygen, of course, is present in abundance on the windswept, open water. So is fuel. Most boats are floating islands of fiberglass, wood, paints, cloth, paper, plastics, and electric wires. All are excellent combustibles. Ignition can occur in the electrical system, engine room, engine exhaust, galley, battery box, appliances, or anywhere a smoldering cigarette is carelessly discarded. Discovering why and how fires get started is the key to prevention.

Problems in the DC Electrical System

Based on the BoatU.S. Marine Insurance claim files, the number-one cause of boat fires—accounting for 44% of all fires—is faults in the DC wiring system. These include chafed wires, wires that weren't protected by fuses or circuit breakers, overloaded electrical panels, improper wire sizes, loose or improper connections, improper battery charging, unprotected batteries, and something called locked rotor condition (see page 64). More often than not, the fire is traced to a shoddy do-it-yourself installation.

Engine and Transmission Overheating

Almost a quarter of all boat fires (24%) result from restricted water flow, oil leaks, and broken hoses. Sometimes these fires are just bad luck, but more often they're the result of insufficient maintenance.

Problems in the AC Electrical System

AC electrical fires constitute 11% of all boat fires. A few AC fires get started in

The Price of Ignoring an Obvious Warning

THIS SAILBOAT was destroyed in a dramatic explosion that blew the skipper out of the pilothouse and into the water. Investigators believe the most likely cause was spilled gasoline from portable containers stored on deck.

The cause put forth by investigators was not cast in stone, however; the boat was too badly damaged to know for certain exactly what happened. Since there are no hard-and-fast conclusions, why even mention the accident? Buried in the account taken by the investigator is a telling admission: "[The owner] said that he had smelled fumes when he arrived the day before and had opened the hatches. He thought he may have also smelled something just prior to the explosion."

Unfortunately, the boat's owner didn't take time to investigate the source of the fumes. The result, as you can see, was catastrophic.

Flare Guns Aren't Toys

MOST PEOPLE would consider having a loaded handgun on the family boat dangerous, especially if there were children aboard. Prudence would dictate that the gun should be unloaded and not easily accessible to small hands. Flare guns are no different. The combination of flare guns and children can be particularly dangerous since a flare gun looks like a toy.

An accidentally fired flare gun can be just as dangerous as a handgun; the flare is hot enough to easily start a fire. That's what happened to one 12-year-old boy who found a loaded flare gun in the cabin of the family sailboat. The gun went off accidentally in the boy's hands and severely burned the boat's interior. Fortunately, the boy wasn't hurt.

But that's not always the case. Two brothers, ages 11 and 13, were helping a BoatU.S.

member unload some items from his 40-foot sailboat when the older brother picked up a loaded flare gun resting on a shelf. Whether the boy toyed with the gun in front of his brother or dropped it is unclear; the result was that the gun went off, and the younger brother was struck in the eye with a 12-gauge meteor flare at close range. The boy spent six days in a hospital and lost some of the vision in his right eye. The owner of the boat said he had kept the flare gun loaded in case it was needed quickly.

Most skippers realize the deteriorating effect of sunlight on things like rope, fabrics, and even gelcoat, but what isn't so widely known is that sunlight, given the right circumstances, can cause a fire. There have been several claims for fires that were started by sunlight reflecting off a bright object, typically a stainless steel sink, and then amplified onto a flammable material. While certainly not as common as fuel or galley fires, this sort of thing happens more often than you might think. In most cases, like the burned overhead liner shown here, damage is relatively minor. A sponge left in the sink on the flybridge caught fire and burned a chart, which eventually did $20,000 damage to the boat and electronics before it was extinguished.

The solution is relatively simple: If you have a sink on board that gets extremely hot when it's in direct sunlight, keep it covered. A fitted cutting board is ideal, but even a dishtowel draped completely over the sink will do the job.

Watch Out for Power Lines

THE SKIPPER OF THIS BOAT was moving his boat around near a marina in a pea-soup fog and backed into a power line that was strung across the back of the marina. As you can infer from the photo, he probably knew instantly he'd made a serious mistake.

Nobody hits a power line on purpose, of course, but almost all skippers who have said that they were aware the lines were in the vicinity. One skipper said the power line was hidden by glare. Another was looking for a quiet place to anchor late one night and said he hadn't realized how far into the cove he'd gone. It's not just sailboats, either; a large sportfisherman in Texas struck a line with its outriggers. All the skippers and crews survived, but most of the boats were destroyed.

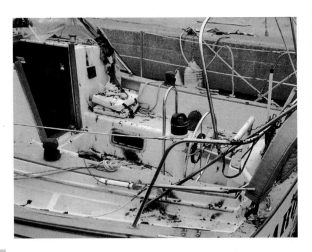

Whenever a chart indicates a power line is nearby, don't take chances. There is no standard minimum vertical distance required for power lines, and vertical distance is almost impossible to judge by eye. Lakes and rivers have varying pool stages or water levels. Saltwater tributaries have tides. Wires with a safe overhead clearance when the water is low may be dangerously close a few hours later. In addition, power lines can sag considerably on hot days. Your boat's mast or outriggers need not touch the lines to be damaged; electricity from high-voltage lines can arc from several inches to a foot or more, depending on the voltage in the wire. When in doubt, don't go anywhere near a power line.

much the same way as DC fires—improper connections, overloaded panels, and improper wire sizes. But fires in the AC system are most likely to occur at the "sliding" connection—the shore-power cord and inlet—where electricity is brought aboard the boat.

Fuel Leaks

At 8% of all fires, fuel leaks may not be the number-one cause of fires on a boat, but they tend to be far more dangerous and more likely to inflict injury than other fires. They also can be difficult to extinguish. Considering that 95% of all fuel fires involve gasoline, it's a good idea to pay careful attention to how gasoline is handled, stored, and moved from the boat's tank to the engine. Diesel fires are less common on boats, but diesel fuel can also be surprisingly volatile.

Miscellaneous

Some fires just don't fit neatly into any category: misdirected flares, kids playing with matches, errant fireworks, and even spontaneous combustion from rags. Most such fires can be prevented by using common sense.

Unknown

Fire investigators have an uncanny ability to determine how fires got started, even when boats have been underwater and/or reduced to a pile of ashes. Alas, fire investigators, however uncanny, are not perfect. One out of every twenty boat fires, on average, is attributed to "unknown" origins.

Stoves

Probably because pressurized alcohol stoves are no longer being marketed (thankfully), fires in the galley are far less common (1% of all boat fires) than they were only a decade or two ago. But when galley fires do occur, they often have the potential to spread quickly and do significant damage.

ONE FINAL COMMENT: The first line of defense against any fire is prevention. The latter isn't something that's done once when the boat is purchased and inspected by a marine surveyor; it must be ongoing. Vibration and damp air can weaken even the best of systems aboard a boat. Hoses split, wires corrode, and fuel tanks rust. Keeping fuel, oxygen, and sources of ignition safely apart should be an ongoing part of a boat's maintenance program.

A fire started by spilled alcohol quickly burned out of control and destroyed this handsome fishing boat. Experts suggest someone has very little time—as little as 25 to 30 seconds—to extinguish a fire before he or she will be forced by heat and smoke to retreat from the boat's cabin.

Troubleshooting 12-Volt DC Electrical Systems

An astounding 44% of onboard fires start somewhere in the jumble of wires that comprise the direct current (DC) electrical system. It's the downside of progress. Only a few years ago, the typical electrical system on a boat might include cabin lights, running lights, a bilge pump, and maybe a VHF radio and depth sounder. Today, a skipper's choice of 12-volt equipment has expanded to include GPS chart plotters, radar, stereos, digital wind instruments, color fish-finders, automatic windlasses, autopilots, fans, hailers, refrigerators, knotmeters, trim tabs, electric stoves, and electric stowaway masts.

Where a single battery and a few wires once powered the boat's electrical system, a contemporary electrical system is likely to have multiple batteries, packing hundreds and even thousands of amps, as well as a vast network of wires strung throughout the boat. Besides an increase in potential headaches, a more complex electrical system carries with it an increased likelihood of a wiring mistake, even a subtle mistake, that could cause an electrical fire. It's no wonder then that the technical staff at the ABYC say they receive more questions about electrical systems than any other topic.

A Primer on 12-Volt DC

Electricity in a DC system flows from a battery through the wires in one direction, much like gasoline flows through a fuel line. Although there are obvious differences, this analogy is especially appropriate because both electricity and gasoline are "fuels," which must be handled properly or a fire could result.

Most onboard electrical fires typically start in one of several ways. A fire can start when a battery is being "refueled" by a battery charger. Fires can also start when the flow of electricity escapes from a wire (analogous to a burst fuel line and referred to as a *short*). This can happen, for example, when a bundle of wires chafes against a hot engine or when a wire is not large enough to accommodate the flow of electricity. In both cases, a boat is *supposed* to have safeguards—fuses or circuit breakers—that will automatically cut off the flow of electricity and avert a fire. All too often, the claim files indicate these safeguards have been compromised or bypassed altogether. When this happens, the flow of electricity cannot be shut off, and a fire is much more likely to occur.

Where DC Fires Are Likely to Occur and Why

Unprotected Batteries The DC system's "fuel tank"—the battery—must be secured and covered. A battery that is allowed to come adrift could move the battery cable across the engine or against some other sharp object with devastating results. And an uncovered battery can easily be shorted by tools, boating equipment, or other gear coming in contact with terminals. A skipper working on his

boat in Massachusetts, for example, dropped a pair of pliers on his battery, causing a mild explosion and spilling burning acetone into the bilge. Although his boat suffered several thousand dollars worth of damage, he was not injured. (This claim is also a good example of why you should wear safety goggles whenever you inspect your batteries.)

Running Wires Directly to the Battery Two heavy cables—not a jumble of wires—are supposed to be routed from the batteries to the electrical distribution panel via a battery switch. (A battery switch is required by the Coast Guard on boats 26 feet and over. It is not required on boats under 26 feet.) The distribution panel is designed to then route electricity to various parts of the boat and to protect the wires in each circuit by using a circuit breaker or fuse to stop the flow of electricity in the event of an overload or short circuit. (A short circuit occurs when an exposed wire carrying current touches anything that's grounded.)

A distribution panel with too few circuits is a common problem on many boats, especially older boats with bare-bones electrical systems. Fuses or circuit breakers are only available for the essentials—running lights, cabin lights, and maybe aux 1 and aux 2. When an autopilot or GPS is added, do-it-yourself electricians will sometimes run wires directly to the battery or, in many other cases, to an existing circuit with other accessories. Both of these shortcuts bypass the safeguards and increase the risk of an electrical fire.

For example, here's a quote from the surveyor's report for one fire claim: "The electrical wiring evidently shorted behind the electrical panel. The wiring got hot enough to melt the insulation and cause fire throughout the electrical system from the battery master switch to the flybridge instrument panel . . . There must have been five things on that one fuse."

This wiring is neat, organized, and labeled. Troubleshooting an electrical problem should be relatively easy.

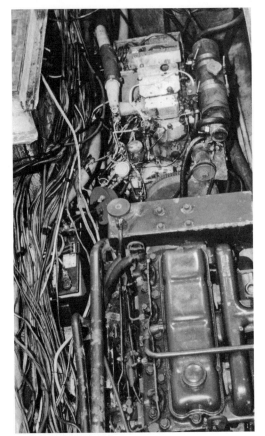

Somewhere in this mess is a fire waiting to happen. (Note the proximity of the wiring to the engines.)

One solution to the problem of too few circuits is to add a second electrical panel with additional space for extra appliances. You (or a marine electrician) can also add a bus bar for use with in-line fuses next to the bus, one for each appliance. Before you add a bus or panel, obtain a copy of the ABYC's E-11 electrical standard (see the ABYC and the NFPA sidebar on page 64). While not a how-to manual, E-11 lays out all the dos and don'ts to safely install and maintain a state-of-the-art marine electrical system.

The second problem that can occur when wires are run directly to the battery is the bypassing of the battery switch. Here's another surveyor's finding:

"The fire appears to have originated in an unprotected circuit for an automatic pilot that was connected directly to the battery terminals. This set of two wires extends between the autopilot at the starboard cockpit seat side panel, down the bulkhead, under the starboard quarter berth cushions, under the companionway stair, and into the battery box where they were secured with ring lugs. The wires were mashed heavily from placement of the closure panel over a drop storage bin."

With a properly connected battery switch, in the event of a sudden problem in the DC electrical system—a whiff of acrid smoke, for example—the skipper can simply shut off the battery switch, instantly stopping the flow of electricity. In the claim above, this was not possible because the autopilot had been wired directly to the battery. Although the use of a fire extinguisher put out the fire initially, the fire reignited. Without a battery switch, there was no way to quickly take away the source of the fire.

Note also that whenever you leave a boat unattended, always turn off the battery switch. Bilge pumps, carbon monoxide detectors, and burglar alarms that must remain on can be connected to the positive battery terminal of the battery switch with protection (usually an in-line fuse) on the wire to the circuit board.

Broken Wires Once wires leave the distribution panel, every place they start and stop creates some type of connection. A connection is a break in the wire, and like any other fuel line, you want a connection that won't leak electricity or deteriorate. A poor connection—one that is loose or corroded—will cause intermit-

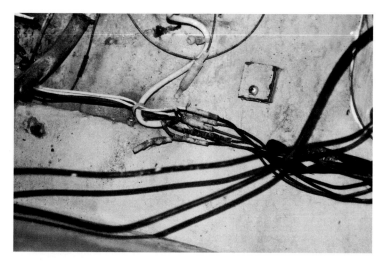

What's worse than having wires running through a boat's bilge? Having wires with connections in the bilge. All the connectors shown here corroded and caused the failure of a bilge pump, among other things. In one sense the boat's owner was lucky; had any 12-volt current leaked into the bilge, fittings would have corroded quickly and the boat could easily have sunk.

tent loss of power, which can be frustrating and also be difficult to troubleshoot. There are also two ways that a poor connection increases the risk of fire. First, it increases resistance, which, in turn, increases heat, sometimes a lot of heat. A loss of power also causes DC motors like bilge pumps to run so hot that they melt.

To be safe, use only crimp-type connectors for the wiring on your boat. The best crimp connectors have heat-activated glue that completely seals the connection. Wire nuts *don't* make a secure connection on a boat, and they're also open at the bottom, which lets in moisture and dirt. One marine surveyor who frequently investigates fire claims calls wire nuts the "mark of Zorro," an indication that the electrical system has been tampered with by an inexperienced, do-it-yourself owner.

Wire problems aren't only found at connectors. Here's another report from the BoatU.S. claim files: "The damage sustained was the result of an electrical fire originating from the starboard engine harness. The fire started at the starboard engine at the cable that runs from the battery directly to the refrigerator, which was not fused. Since this wire was tied in with the main harness, further damage was done."

It is important to route wires as far away as is practicable from exhaust pipes and other heat sources. Even engine wiring should be routed to avoid hot spots such as the exhaust and turbochargers. The reason wires must be kept well clear of the engine, as the claim above indicates, is to prevent them from being burned through, causing a short with the potential for fire.

The largest "wire" in the 12-volt electrical system is the battery cable, which is installed between the battery and starter without overcurrent protection. This cable can put out between 2,000 and 3,000 amps—the system's entire charge—on a dead short, which instantly produces tremendous heat. As a skipper in New York learned in one claim, these cables must be kept safely away from sharp edges

Starter cables carry a lot of electricity and aren't required to be fused within 6 feet of the battery. This cable wasn't supported with cable clamps in the engine room, and it abraded against a spinning shaft. The subsequent fire began destroying the engine control cables, and after the skipper shut down the engine, the engine restarted. The kill switch wiring was damaged, and the engine had to be stopped by choking the air supply.

Why should a fuse be next to the power source? Picture a hose ready to burst from too much pressure. You can't save the hose by turning off a valve halfway down the hose; to be effective, the valve would have to be at the source. The photo shows two bilge pump wires that chafed where a cable tie held them against a bilge pump hose. Since the fuse was on the bilge pump, when the wires shorted a few feet away, the fuse couldn't protect them. The wires ignited the hose and the boat was damaged.

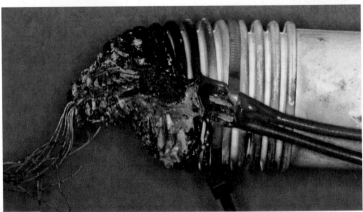

and hot engine parts that could destroy the wire's insulation and cause a short. Even though in this particular claim, the boat itself did not catch fire, the outdrive, trim tabs, engine gauges, and water pump sustained considerable damage, all because the battery cable had been rubbing against an exhaust elbow.

When securing wires to your boat, use clamps every 18 inches. Metal clamps must have smooth, rounded edges so they don't damage the insulation. Plastic or rubber liners offer the best protection. Never use metal sta-

The electronics in the bottom of this console were installed by the manufacturer to ABYC standards, and look fine. The ones in the top were installed later by someone else. Notice any difference?

Here's what happened: When the 12-volt positive wire for the burned equipment was installed, the boat's battery switch was bypassed. The wires chafed against the console, the battery's current shorted to the cabinet, and the electronics were permanently damaged.

ples that could penetrate the insulation. Nonmetallic clamps are acceptable in most parts of the boat, but not over the engine, shaft, or any other machinery that might damage the wire.

Wires that pass through a bulkhead or other structural members must be protected against chafe. In one claim involving a sailboat in North Carolina, wires that were routed under cabinet doors chafed and eventually started a fire that destroyed the boat. The wires should have been routed away from the doors. When wire must pass through a bulkhead, a couple of turns with electrical tape (and an occasional visual inspection) will go a long way to prevent chafe.

Improper Wire Sizes Wires that are too small to carry the intended load can "burst" and have been the cause of many onboard electrical fires. The longer the run of wire, the larger the wire you must use. Anytime you add new wiring, consult a wire gauge chart to ascertain the correct size. With most appliances, the manufacturer will supply the wire size. If they don't, measure the distance from the source (distribution panel or terminal strip) to the appliance (radio, lights, etc.) and back, then use a wire gauge chart to determine the correct wire size. When using a wire gauge chart, it's safest to be conservative and anticipate a 3% voltage drop. Also be sure to color-code the wires according to the ABYC guidelines.

Conductors Sized (AWG) for 3% Voltage Drop at 12 Volts

Current (amps)[1]

Length (feet)[2]	5	10	15	20	25	30	40	50	60	70	80	90	100
10	18	14	12	10	10	10	8	6	6	6	6	4	4
15	16	12	10	10	8	8	6	6	4	4	4	2	2
20	14	10	10	8	6	6	6	4	4	2	2	2	2
25	12	10	8	6	6	6	4	4	2	2	2	1	1
30	12	10	8	6	6	4	4	2	2	1	1	0	0
40	10	8	6	6	4	4	2	2	1	0	0	2/0	2/0
50	10	6	6	4	4	2	2	1	0	2/0	3/0	3/0	3/0
60	10	6	6	4	2	2	1	0	2/0	3/0	3/0	4/0	4/0

1. Current (amps) determined by adding the total amps on a circuit.
2. To load and back.
Source: Ancor Marine Grade Products and ABYC

Lack of Overcurrent Protection In one claim, all of the battery's current shorted to the console; with no fuse installed, the electronics suffered permanent heat and smoke damage (see bottom photo opposite). Had any flammable equipment been in the cabinet, the owner would have been towing a flaming boat down the road.

The ABYC and the NFPA

MOST, BUT NOT ALL, of the specific recommendations in this chapter can be found in standards pertaining to AC, DC, and fuel systems published by the American Boat and Yacht Council (ABYC) and the National Fire Protection Association (NFPA; the world's leading advocate of fire prevention). For more information, see the Resources.

A large distribution panel does not guarantee that all of the wires in the system are protected. While a circuit breaker or fuse is critical, it will only protect the main wire, not the smaller wires or the electrical device itself. According to the ABYC, each device must have its own fuse located on the positive wire within 7 inches of the power source. If the device—say a VHF radio—were to short, it would be protected.

Locked Rotor One of the more unlikely culprits in an electrical fire is a small DC motor, such as a bilge pump, water pressure pump, trim tab motor, or bilge blower. Unlike motors used ashore, a boat's DC electric motors are not required to have built-in thermal protection, so even the smallest pump has the potential to start a fire in a locked-rotor condition.

A locked-rotor condition exists when the shaft stops spinning but the motor continues to be energized. An example of this would be a bilge pump that has become clogged with debris. If the pump is not fused properly, and the fuse or circuit breaker does not blow or trip, the pump will continue to build up heat, which can cause a fire. In one claim, a boat that was being stored for the winter caught fire when both the bilge pump rotor and float switch froze in the ON position and continuously energized the jammed (locked rotor) bilge pump.

The best defense against a locked rotor is to install pumps according to the manufacturer's instructions. (Remember, longer runs of wire will change the requirements for wiring size.) Unfortunately, many boats have several appliance motors, such as windshield wipers, that have been wired through a single circuit at the panel board. Others, especially bilge pumps, are wired directly to the battery without a fuse. In either case, the pump is not protected and will not shut off when the rotor becomes jammed.

Note that aside from the fire risk it poses, a bilge pump with a locked rotor can also cause rapid and serious stray-current corrosion problems (see the Galvanic Series sidebar on page 70).

Using Cheap Battery Chargers Electricity for a battery charger is supplied by 110 volts, AC power. In the best of all possible worlds, electricity flows to the battery until it is fully charged, then it is either reduced to a trickle charge, or better still, shut off. Many cheaper chargers, however, will continue charging away with the potential to fry (and ruin) the battery or even start a fire. In one case, "The fire originated inside the boat as a result of electrical sparking that occurred when the battery was subjected to a charging current for an extended period of time."

The safest battery chargers, from a fire prevention standpoint, should be fused at the ends of the battery wires and should also have an Underwriters Laboratory (UL) marine listing. When a battery charger is only fused at the charger, the wires between the battery charger and the battery are not protected. The UL marine listing, among other things, means that a battery charger will drop to a much safer trickle charge.

The AC Electrical System

While the DC system has the dubious distinction of causing the majority of onboard electrical fires, it's the AC system that gets the prize for causing the most expensive fires. On average, the cost of repairs after an AC fire is eight times greater than that for repairs that follow a DC system fire. The likely reason is that more and more boats with AC systems have become the equivalent of expensive second homes, with luxuries like air-conditioning, refrigerators, microwaves, televisions, DVD players, and even washers and dryers.

While the appliances may be similar, the system that brings AC power aboard a boat is significantly different from the AC system in a house. When AC electricity is brought into a house, every connection up to and in the panel board must be securely bolted. With a boat, electricity is routed through a gauntlet of adapters and "sliding" (plug-in) shore-power connections that depend on friction to maintain contact. These connections are ideal spots for poor contacts that can start an AC electrical fire.

These wires were lying on top of the engine. Due to vibration, they eventually chafed through and shorted, starting a fire.

Here's a good example of why household wiring (Romex) shouldn't be used in a boat's electrical system. This boat had just crossed to the Bahamas for a leisurely vacation cruise when the owner noticed the depth sounder was acting erratically. A few seconds later he smelled smoke. The owner stopped the engines, dashed below, and discovered that smoke was pouring out of the forward cabin. His friend, still on deck, yelled that she could see flames. After radioing a hasty Mayday, they jumped into the boat's inflatable. Within minutes, the $250,000 boat was engulfed in flames and soon sank.

Though the boat had burned to the waterline, investigators were able to determine that sometime during the boat's life, someone had used solid household wire, which is less flexible than wires used on boats, for a circuit. The wire work-hardened and eventually broke due to the boat's constant motion. It then shorted, causing a fire inside the locker.

Power from the dock is brought aboard by a shore-power cable via an inlet on the boat, and by necessity, the cable and inlet must fit snugly. However, as they are connected and disconnected during normal use, the surfaces wear against each other. In addition if the cable isn't properly supported, it puts a strain on the sockets. Over time, insufficient contact and/or corrosion can result in increased resistance, which generates excessive heat. You can detect this condition by placing your hand on the shore-power cord plug. Some warmth is normal, but heat that makes it difficult to hold the plug under load means it's time to replace the shore-power cable and/or the inlet. Burn marks at the connection, however subtle, are another red flag that you must not ignore.

Marina receptacles don't last forever either. If your marina has dock receptacles that are loose, cracking, badly weathered, and/or get hot when they're being used, you should complain loudly until they correct the problem. (And in the meantime, don't use the receptacle.)

Marina Voltage Drop

When a motor fails to receive full voltage—especially a large motor under heavy load—it can overheat, creating a fire hazard. Loose connections between the boat and dock are one reason a motor may not receive full voltage. The marina is another. As one fire investigator said, "It is a well-known fact that some marinas are not wired according to the electrical codes. Just because you match the plug on the dock doesn't mean you're getting the proper voltage." Problems with the marina's electrical system are most likely to occur when there are several boats on a single dock drawing heavy loads simultaneously.

Input Meters: How Much Electricity Is Coming Aboard?

For the boatowner, the bottom line is knowing whether or not the boat is receiving the advertised voltage. The solution is an input voltage meter, installed at the electrical panel, which tells the skipper exactly how much voltage is coming aboard. Especially when visiting a strange marina, make it standard practice to turn off all your circuits, then read the voltage before the equipment is turned on. This not only prevents fire, it will also prevent damage to the boat's equipment caused by incoming voltage that is too high or too low. Look at the labels on AC motors to find out what voltages they require.

As a general rule, the electricity input panel should never read below 108 volts. If the electricity coming aboard is sufficient—within a few volts of 120— appliances may be turned on. If the voltage then drops below 108 volts, however, turn off the appliances and shut down the AC system until the problem (typically with the marina) is identified and corrected.

Many boats come equipped with voltage input meters. If not, one should be installed properly, according to ABYC and NFPA standards, at the electrical panel. Like any electrical installation, a shoddy installation presents both a fire and shock hazard.

Polarity

When electricity is brought aboard the boat from shore, polarity can sometimes be reversed if the marina is not wired correctly. When this happens, the previously hot black wire becomes the more benign grounded wire, and the previously neutral white wire can pack a 120-volt wallop. This is an obvious shock hazard to anyone tinkering with an appliance or the electrical system, but it also presents a fire hazard if the boat has single-pole circuit breakers.

When polarity is reversed on boats with single-pole circuit breakers (typically older boats), the circuit protection is on the wrong side of the system, which means that wiring is not protected in the event of a short. The solution is to upgrade the system with double-pole main circuit breakers, which protect both the white and black wires.

Generators

Assuming proper installation (i.e., connections to the electrical distribution system routed through a selector switch and power feeders sized to at least accommodate the generator's maximum rated output), a permanently installed generator does not present the same risk of fire as AC from a shore-power outlet. Loose shore-power connections, reversed polarity, and insufficient voltage are not problems with a marine generator. Because of carbon monoxide concerns, portable generators should not be used on a boat.

AC/DC: What You See Is Not Necessarily What You Get

Once the 120 volts is aboard, the AC wiring system looks similar to the boat's DC wiring system. As with wiring a DC system:

- Protect AC wires wherever they pass through a bulkhead.

- Be sure connections are tight.

- Use similar metals at connections to prevent corrosion.

- Keep wires above the bilge and properly supported at least every 18 inches.

- Use only tinned wire.

- Be sure the wires in the AC system are properly fused and large enough to accommodate the flow of electricity. To prevent both shock and fire hazards, *all* AC wires should have a minimum rating of 600 volts. A boat in Massachusetts caught fire because the undersized wiring could not handle the combined load of two portable heaters, a refrigerator, and a battery charger.

To reduce the chances of an inadvertent mix-up of AC and DC wires, which could cause a fire or a fatal shock, ABYC standards require that the two systems be in separate harnesses on new boats, which keeps the two systems safely apart. While it is not required by the standards, the two systems should also have separate circuit panels.

Although a boat's AC wiring is similar to its DC wiring, the boat's AC wiring is still much different from the AC wiring in a house. Electrical systems in a house can use solid-strand (Romex) or seven-strand wire, but this is not the case aboard a boat. Wires (both AC and DC) on a boat must have at least sixteen strands to withstand the vibration and "working" of the boat.

While a boat's AC wiring may be more resilient, it is not as well protected as house wiring, which is always sheathed and usually hidden behind walls. On a boat, the AC and DC insulated wires may meander, with no additional protection, through machinery spaces. A sagging AC wire that chafes against a sharp corner or hot surface, in addition to being a fire hazard, has the potential to give a lethal shock.

The Green Grounding Wire

When a boat is afloat, the AC electrical system relies on the green grounding wire in the dock's AC system to protect against electrical shock. If that green wire is not properly connected throughout the system, current from a short circuit can find its way into the water with the potential to electrocute someone in the water who comes too close to the boat.

The same potential for injury exists when a boat is stored ashore. If the green grounding wire has been disconnected, electrical current that is leaking from metal fittings under the boat will find a path to ground whenever someone touches a metal fitting, such as a through-hull, shaft, or rudder. The message? Don't disconnect the green grounding wire!

Poking Around Your
AC and DC Electrical Systems

Here are a few things you can do to safeguard your boat:

- Use an infrared temperature gun (these cost about $50 to $75, depending on features) to test for excessive heat at connections. A temperature that is hotter than others indicates a trouble spot, typically a loose connection. Electricity can arc at a loose connection, which creates an enormous amount of heat and is an obvious fire hazard.

- Use copper, not aluminum or steel, for studs, nuts, and washers. Dissimilar metals have the potential to cause galvanic corrosion. Regularly check all connections for indications of corrosion. Problems ranging from a poor contact to arcing may result from a poor choice of washers.

- Replace worn shore-power "sliding" (plug-in) connections that are loose and generating heat. (Use your hand or, better still, an infrared temperature gun to detect heat.) Though either the cord or inlet can deteriorate, experts say it's the boat's inlet that is most often the culprit in a fire. Even if you don't detect heat, it is a good idea to check the plug occasionally for telltale burn marks.

- Use a voltage input meter to monitor the amount of electricity coming aboard from the marina. It will prevent damage to the motors from too little voltage and could also prevent a fire caused by overheating. Do not operate air conditioners or other motors if voltage drops below 108 volts.

- If your marina has dock receptacles that are loose, cracking, badly weathered, and/or get hot, you should complain loudly to management until the problem is corrected.

- Use double-pole breakers and polarity indicators to reduce the risk of fire and shock caused by reversed polarity. You can permanently install polarity indicators or use a portable model.

- Always protect wires from rough edges, such as cabinets and bulkheads.

- Support wires every 18 inches using the correct size of nonmetallic clamps to hold the conductors firmly in place, or you can use metal straps with smooth, rounded edges. Insulated straps are preferable. Do not use a metal staple to secure wiring; its sharp edges can abrade the insulation.

- With the exception of the automatic bilge pump and alarms, route all DC circuits through a battery cutoff switch.

The Galvanic Series

THE TABLE AT RIGHT IS A SHORTENED VERsion of the galvanic series table, which lists a range of metals from cathodic to anodic. Galvanic corrosion arises when dissimilar, electrically connected metals are immersed in an electrolyte (like salt water). A current is generated, leading to the destruction of the anode (the less noble metal) and the protection of the cathode (the more noble metal). Using the table, you can get a fairly good idea how vulnerable a fitting might be to galvanic corrosion. A fitting made of a metal at the bottom of the scale will waste away in seawater if it is in direct contact with a fitting made of a metal at the top. Fittings will be damaged more quickly in salt water than in fresh water, but it is also possible for galvanic corrosion to take place when dissimilar metals are out of the water. The farther apart the two metals are on the scale, the more likely the anodic metal will be damaged.

Note: Galvanic series tables are frequently published that seem to disagree slightly. For example, brass may be listed ahead of bronze, or vice versa. This has to do with variations of the alloys, as well as the electrolyte.

Cathodic	graphite
	Monel
	stainless steel
	bronze
	brass
	copper
	tin
	mild steel
	aluminum
Anodic	zinc

Be aware that stray-current corrosion, caused when a leak from a hot wire allows current to find a path to ground through bilge water, damp areas of the boat, or seawater, can occur in any metal fitting that feeds a current into the water—regardless of the composition of the metal and regardless of its position in the galvanic series table relative to other metals; the direction of the current determines which metal will corrode.

- With the exception of an automatic bilge pump, do not route wires near the bilge.

- Do not use one fuse for two or more appliances.

- Periodically spray the contacts on shore-power cords with an electrical contact cleaner, such as LPS 1, to inhibit corrosion. (Note that WD-40 or silicone sprays are not appropriate because they leave a film that increases contact resistance.)

- Never use solid-strand and seven-strand wire on boats. Although these wires are fine for a house, wires aboard a boat must have multiple strands, at least sixteen, for added resiliency when the boat vibrates and works. Tinned wire works best, as it is more resistant to corrosion than copper.

- Be careful not to cut strands when stripping wire prior to crimping.

- Use ring or captive spade–type crimp wire connectors rather than spade-type connectors. Captive connectors are less likely to be disconnected by vibration. Ring and captive-spade connectors must be the same size as the screw or stud.

- When crimping a connector, don't be afraid to check it by giving it a tug; if it's loose, you need to use a better crimping tool.

The Problem with Portable Electric Heaters

A fire hazard in a house is also a fire hazard on a boat. Smoking in bed, for example, is hazardous no matter where you are. The same is true of disposing oil-soaked rags, storing gasoline, replacing frayed wires, using undersized extension cords with large appliances, etc. Conversely, you might also assume that when something is safe in a house, it must be equally as safe on a boat. Yes?

Um, no.

There is at least one potential hazard aboard a boat that is not generally recognized because it is so widely used in a house: the portable electric heater. Portable electric heaters, the same glowing boxes of warmth that are frequently used to extend the boating season in late autumn and early spring, are more of a risk when they are used aboard a boat. The reason is due in part to the design of the heaters but also to the limitations of the AC electrical systems on most boats.

Because they draw a lot of current, portable heaters have special requirements for size, type, length, and condition of wiring. A house, which must be built to

As shore-power cords age, the sliding connections corrode and become worn so prongs no longer fit as snugly. The result is arcing, which produces heat, typically at the inlet connection. In this case a high-amperage appliance—the heater—was left on for several hours and generated enough heat at the inlet to start a fire.

Two suggestions: (1) Don't leave a heater or any other high amperage appliance operating when you're sleeping or away from the boat; there are too many ways a fire can start. (2) Examine your shore-power cord plug for black or brown discoloration, which indicates excessive heat. You can also feel the heat at the power cord connection—it's almost too hot to hold—when a high-amperage appliance is being used. Either way, excessive heat means the cord and/or the shore-power inlet needs replacing.

A Portable Electric Heater "Tip"

ASIDE FROM THE CONSIDERABLE POTENTIAL for problems in the boat's electrical system, there is another good reason why portable electric heaters should not be left unattended on a boat. The owner of this boat was doing some fitting out work in early spring when he left for a few minutes to run up to the marina store. Since he would only be gone a short time, he left on the heater he had been using down below.

When the owner returned, he noticed puffs of black smoke drifting out of the hatches. Putting two and two together, he quickly unplugged the shore-power cable, which shut off the heater and reduced the volume of smoke. He was then able to enter the boat and snuff out the smoldering woodwork.

In the few minutes he was gone, his boat was damaged to the tune of $26,000. From the surveyor's report, it appears that his 20-year-old electric heater had tipped over, perhaps when the owner stepped ashore, and had ignited the boat's woodwork. Heaters are supposed to have tip-over switches, but some older models, like the one shown, were made without the switches. The bottom line: Unplug any heaters when you leave your boat. And if you'll be spending the night aboard, using an extra blanket is the safest way to stay warm while you're asleep.

meet strict electrical codes, normally meets those requirements. A boat's AC system is built to voluntary standards, and while most boats meet those standards, some do not. And even the ones that do, won't have electrical systems that are as tightly built as their counterparts in a house. Placing several high-amperage appliances on the same receptacle, using extension cords, or using a combination of both can overload a boat's electrical system and greatly increase the chances of an electrical fire.

An imported fiberglass trawler in Maryland, for example, burned to the water-line after its owner went to dinner and left a portable electric heater going full blast in the main saloon. The heater was plugged into a 120-volt outlet along with a battery charger. The outlet eventually melted and started a fire that destroyed several other boats.

In a similar claim, a fire started aboard a 41-foot sailboat in Florida while the boat's owners were taking showers at the marina. Two electric heaters at the same outlet had been left on at their highest settings. According to fire investigators, neither of the safeguards—the circuit breaker on the boat or the circuit breaker on the dock—tripped and broke the circuit.

Tip-Over Switches

The AC electrical wiring is only part of the problem. Heater design can be another. Many heaters don't have wide bases for stability, or more important, *tip-over switches* to automatically shut off the heater if it gets knocked over. The BoatU.S. Marine Insurance claim files contain several accounts of heaters that were knocked over by boat wakes and ignited a carpet or woodwork. In one claim in Georgia, a heater tumbled off the dinette and ignited the carpet and woodwork while the owner was ashore. Eight other boats and the shed that covered the slips were also destroyed.

Four Rules for Using Portable Electric Heaters Safely

1. *Never* leave on a portable electric heater while you are away from the boat or when you go to bed.

2. Use only an electric heater with a tip-over switch that will automatically shut off the heater if it gets knocked over. Don't use older heaters with frayed cords.

3. Never use another high-amperage appliance on the same receptacle with a portable electric heater.

4. Never use an extension cord with an electric heater.

Propulsion System Fires

Most people tend to think of an overheated engine as nothing more than a smoky nuisance; expensive, maybe, but certainly not a threat to the boat itself. Consider, however, that only about a quarter of the energy that's produced by combusting gasoline (slightly more for diesel fuel) is used to move the boat. The rest becomes heat—*a lot of heat*—which is usually ushered safely overboard via the boat's cooling system. The key word here is *usually*. A study of the BoatU.S. Marine Insurance claim files found that nearly a quarter of all boat fires were caused by the cooling system failing to do its job, with the result that all that heat built up somewhere in the boat's propulsion system—the engine, transmission, or turbochargers.

First, a primer on how a cooling system is supposed to work. Almost all marine engines rely on seawater (also referred to as raw water) for cooling. Some use *only* seawater for cooling, while others have a system similar to an automobile's, which circulates coolant in a closed system inside the engine. But since radiators aren't practical on a boat, these systems must also rely on seawater to cool the coolant.

And if the seawater fails to keep flowing—for example, the water pump fails or the water intake or exhaust passages become clogged—the exhaust components of a marine engine will get blistering hot surprisingly quickly. Within seconds of a blockage, rubber hoses connected to the boat's exhaust discharge will melt and begin smoking, which isn't surprising when you realize the exhaust gas temperatures without the benefit of cooling water can be well over 1,000°F. If the engine keeps running without cooling water, the hoses will ignite, burning nearby wires and possibly the engine cover. (This is when you'll be glad your gasoline lines are USCG Type A-1, which means they can withstand at least 2½ minutes of flame before spewing gasoline into the mess.)

If you haven't noticed the smoke before now, you certainly will when you look back to see why the boat is losing power. During a high-speed run, one skipper's starboard engine began to overheat when the intake clogged and the flexible boots from the exhaust and shift cables began smoking. He never noticed his temperature gauge climbing, and only knew there was a problem when the boat started slowing, and he glanced back and saw a lo-o-o-ong trail of black smoke. By the time he shut down the engine, the block had cracked and the heads were damaged. During the subsequent inspection, gunk was found to be clogging the intake hose. There was no intake strainer for the engine.

Most systems use a rubber impeller–type pump to suck cooling water into the engine. These pumps will suck up water, and if you're not careful, weeds, mud, and sand as well. It is essential to stop gunk from getting into the system. To do this, some inboards have a scoop strainer outside on the hull and all should have an in-line strainer in the raw water intake line. Routine inspections of the latter should take only a minute or two. Care must be taken with scoop strainers to prevent growth—barnacles, zebra mussels—from inhibiting water flow. This can be done by applying bottom paint in the spring and/or using a scraper (and a diving mask and flippers) during the season.

However, a strainer won't help much if it is overwhelmed. A number of engine fires, like one awhile back in Alabama, have been caused after a boat ran aground, and an impatient skipper kept shoving the throttle into forward and reverse to free the boat. The props stirred up all kinds of junk, some of which, despite the strainer, got sucked up into the cooling system. The irate skipper persisted, and soon his boat was aground *and* on fire. This situation happens frequently—but it shouldn't. If you can't get off immediately using your engine, it's time to wait for the tide (be patient!) or to swallow your pride and call for professional assistance.

Another way a cooling system becomes blocked is when aging rubber impeller vanes dry out and crumble, causing the pump to fail. Not only will the pump no longer operate (this is bad), but the broken vanes can find their way into cooling passages (this is worse!). Broken vanes are much more likely to happen with older impellers; the best insurance is to replace an impeller every 100 hours or two years, as recommended by manufacturers. Note that over-heating can age an impeller prematurely. Should your boat overheat for any reason—a clogged intake, for example—it's a good idea to replace the impeller. Think of it as cheap insurance.

Exhaust Manifolds

Perhaps the biggest trouble spot in a boat's cooling system is the manifold. A skipper in Indiana discovered his manifolds were shot when a water-skier he was towing yelled that he could see smoke coming from the cowling vents on the side of the boat. The driver wisely shut down the engine. The surveyor's report speculated that by the time the boat was stopped, the manifolds were red-hot, which would explain why, when the skipper made the mistake of opening the cover to see where the problem was, the engine cover ignited. It was later found that the exhaust manifolds were so clogged with corrosion that only a tiny trickle of water had been passing through. Note that he might have discovered the problem much sooner if he'd made it a practice to check his boat's exhaust routinely.

An exhaust manifold keeps exhaust gases and cooling water separated so that water goes directly overboard through the exhaust without getting into the engine. (Keeping them separated until they enter the risers is critical; water that finds its

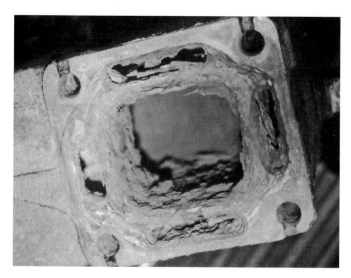

Exhaust manifolds lead a tough life. Water (especially salt water) and hot exhaust gases can corrode the inside passages until they are so restricted that the engine overheats, sometimes severely. Manifolds must be removed periodically and checked for blockages.

way into the gas-only section could then enter the cylinders with predictably grim results.) But the now-hot cooling water has one more job to do before it's pumped back overboard—cool the manifold. Without water, a manifold gets red-hot, which can ruin your engine, not to mention an afternoon of waterskiing.

Manifold Maintenance Manifolds lead a tough life, enduring hot gas, corrosive acids, seawater, and vibration, followed by days and even weeks and months of idleness. All of this mechanical debauchery leads to rust and corrosion, which eats away at the metal and clogs water passages. Considering all they endure, it's a wonder that manifolds last as long as they do, which isn't very long. Boats in Florida that are used frequently may get a scant two or three years out of the risers and a little more for the manifolds, while those in the Great Lakes may last two or three times longer.

When a boat is used in salt water, flushing the raw-water cooling system with fresh water after each use and prior to storage will slow corrosion and prolong the life of the exhaust manifold and risers. There are several flushing options available, depending on how the cooling system is arranged. Inboard/outboard outdrive units and outboards have similar intakes, and both can be flushed using muffs that attach to a freshwater garden hose and are cupped over the water intake ports. Inboard engines with through-hull intakes, on the other hand, can be flushed through an in-line T arrangement along the intake hose or with an engine flush-out valve. All of these gizmos are readily available commercially.

Even with the best care, however, manifolds and risers won't last forever. You (or a mechanic) may get a hint of trouble by using an infrared pyrometer to detect excessive heat that is created at clogged passages. You can also look for corrosion seeping out at the joint between the manifold and riser, which indicates that the gasket has failed. If water is leaking out, there's a good chance it is also leaking inside at the joint to the gas-only chamber. Finally, if you hear a knocking sound, it could be an indication that (1) water has been seeping into the cylinders, and (2) you need a new engine.

While not foolproof, one way to gauge the overall health of your cooling system is to inspect the water coming through at the exhaust whenever the engine is started. Learning to recognize a healthy flow of water will make it easier to recognize a developing problem. Another technique is to keep your eyes glued to your engine's temperature gauge. But since you also have to steer and watch for other boats (Rule 5!), your attention is likely to be elsewhere. The solution is an overheat alarm, similar to the ones found on many boats to monitor low oil pressure. If the cooling water temperature goes up too much, the alarm goes off. Position the alarm near the helm and be sure it is LOUD, so you will be able to hear it. There have been instances where the overheat alarm wasn't heard until *after* the skipper noticed smoke and slowed the engine.

The only surefire way to know the condition of a manifold is to remove it every couple of years for boats used in salt water, and a little less frequently for those used in fresh water. Consider this inspection as another part of an engine's routine servicing. Because you usually have to fumble with fittings that are in the way, the job of removing a manifold usually stretches into an afternoon or even longer. In most cases, the casting can be cleaned, pressure checked, and reinstalled for more years of useful service. If you do find that the time has come to replace the manifold and/or riser, be assured that the money is well spent.

A word of caution is in order here: Exhaust hoses disconnected from the engine will leave the boat open to the outside. They must be tied securely above the waterline to prevent water from flowing into the boat. Each year, owners and even professional mechanics have sunk boats because they were careless with open ports.

An alternative to removing the manifold periodically is to convert your raw-water cooled engine and manifold to a freshwater cooling-system using a conversion kit. A freshwater cooling-system will increase overall engine life, and you won't have to worry about raw-water corrosion in the manifold. Note, however, that the risers on top of the manifolds will still need to be raw-water cooled.

Other Hot Mechanicals

Aside from the engine itself, there are two other components in the engine room that can start a fire: the transmission and turbocharger, which together account for 4% of all boat fires.

Marine transmissions are frequently called on to work at peak loads for hours at a time. One fire was started by a misaligned transmission that overheated and spewed transmission fluid (which is flammable) all over itself. Since the boat had no temperature gauge for the transmission, the skipper never knew he had a problem until the transmission began to seize, and the boat lost power. The fire was put out by the boat's automatic fire extinguishing system, but not before ruining the transmission.

It's a good idea to check transmission fluid levels as well as look for leaks at regular intervals. Some transmissions on larger boats have fluid coolers, which work just like an engine's heat exchangers. Passages in the seawater side can become blocked with gunk or barnacles, and the resulting lack of water can quickly overheat the transmission. The solution is to keep the strainer clean, and open the heat exchanger occasionally to make sure passages aren't restricted.

Turbochargers (mostly in diesel engines) increase heat, adding another 150° or so to a diesel's already hot internal temperatures. Because of the added heat, turbo manifolds can sometimes become red-hot. Flammables (and fingers!) must be kept well away. According to the NFPA, combustible surfaces adjacent to turbocharged diesel exhaust systems should not exceed 225°F. Thermal "blankets" are used frequently to shield combustible surfaces from the intense heat.

Turbochargers require a constant supply of cooling oil to keep temperatures down. If a seal ruptures and no oil reaches the turbo, which spins at up to 100,000 revolutions per minute (rpm), it goes into meltdown, shooting out flames that can burn the insulating blanket and anything else nearby. It's ugly. One skipper was motoring along at cruising speed, noticed a drop in rpm, and looked around to see smoke pouring out of the starboard exhaust. He quickly checked the engine room, and after peering through the smoke, saw that the turbocharger and air filter were on fire. It required three extinguishers to knock down the flames.

Since turbos are often covered by insulation, which is difficult to remove, checking them is sometimes overlooked. It shouldn't be. Look for insulation that's oil stained or badly scorched—a sure sign that the turbo needs attention (and the insulation needs replacing).

Keeping Fuel Out of the Bilge: Gasoline

From a surveyor's report: "The vessel is so severely damaged that an accurate cause would be difficult to determine. We can, however, assume that since there was raw gasoline in the bilge, that the fuel entered the bilge, either by improper fueling procedures by the insured or from a leak in the system."

Help Your Engines and Transmissions Keep Their Cool

- *Make sure cooling water can get in.* Inspect your hull-mounted scoop and engine room strainer frequently to make sure there's nothing to obstruct the flow of water. Sterndrives often have small intakes that can be easily clogged with marine growth.
- *Make sure cooling water can get out.* Manifolds have a limited life, and eventually rust begins to narrow the passages. Remove manifolds every couple of years to check for blockages.
- *Maintain your seawater pump.* Rubber impellers wear with time, and old vanes can break off causing the pump to fail, and worse, clogging the system.
- *Check fluid levels regularly.* Engines and transmissions depend on oil to lessen friction and heat. Look also for leaks and correct them before you're faced with a meltdown.
- *Check turbochargers for leaks and signs of overheating.* Make sure flammable materials are not close enough to ignite.
- *Make sure your engines have temperature gauges that work.* Overheat alarms are a terrific investment; they can alert you to a potential problem when your attention is elsewhere.

Here is one reason to inspect your fuel system periodically: gasoline leaking from a carburetor fuel line (inset) ignited, and the boat burned to the waterline.

While not as common as a few decades ago, a gasoline explosion is by far the deadliest type of "fire" on a boat. As recently as the late 1980s, fuel hoses deteriorated more readily because they hadn't been upgraded to handle alcohol blends, and boatbuilders were less likely to adhere to ABYC and NFPA standards for fuel tanks and fuel systems. Fortunately times have changed. One thing that hasn't changed, however, is gasoline itself. Gasoline vapors are still heavier than air and still highly flammable. There is always the possibility, with any gasoline engine, that some fuel can find its way to the bilge. And gasoline in the bilge is bad news. The longer it accumulates undetected, the more violent the explosion it causes. Even a half-cup of spilled gasoline can blow a boat to pieces.

In some cases of gasoline explosions, gasoline was spilled carelessly as the boat was being refueled. In other cases, fire investigators found that gasoline had leaked from a corroded fuel tank, a loose fitting, or a split hose. Whatever the source of the spilled fuel, most of these accidents could have been prevented by carefully inspecting the fuel system at least twice a season and by getting down in the bilge and sniffing for gas vapors before starting the engine.

Troubleshooting the Fuel System

Inspect every component in the fuel system thoroughly each season for indications of failure or an incipient leak. According to fire investigation experts, the most likely point of failure in a boat's fuel system is the fuel tank, followed by the fuel fill system, fuel filters, fuel lines, and fuel pump.

Fuel Tanks A gasoline tank weighs hundreds of pounds when filled; therefore, it must be well supported, such as with blocks, chocks, straps, and fiberglass tab-

Corrosion on aluminum fuel tanks typically begins where the tank bottoms have been exposed to water over a long period of time. Pinhole leaks form, allowing fuel to leak into the bilge. Look for telltale patches of white powder, indicating the onset of a serious corrosion problem.

bing, to prevent it from shifting. To avoid corrosion problems, a metal tank must sit well above the bottom of the bilge and always have air, not bilge water, beneath its bottom. Metal tanks should never rest on wood or carpet fabric, since both retain moisture that will corrode the tank.

Tanks must be bonded with a wire between the tank and an engine ground so that static electricity can pass harmlessly to earth before it sparks. Fittings must always be at the top of the tank. Breather vents must be clear so that dangerous fumes can spill overboard. (There should be a loop in the hose going up from the vent opening to keep water out of the tank.) Finally, don't overlook the fuel gauge transmitter that sits on top of the tank; it has a large gasket that may crack or soften with age and need to be replaced.

Although all fittings and connections in the fuel system must be accessible, the tanks themselves may not be; many are buried under decks or foamed in place. Although you can pressure test your tank, your best deterrent for detecting a leak in an inaccessible tank—even if you have a fume detector—is a vigilant nose.

Fuel Fillers The flexible hose used to connect the fuel filler with the gas tank must be double clamped. In addition, a bonding wire to prevent static discharge must be used between the fill pipe and the tank top. Leaks can occur from several sources. One possible source is at the end of a bonding wire that has been tucked under the hose. Another source is loose clamps or hoses secured with only one clamp. Also, check the hose itself. When a hose is reinforced with wire, the wire can rust and puncture the hose, creating a leak.

Fuel Filters Fuel filter leaks can occur because of deteriorated gaskets or incorrect installation by a sloppy mechanic. In some cases, compounds, which are more prone to leaking, have been used to bed the filter instead of a gasket.

Filters may also leak if the brass bowl is cracked or if the drain plug or housing is badly corroded.

Fuel Lines Three types of fuel lines are typically found on marine gasoline engines: flexible hose (USCG Types A1, A2, B1 and B2), steel lines (on the engine), and copper tubing. Because of vibration, the Coast Guard requires that metal fuel lines be connected to the engine with a section of flexible fuel line. Check all joints for leaks (use your finger and look for stains under or around the fitting) and make sure the lines are well supported with noncombustible clips or straps that have smooth edges.

Wipe flexible hoses with a dry rag to see if there is an odor of gasoline. Flexible hoses deteriorate over time and must be replaced, but only with Coast Guard–approved SAE J1527 hose. Of the A and B types, Type A is more fire resistant than Type B hose and must be used at the fuel pump and carburetor where more than 5 ounces of fuel could spill if the hose is cut. Type 1 has less permeation loss than Type 2 and is a better hose. Every flexible hose should be clearly marked "USCG." If not, replace it immediately.

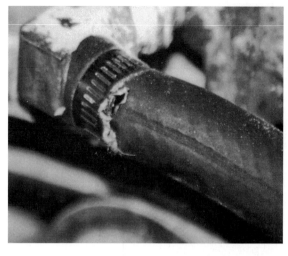

Antisiphon Device Any engine that has a carburetor fuel inlet connection below the top of the gas tank must have an antisiphon device to prevent fuel from being spilled back onto the flames should there ever be a fire. Unfortunately, in the interest of more speed or a smoother running engine, antisiphon devices are sometimes removed by owners or mechanics. Besides being illegal, removing an antisiphon device is dangerous. A good mechanic should be able to install an antisiphon device that will not affect engine operation.

Fuel Pumps Fuel pumps are operated either mechanically or electrically. Electrical models must be within 12 inches of the engine and wired through the oil pressure switch so that the pump will stop operating if the engine stops. A

Hoses that carry fuel are different from other hoses; they're typically stronger and specifically designed to withstand the effects of constant exposure to gasoline and diesel fuel. The nonapproved hose in this photo split. Fortunately it was discovered before it caused any problems.

If your mechanic tells you an antisiphon device is a nuisance, show him this photo. The boat was destroyed because gasoline leaked from a tank onto the engine and started a fire.

28-foot cruiser in Florida had an electric pump that was operated manually by a toggle switch at the helm. When fire destroyed the boat, a fire investigator discovered that the manually operated electric pump not only caused the fire but continued to pump gasoline into the burning hull until the batteries were finally destroyed.

Periodically remove and clean the fuel pump's filter bowl and filter screen, but be careful not to spill fuel during the process. Also, make sure the bowl is centered and flat when it goes back on. The gasket may absorb gasoline, which will cause it to swell. When this happens, the bowl will not seat properly and will leak.

If you ever need to remove the pump for servicing, be careful that fuel does not leak into the bilge. The diaphragm is the component that needs the most attention, as it hardens with age and can rupture. Rebuild kits are available, but the job is best left to a qualified mechanic. Auto fuel pumps must not be used on boats. These pumps do not send the gas back to the engine. Guess where the gas goes? (Answer: the bilge.)

Ignition Protection By law, electrical components in a gasoline engine space must be ignition protected so that they will not produce sparks that could ignite stray gasoline vapors. Unfortunately, when mechanics rebuild or replace some of the engine components—the starter motor, alternator, or distributor—the replacement components are no longer ignition protected. Whenever you need a component replaced, stress the importance of ignition protection to the mechanic.

Fueling Procedures

According to the claim files, many gasoline fires and explosions occur because of carelessness at the gas dock. Occasionally (more often than you might expect) someone pumps gasoline into something other than the gasoline tank. An insured boatowner in New York filled his water tank with gasoline. In another claim, a dock attendant in Texas pumped gas into an insured boatowner's fish rod holder. Both of these mistakes resulted in explosions and serious injuries.

Besides making sure the tank is marked "GASOLINE" (not "WATER" or "WASTE"!) before inserting the hose nozzle, close ports and hatches on the boat to prevent vapors from wafting below. Carry portable tanks ashore for refueling. Turn off main battery switches and shut down any electrical equipment connected directly to the battery. Extinguish all open flames. Finally, send the crew ashore while the boat is being fueled.

When you refuel, be aware that simply squeezing the pump trigger until gasoline spews out of the vent is illegal and can result in a considerable fine. Always leave about 5% of the tank empty so that the gasoline has room to expand. Overfilling the tank also causes gasoline to sit in the fill pipe and fuel vent lines, which are not designed to store gasoline.

Gasoline Gone Astray

FUELING A GASOLINE-POWERED BOAT should always be done slowly and deliberately, preferably by the boat's owner. A couple of summers ago, a father had his teenage son refuel their boat while he took care of other matters. The son placed the hose nozzle into a rod holder and pumped gas into the bilge. After briefly trying to start the engine, the son said he smelled gasoline. The father assumed the engine was flooded. It wasn't until the second attempt to start the engine that they realized their mistake when an explosive flash traveled through the bilge and out the forward cabin. Miraculously, the two were only singed, but the boat burned and was a total loss.

   In addition to such incidents, BoatU.S. claim files contain a surprising number of accounts of gasoline being poured into diesel tanks and diesel being poured into gasoline tanks and both fuels have been poured into water tanks, waste tanks, and fish rod holders. This can have both explosive and catastrophic results.

   To prevent confusion, clearly mark deck fills as "GAS" (or "DIESEL"), "WATER," and "WASTE." Give attendants specific instructions; ask for gasoline or diesel, don't just say "We need some fuel." But the best defense against mistakenly shoving a nozzle into the wrong fill is for *you*—the boat's owner—to always handle the nozzle. Don't leave the job to a guest or relative while you go off and look for your wallet.

Before starting an engine, reopen ports and hatches and turn on the bilge blower for at least 5 minutes. It is also wise to open the engine hatch and use that marvel of human anatomy—your nose—to sniff for gasoline vapors. This is critical!

Simply operating the bilge blower can, in certain situations, actually increase the chances of an explosion. "After fueling, I started the bilge blower and let it run for several minutes. I then started the engine. It ran normally for three to five seconds and I heard a loud 'poof.' The engine stopped. At first I saw no flames but there was lots of thick black smoke." If fuel has spilled into the bilge, the gas-air mixture could be above the upper explosive limit (which means there is too much gas in the air to cause an explosion). By using the blower, you introduce more air, which alters the gas-air ratio, bringing the mixture down into the explosive range.

Although certainly useful, fume detectors are not infallible and are not as

What If You Find Spilled Gasoline in the Bilge?

WITHIN THE SPAN OF A FEW DAYS, there were two explosions on opposite sides of the country—one in Seattle, Washington, and one in Weirs Beach, New Hampshire—that destroyed two boats and sent four people to the hospital. In both cases, the explosions were caused by people using wet-dry vacuums to clean up spilled gasoline. One eyewitness in Weirs Beach stated that the explosion had occurred within seconds of the vacuum being turned on.

Although neither boat was insured with BoatU.S., there has been at least one similar accident documented in the BoatU.S. claim files that involved the use of a wet-dry vac. Did these skippers think that the vacuums were ignition protected? It's likely they didn't give it much thought at all, which is exactly the *wrong* approach to cleaning up spilled gasoline.

What should you do if you discover spilled gasoline in the bilge? If you're at the gas dock, *larger quantities of gasoline should only be dealt with by professionals*. Get off the boat and call 911. Don't operate anything electrical, including the blower; it won't eliminate spilled gasoline. Although you might be sorely tempted to disconnect the battery cables before leaving, DON'T. They could spark. (If you just refueled the boat, the battery switch should already have been turned off.)

If you're out on open water, the first order of business is to shut off the battery switch. The safest way to summon help is with a cell phone. A VHF radio is not required to be ignition protected, which poses an obvious risk if the cabin is reeking of gasoline. If the VHF is well away from the fumes and you decide it is safe, shut down all circuits except the one for the VHF before turning the battery switch back on.

If you can't call for help with a cell phone or VHF, flares are obviously out of the question, unless you are well away from the boat in a dinghy. About the only other thing you can do safely is turn your ensign upside down and wave your arms to alert passing boats. If the situation is such that you decide to abandon ship, don't go far; someone happening along will have no idea your boat is a floating bomb.

The owner of the Seattle boat learned a painful lesson: don't use a wet-dry vac to clean up spilled gas!

reliable as your nose. A sensor in one part of the bilge may not detect vapors in another. A boatowner in Arkansas learned this the hard way after a fume detector gave him a "green light." He turned the key and almost instantly heard an explosion.

Stalled Engines

"We started the engine and headed into the marina. I went forward to drop the staysail. My wife was at the helm and advised that the engine was not holding rpm. I went back and shut off the engine. After adjusting the throttle, I tried to restart the engine and at that point, there was a small explosion followed by a lot of smoke."

Because "hot spots" were found under this vintage sailboat's old side draft carburetor, the surveyor investigating the fire suspected (it was never proved) that the carburetor had flooded and spilled gas into the bilge. Whatever the cause, any engine that stalls mysteriously could be leaking gasoline into the bilge. Maybe a hose split or a gasket is leaking, and the fuel that is no longer getting to the engine is spilling into the bilge. If you experience an untimely stall, follow the same start-up procedures as a cold engine: open the hatch and sniff below for spilled gas.

Keeping Fuel Out of the Bilge: Diesel

Diesel engines have a well-deserved reputation for being safer than gasoline engines. Unlike gasoline vapors, which are highly volatile, diesel fuel is relatively tame and will not explode. And while a gasoline engine must rely on a high-voltage electrical system to ignite the fuel, a diesel uses a seemingly more benign compression ignition system.

Despite its well-publicized safety advantages, however, a diesel is occasionally found to be the culprit in an engine room fire. And it's no accident that the NFPA standard for boats (NFPA-302) applies to both gasoline and diesel engines. Unfortunately, many boatowners have the mistaken idea that their trusty diesel, while safer, could never cause a fire. That's not the case.

In one claim in the BoatU.S. files, the faint smell of something burning prompted the skipper of *Molly B*, a 36-foot sailboat, to open the engine hatch and poke around for signs of trouble. When he found nothing, he closed the hatch, blaming the smell on carelessly spilled oil. A short time later, just as *Molly B* was pulling into its slip, someone noticed smoke drifting out of the companionway hatch. The skipper went below and grabbed an extinguisher, but before he could open the engine hatch under the companionway, he was driven from the cabin by heat and smoke. An attempt to fight the fire from the cockpit proved fruitless; the boat eventually burned to the waterline.

The owner suspected the fire had been caused by a cigarette left carelessly on

Turbocharged Diesels

WHILE IT'S TRUE that operating a diesel engine is generally safer than a gasoline engine, diesel certainly isn't without its share of potential hazards. This is especially true of turbocharged diesels, which have normal operating temperatures of up to 1,100°F. If one of these diesels overheats, as engines sometimes do, the temperature will rise even higher. This boat burned and sank after a small hole in the muffler shot an intense amount of heat, perhaps even a flame, onto a thermal blanket.

As much as any gasoline engine, turbocharged diesels need to be inspected routinely for signs of trouble. Exhaust systems are often difficult to reach—a mirror can help—but a hole or even a spot of dark rust anywhere is an indication that it's time for a replacement. The following are a few more things to look for:

- Check the condition of thermal blankets. Fires have started because older thermal blankets became soaked with oil from tiny leaks. When this happens, it's only a matter of time—probably not much time—before the blanket and boat catch fire. Replace blankets periodically and fix leaks promptly to avoid fires.
- Replace hoses that are leaking or otherwise suspect.
- Be sure that all surfaces less than 18 inches above the turbos have metal sheathing, *not* the foil-covered foam plastic insulation that is commonly found on boats.
- Protect wood and fiberglass deck beams, which can and do catch fire.
- Secure all hoses—whether oil, fuel, or water—well away from the exhaust system; use metal straps since plastic will melt.

the bunk. Certainly the sailboat's reliable little diesel could not have been the culprit. But a fire investigation specialist used fire patterns as well as observations made aboard sister ships to conclude that *Molly B* burned because an aluminum heat shield between the fuel line and the manifold was missing. The shield was present on the sister ships but had not been installed on the burned boat. Both ABYC and NFPA standards require that shielding, water jacketing, lagging, guards, or engine enclosures be used whenever combustibles could come in contact with hot surfaces. In addition, both standards require that hangers and brackets used to support a metal exhaust system be noncombustible within 6 feet of the engine connection.

A Quick Lesson in How a Diesel Works

Diesels produce hotter internal temperatures than gasoline engines. The reason is compression. Air drawn into the cylinder is compressed to 500 pounds per square inch (psi) or more, which raises the temperature in the cylinder to between 850°F and 1,000°F. Rather than using a spark plug, atomized fuel is injected into the heated cylinder and instantly burns. The additional heat raises the pressure another 250 psi and shoots the piston down. In some diesel engines the temperature is raised to well over 1,000°F.

Fuel Lines

To overcome the high pressure in the cylinders, diesel fuel must be injected at an even higher pressure (1,500 to 5,000 psi, depending on the system). On some diesels, fuel feed lines carry pressurized fuel up to the injectors. On others, such as GM diesels, pumps pressurize the fuel within the injectors.

If you have a diesel system, periodically inspect the pressurized fuel lines for signs of a leak. There have been claims involving nothing more than a tiny pinhole leak that sprayed fuel onto a hot exhaust manifold.

Fuel return lines, another feature unique to diesel engines, contain heated residual fuel and should not be taken lightly. Heated diesel fuel is readily combustible. The ABYC says, "Non-metallic hose used for fuel return lines shall be USCG Type A1 hose." Type A1 hose (indicated on the hose) offers the highest resistance to fire and permeation. Using a lesser-grade hose can quickly make a bad situation much worse.

A boatowner in Florida moved up to a larger and better boat but failed to move up to a better mechanic. The mechanic, an old friend of the owner's who usually worked on outboards, used clear plastic tubing for what he casually referred to as a diesel "overflow line." The tubing soon failed and sprayed hot fuel onto the engine. A passing boat alerted the skipper to smoke spewing from the engine hatch, but the warning came too late; the boat was soon engulfed in flames.

All lines are subject to engine vibration, which can cause loose connections and leaks throughout the fuel system. Besides inspecting lines and connections periodically, keeping bilges clean can give you an early warning of a leak. The appearance of fuel in the bilge should prompt an immediate inspection of all fuel lines.

Galley Fires

There's good news and bad news for anyone who cooks meals on a boat. The good news is that galley fires are not as common as they once were back in the heyday of pressurized alcohol stoves. Given their ongoing problems—spilled alcohol and flare-ups—it's no coincidence that West Marine and BoatU.S. no longer sell pressurized alcohol stoves. The bad news is that, on average, a galley

The fire that destroyed this boat was started by burning alcohol that spilled on the stovetop. It was originally a small fire, which, according to eyewitnesses, the boat's skipper tried—unsuccessfully—to extinguish with water.

Water can extinguish a fire, but may only dilute an alcohol fire. The fire can then expand from the top of the stove, and will be even more difficult to see and extinguish. An extinguisher is a better choice than water when it comes to fighting an alcohol fire.

is still not nearly as safe as a kitchen. The typical galley is cramped, surrounded by flammables, and is bounced up and down by waves. And when a fire does occur in the narrow confines of a boat's cabin, the smoke builds up quickly.

In one claim, at the end of her first-ever day of boating, the skipper's new girl-friend was eager to make a good impression and offered to cook dinner. First, she heated some oil in a pan and then threw in a frozen fish. The fish splattered the oil, which burned her hand. She yanked her hand back, knocking the pan over and spilling oil onto the burner and down the side of the stove. Flames jumped up and ignited paper towels and the curtains. In a matter of seconds, flames reached the overhead liner and thick, black smoke filled the small cabin. Clearly, this wasn't the sort of impression she was hoping to make.

Meanwhile, the skipper smelled smoke and stuck his head below. An attempt was made to put out the fire, but it was too late. Smoke had made it impossible to see or breathe. They abandoned the burning boat.

Combustibles must be kept safely away from a stove. NFPA standard 302 for recreational boats says that materials and curtains above and surrounding the stove shall be resistant to fire. Unfortunately, this is a voluntary standard, and even if a manufacturer has complied, curtains, paper towel racks, etc., may have been added later. Make curtains safer by using tracks on the bottoms as well as the tops. Store cloth pot holders, wood spoons, plastic salt and pepper shakers, etc., well away from the stove. In the claim above, the only thing that should have been near the stove—a fire extinguisher—wasn't.

Even in the largest galley, both the safety standards and manufacturer's instructions stress that it is a bad idea to leave a lighted stove unattended. This is a bad idea in a boat or house. A skipper in Connecticut left bacon cooking on low heat while he went on deck to enjoy his coffee. In the minute or two he was gone, a fire started below (from spilled alcohol) that destroyed the boat.

In a similar claim, a skipper in Michigan lit his stove to warm the cabin (unwise) and went to fetch some tools (very unwise). When he returned, the boat was engulfed in flames. Aside from leaving the stove on while he was away, using a stove as a source of heat is also a bad idea. For one thing, an open burner without a pan to dampen the flame can ignite nearby materials. And in the confined spaces of a boat, carbon monoxide (CO) from an open flame accumulates quickly. One member in a cold Alaskan anchorage was nearly overcome by CO after he shut off the propane stove being used for heat. The oven's pilot light was accidentally left on overnight while the boat was closed up. A CO alarm saved his life.

Cooking Fuels

Besides cabins crammed with flammables, onboard chefs have another potential hazard: the stove itself. Unlike a stove in a house, a stove aboard a boat is not so user-friendly. Older stoves that use alcohol as fuel must still be lighted using priming techniques, which seem archaic in this era of microchip technology. And while other fuels are easier to use than alcohol, they are highly flammable and must be respected.

Alcohol Stoves

Alcohol is a low-viscosity, nearly invisible, volatile liquid, which means that it is easy to spill, hard to see, and if handled improperly, dangerous. While not nearly as common as only a few years ago, alcohol stoves are still in use on older boats. Pressurized stoves have to be primed, which frequently leads to flare-ups and occasionally fires. A stove fire in Maine is typical: Alcohol in the primer cup was lighted but the flame remained an unsafe 10 inches high for several minutes. The skipper decided to pour water on the flame and start over. What he didn't realize was that water may only dilute the alcohol, which continues to burn. In this case, the water carried burning alcohol behind the stove. A few minutes later smoke started pouring out from somewhere down in the hull. The captain wisely hustled his kids out of the cabin, but when he returned to fight the fire, the cabin was filled with thick smoke. The boat was a total loss.

Nonpressurized alcohol stoves with wicks, which have largely replaced their pressurized counterparts on boats, are safer, if for no other reason than that they don't require priming. There are also no fuel lines or connections to worry about and almost no moving parts; the flame is controlled by adjusting the opening at the top of the canister. Other than keeping combustibles safely away, there would seem to be little danger in using a nonpressurized stove. But that's not quite the case.

While nonpressurized stoves are less likely to cause a fire, they are more likely to cause injuries. The reason is that liquid alcohol is only slow to ignite when it's at room temperature; when it's heated sufficiently, *vaporized* alcohol is extremely volatile.

A BoatU.S. member in Florida was boiling water for coffee when his canister went out. Thinking that it would be cooler, and therefore safer, he opted to fill the unused canister. Unfortunately, the second canister had also become heated by the operation of the first, and when he tried to light it with a match, the vaporized

Two Boats, Two Fires, One Fuel: Alcohol

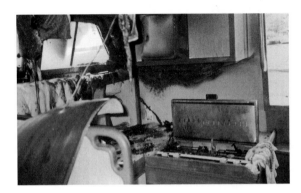

ALCOHOL IS WIDELY CONSIDERED to be a relatively benign cooking fuel—safer than LPG—since alcohol won't explode. The reality is that BoatU.S. has received more claims from the use of alcohol than from LPG or any other cooking fuel.

In the galley fire shown above, the boat's new owner had been trying to light the burner on his boat's pressurized alcohol stove and finally, thinking it wasn't lit, gave up and left to keep an appointment ashore. When he returned a short time later, he was greeted by the fire marshal.

The man had recently bought his boat and was unfamiliar with the finer points of operating the stove. While he may not have been successful at lighting the burner, he had been successful at lighting a primer flame, which dribbled down the back of the stove and eventually ignited the woodwork. Alcohol is a low-viscosity, nearly invisible, and volatile liquid that is easy to spill and hard to see.

And when it is first lighted, alcohol creates a pale blue flame that is also difficult to see on a bright day.

Luckily, a passerby saw smoke and alerted the fire department, which extinguished the fire before much damage was done.

In another fire (below), this one involving a nonpressurized alcohol stove, a woman had been cooking dinner and was refilling a canister when the vapor ignited and burned 45% of her face and body. Heated alcohol is extremely flammable, and a canister *must* be cooled *completely* before it is refueled and lighted.

With any stove, be sure you read the owner's manual before striking a match. Even if you've owned the stove for many seasons, it's a good idea to reread the stove's manual occasionally. Aside from telling you how to operate the stove safely, an owner's manual gives you important details on its maintenance.

A passing wave can easily throw an unsecured portable propane stove off a counter with predictable results. The fuel canister on this stove was not sufficiently tightened, causing butane to leak. The resulting fire burned the boat's overhead but was controlled with a fire extinguisher before serious damage was done.

alcohol flared up in his face. He suffered minor burns, and the boat's cabin was damaged slightly.

Kerosene Stoves

Like alcohol, kerosene stoves need to be primed—a tricky business no matter which fuel you use. Unlike alcohol, burning kerosene cannot be extinguished with water. Kerosene also burns hotter and is dirtier, especially if a cheaper grade of kerosene is used.

Propane Stoves

There is much to recommend a propane (liquefied petroleum gas—LPG) stove: the hot flame cooks food quickly, operation is clean, and propane refills are readily available in most areas. The drawback, as most skippers are aware, is that propane is heavier than air and will settle into pockets in the bilge. Once in the bilge, it has a tendency to linger, and propane is extremely flammable.

Thanks to a BoatU.S. underwriting policy requiring safety inspections that assure boats comply with ABYC and NFPA-302 safety standards, propane explosions have been almost nonexistent in the BoatU.S. Marine Insurance program. One of the few that did occur was due to a corroded copper feed line protected by a neoprene sleeve. The sleeve was placed over the entire length of the copper line, which probably caused the corrosion and also hid the leak until it was too late. The sleeve should only have been used where the line passed through a bulkhead.

Periodically inspect any cooking system, especially propane, for leaks (see the Inspecting Your Propane and CNG System for Leaks sidebar on page 92). Also inspect tank lockers to make sure overboard drain holes have not become blocked. Close tank cutoff valves whenever the stove is not in use. Finally, anytime the wind or a boiling pot puts out the cooking flame, it is important to sniff the bilges for gas before relighting the stove. (An additive in the propane gives it a distinct odor.)

Do not store portable propane or butane cooking stoves that use disposable canisters below on a boat. The canisters can't be vented overboard, and the materials aren't marine grade. A forgotten canister buried in a damp locker is a time bomb.

Compressed Natural Gas (CNG)

CNG, though increasingly difficult to find, has the advantage of being lighter than air and dispersing quickly, which reduces the chances of an explosion. It is stored in high-pressure cylinders similar to scuba tanks. As with any cooking fuel, periodically inspect CNG stoves, tanks, and piping for leaks. Never use CNG tanks with propane stoves, and vice versa.

Electric Stoves and Microwaves

From a safety standpoint, electric stoves and microwaves are the way to go. They have no fuel lines, connections, canisters, and tanks, and they never require priming. Unfortunately, these stoves can't be used away from dockside electricity unless the boat has a permanently installed generator.

Other Fuels

Charcoal stoves hung on the stern rail at anchor are probably safe, as long as skippers are prudent and keep all combustibles safely away. If the boat is not able to swing into the wind at anchor, a charcoal stove should not be used, lest sparks get blown back onto the boat.

Marina Dry Stack Fires

In the past few years, there have been several devastating fires at dry stack storage facilities that involved the complete destruction of hundreds of boats. Every boat in an enclosed storage rack in Virginia Beach, Virginia, was destroyed one night in a fire that was already out of control by the time it was discovered. A little farther north, a similar fire at a marina dry stack facility in Pasadena, Maryland, was equally destructive. These fires underscored the one significant

---

Inspecting Your Propane and CNG System for Leaks

WITH THE STOVE'S COOKING VALVES closed and the valve at the tank open, note the pressure on the gauge at the tank, then close the tank valve. The pressure should remain constant for at least 10 minutes. If the pressure drops, locate leaks by applying a soap-and-water solution at all connections. Repeat this test for each tank in multitank systems.

NEVER USE A FLAME TO CHECK FOR LEAKS. NEVER USE SOAP CONTAINING AMMONIA.

If you find defective parts, it is important that you replace them only with materials that are suitable for use with a hazardous liquid. Probably your best bet is to contact the stove's manufacturer.

Preventing Galley Fires: A Checklist

- Keep a Type ABC fire extinguisher (see page 96) close at hand to the galley and make sure you can get to it if there is a stove fire.
- Don't store pots and pans (or worse, a fire extinguisher) behind the stove so you have to reach over the stove to get it.
- Make sure there are no flammable objects like curtains near the stove.
- Do not leave a marine stove unattended—unlike your kitchen stove, a passing wake can toss something flammable into the flame.
- Make sure you're familiar with the lighting and use of your marine stove—read the directions!
- Trust your nose. Whenever you smell fuel, check it out before lighting the stove.
- Check installations periodically for chafed hoses and leaking fittings.
- Nonpressurized alcohol stoves must be completely cool before refilling. Be sure to clean up any spilled fuel before lighting.
- Burning alcohol can be hard to see. Place a pot on the burner to make it easier to see the flame. Make certain the flame is completely out before you leave.
- Use a fire extinguisher or a fire blanket to extinguish alcohol flames. Although they can be extinguished with water, the flames could also be displaced and float on top of water.
- Any stove with a remote fuel tank should have a shutoff valve near the tank. Make sure the valve doesn't get buried behind clothes or boxes of food. Keep the valve closed when the stove is not being used.

drawback to this otherwise handy way of storing boats.

Unlike boats that are kept in slips or are blocked side by side ashore, boats in storage racks are stacked up vertically, like firewood, with plenty of air underneath and above. An isolated fire on a single boat can spread with frightening swiftness, first to the boats directly above, then to surrounding boats. If the fire isn't discovered almost immediately, it can grow exponentially with the likelihood that the storage rack will already be an inferno by the time firefighters arrive. According to the claim files, this is true whether the boats are on a rack in open air or enclosed in buildings.

If you leave your boat in a dry storage rack or a covered storage shed with other boats, it is especially important that your marina adhere to NFPA standard

The aftermath of a dry stack storage fire.

303 for marinas and boatyards. This standard is meant to eliminate, or at least greatly reduce, the chances of a "spark" causing a fire. Some marinas have sprinkler systems, which are included in the NFPA standards and are obviously a huge plus in a fire.

Boatowners who opt to leave their boats in storage racks should ask about sprinkler systems and make sure that the marina is following the other key points in NFPA-303:

- Batteries shall be disconnected or the master battery switch turned off.

- The use of portable heaters in a boat storage area shall be prohibited except where necessary to accomplish repairs, in which case they shall be used only when personnel are in attendance. No open flame heaters of any sort shall be used.

- The use of blowtorches or flammable paint remover shall be prohibited.

- No unattended electrical equipment shall be in use aboard boats.

- All portable power lines, such as drop cords, shall be prohibited from any boat in an in-out dry storage building. Portable battery chargers shall also be prohibited aboard any boat.

Your Boat's On Fire . . . Now What?

In a claim from the BoatU.S. files, an owner and his two friends were nearing the last leg of a long trip from Yorktown, Virginia, to Watkins Glen, New York, aboard a 46-foot sportfisherman that he'd bought barely three weeks before. They were making good time across Oneida Lake when one of the crew left the flybridge to go below. He quickly reappeared on the flybridge: "We've got a problem," he informed the skipper, "smoke!" The skipper quickly brought the engines to idle, and one of the crew tried briefly to extinguish the fire. Within a minute or two, he was overwhelmed by fumes and had to abandon the effort. After trying unsuccessfully to send out a Mayday on the VHF radio, the captain ran to the foredeck, set an anchor, and hailed a passing boat by waving a life jacket. Meanwhile, a volunteer fireman saw the smoke from shore and dispatched a fireboat. By the time the fire was brought under control, the boat had been destroyed.

A fire requires quick and decisive action on the part of the crew to get the blaze under control. Fire extinguishers need to be properly mounted and *accessible*. In the Oneida Lake case, after emptying one fire extinguisher on the fire, the crew tried to find the second extinguisher. Can you quickly spot the fire extinguisher in this picture of what they saw? (Hint: Look for the letters "BC.") Neither could they.

Later investigation determined that the electrical panel was the source of the fire. The captain's urgent Mayday call conveys the danger of all fire outbreaks on boats. Unlike fires ashore, where there are usually several escape routes to safety, there are few places on a burning boat to hide from the heat and noxious fumes. Add to that the anxiety of standing above many gallons of explosive fuel, and your first decision should be whether to fight the fire or abandon ship.

If you decide to fight the fire, it is imperative that every move be made quickly and correctly; there is rarely, if ever, a second chance. A crew that reacts initially with confusion and indecision is likely to panic as the fire spreads.

The next decision is which type of extinguisher to use; using the wrong extinguisher to fight a fire is like trying to dig a hole with a rake. Success will depend on understanding the fundamentals of fire classification and providing the most efficient fire extinguishers in the locations where they are most likely to be needed.

The ABCs of Fire Classification

Class A fires consist of *all* combustible solid materials, such as paper, wood, cloth, rubber, and many plastics, including the fiberglass-reinforced plastic used for decks and hulls.

Class B fires consist of *all* flammable liquids, including stove alcohol, grease, gasoline, diesel, kerosene, oil, oil-based paint, teak oil, paint thinners, acetone, varnishes, and flammable gases or fumes.

Class C fires consist of energized electrical equipment. Class C fires are identified for their potential to electrocute or shock anyone using water-based extinguishing agents. Turning off the electricity will change the status of a Class C fire to a Class A and/or B fire.

Note that Class A, B, and C categories are not subdivided any further, so it may be easier to think of them as (A) solids, (B) liquids, and (C) electrical fires; there's no need, for example, to waste time distinguishing between alcohol or kerosene when your stove's on fire.

Selecting Extinguishers

All fire extinguishers are rated according to the extinguishing agent's effectiveness in controlling one or more classes of fire. For example, ABC-rated extinguishers, commonly called multipurpose or tri-class extinguishers, are capable of fighting all three classes of fire. Numbers preceding the letters (on portable units only) indicate an agent's relative effectiveness in extinguishing that particular class of fire. For instance, a 10 BC dry chemical extinguisher is twice as effective in putting out a fire as a 5 BC unit. Multipurpose 1A-10 BC dry chemical extinguishers are becoming more popular as an alternative to the common 10 BC extinguishers because of the additional Class A rating, especially since the additional cost is minimal (less than $5).

In general, dry chemical extinguishers, which use a chemical powder to smother the source of the fire, are the favored choice in the boat's cabin. Not only is a dry chemical extinguisher more effective, it is easier for an inexperienced user to direct the discharge plume to the base of the flame from a safe distance. Conversely, extinguishers with gaseous agents (CO_2, Halon, and Halon replacements FE-241 and FM-200), which react with the surrounding oxygen, aren't as effective in a cabin, especially a larger, more open cabin, because the gases are often dissipated before the fire is extinguished. But, as we'll see, in the tight confines of an engine room, a gaseous extinguisher's ability to dissipate extinguishing agents is its biggest plus.

The ABC units have the drawback of being highly corrosive and often ruining equipment, but because the priorities are safety and the overall effectiveness of the extinguishing agent, the ABYC recommends that ABC multipurpose extinguishers be used in most instances on boats under 65 feet. The ABC extinguishers not only reduce any confusion about what to use and where (saving time), they also cover the possibility that, for example, any Class B fire that spreads from the stove to the curtains (Class A) can be fought with the same extinguisher.

A Subtle, but Costly, Distinction

A 42-foot powerboat was cruising offshore when a crew member reported a strange smell coming from the engine compartment. The owner grabbed a dry chemical extinguisher from the galley on his way to the enclosed compartment, opened the access door, and was immediately driven back by smoke. He tried to direct the stream of dry chemical inside the compartment, but because of the smoke, couldn't locate the source of the fire. By then the fumes had also engulfed the main saloon, and he was driven back. From the cockpit, he saw flames coming out of the engine compartment's starboard ventilation ducts, so he directed another dry chemical extinguisher into the duct openings; the fire died momentarily but quickly resumed and grew rapidly. The boat soon had to be abandoned, and it burned to the waterline.

The same dry chemicals that are so effective in a boat's cabin aren't much use when a fire breaks out in the engine compartment. The reason has to do with how the two types of fires are fought.

A fire port.

Engine fires typically begin with a warning—a burning smell, a loss of engine power, or smoke pouring out the vents—followed by someone throwing open the engine hatch. This is *not* the proper response, however, as the sudden rush of oxygen can quickly make a bad situation much worse. The smoke pours out, the oxygen pours in, the flames shoot up, and the whole mess quickly gets out of hand.

The solution is to leave the hatch closed and fight the fire either with a fixed extinguisher in the engine compartment (actually this would already have been done) or with a portable gaseous extinguisher discharged through a fire port (a small opening into the engine compartment) on deck, which is why dry chemical extinguishers of any class are inappropriate. Blindly spraying a chemical extinguisher through a fire port will do little or nothing to extinguish an engine room fire because the chemical isn't being directed toward the base of the flames. A gaseous extinguisher, on the other hand, extinguishes the fire by affecting the oxygen supply. The same extinguisher that wasn't effective in the wide-open spaces of a boat's cabin will be much more effective in a cramped engine compartment.

For this reason, among others, the ABYC recommends that either a portable gaseous extinguisher be provided near the engine compartment (outside), preferably with a fire port, or a fixed gaseous extinguisher be used inside the engine compartment. In the event of a fire, either option eliminates the need to open the hatch.

A Few Words of Praise for Fixed Systems in the Engine Room

Overall, the most efficient fire protection system is the safest. Claim files show that fires begin in the engine compartment for numerous reasons: constant pounding and vibration loosens wiring terminals and causes chafe, engine exhausts overheat, water pumps fail, fuel leaks—the list goes on. An automatic system, activated by a rise in temperature, can discharge and extinguish a fire almost instantly—long before someone can smell the smoke and react with a portable extinguisher. This is especially relevant if you sometimes cruise short-handed. The automatic system kills the fire earlier and minimizes damage. And since Halon and its replacements will not damage internal engine parts, it is often possible, after locating and correcting the problem, to restart the engine after a fire and return to port.

Engine Fires: An Experiment of Sorts

United States Power Squadrons D/LT/C Joseph W. Cartwright, SN, and Chris Muir, safety officer for the North Olympic Sail and Power Squadron, wrote about a dramatic demonstration that was conducted by the United States Power Squadrons (USPS), District 16, in Bellingham, Washington. It should interest anyone with a gasoline or diesel inboard.

The demonstration was certainly well thought out. Rather than set a match to a pile of old lumber and then squirt it out with an extinguisher, the Squadron built a replica of a 25-foot powerboat's aft deck, complete with an engine hatch, cleats, flagstaff, and a USPS ensign. They then filled a 30-square-inch pan with 3 quarts of diesel fuel and 1 quart of gasoline, tossed in a match, closed the hatch, and left it to burn for what must have been a painfully long minute (the time they estimated it would take to discover the fire and locate an extinguisher).

The intrepid demonstrators then pulled open the hatch expecting to see a fire that looked like, oh, a pile of burning lumber. What they saw instead was—whoooosh—a yellow wall of flame. Chris Muir said the fire was fueled by the sudden rush of oxygen. A volunteer grabbed a Type B, 2½-pound dry chemical extinguisher—the kind that meets minimum Coast Guard requirements (and the kind you probably have on your boat)—pulled the pin, aimed the nozzle at the base of the flame, squeezed the pin, and swept the nozzle back and forth slowly until the extinguisher was empty. This is the textbook way to fight a fire, and it usually works. With this "engine fire," however, it was a dismal failure; the fire kept right on burning. The good news is that they were able to put the fire out using the same technique and a larger B-1, 5-pound 10 BC extinguisher.

The dramatic demonstration proved that bigger is definitely better when it comes to fire extinguishers. *At least* one 5-pound extinguisher should be kept aboard, and a 10-pound extinguisher would be even better. In a follow-up test,

The District 16 fire.

the fire was allowed to burn for 2 minutes before the extinguisher was used. In the second test, a 10-pound extinguisher had to be completely emptied before the fire was extinguished. The larger extinguishers deliver much more agent in the same amount of time.

The demonstration also proved that installing a fire port (remember, it must be used with a gaseous extinguisher) or an automatic fire extinguishing system (also gaseous) is invaluable should an engine fire ever occur. Fires thrive on air, and the *chimney effect*—flames shooting up from the bilge toward open air—means the fire will be much, much harder to extinguish once the hatch is opened.

Spontaneous Combustion of Charcoal

While the BoatU.S. claim files have been used many times to provide insight into how fires get started on boats, there has been at least one instance where they were used to prove how a fire can't be started. It all began when a BoatU.S. member sent an e-mail asking if BoatU.S. Marine Insurance staff had ever received a claim for a fire that was caused by the spontaneous combustion of charcoal. It was a good question, since just about everybody has heard that storing charcoal on a boat is risky. But after examining hundreds of claims for onboard fires (this was already being done for another project), BoatU.S. confidently told the member that it hadn't.

A short time later, he posted the response on one of the BoatUS.com message boards, and the fireworks started. Someone replied that BoatU.S. was guilty of giving bad "advice," even though BoatU.S. had only answered a simple question. This guy was clearly peeved and felt strongly that charcoal must be kept dry and stored in an airtight container.

BoatU.S. didn't necessarily disagree, but the question—a big question—still begged to be answered: With all the charcoal being used on boats, why hadn't there been any claims? Do all BoatU.S. members diligently store their charcoal in airtight containers?

The Case for Spontaneous Combustion The claim files had already been consulted, so the next stop in the quest to get answers was that bottomless sea of information, the Web. Sure enough, there, hidden among those lovable pop-up ads, were hundreds, maybe thousands of hits for charcoal/spontaneous combustion, including many that advised about the possibility of fires. A warning from a local New York fire department was typical: "Keep damp or wet coals in a well-ventilated area. During the drying process, spontaneous combustion can occur in confined areas." A barbecuing safety page further recommended, "Store charcoal in a metal container with a tight-fitting lid." Just how many sites warn of the dangers of charcoal and spontaneous combustion is anybody's guess, although one website reported that there were 562 charcoal/spontaneous combustion warnings at various websites.

A word or two about the Web is in order here. Like information anywhere, you first have to consider the source whenever you're doing research. Not all sites are hosted by organizations you're likely to have heard of, and some of the "warnings" are equally as suspect. In the case of charcoal combustion, however, the warnings were from reputable sites, including many local fire departments. What was lacking at any of the sites, however, were verifiable, firsthand accounts of charcoal combusting spontaneously. With other well-known types of accidents, such as collisions or fuel fires, there are many such accounts, most often reported by local newspaper and television station websites.

The Case against Spontaneous Combustion   The most compelling argument against the spontaneous combustion of charcoal was presented by P. J. Pagni, a professor at the University of California, Berkeley, at a symposium on fire safety science in 2002. The symposium was sponsored in part by the NFPA and was held at Worcester Polytechnic Institute in Worcester, Massachusetts, which posted the paper on its website. Pagni's research found that the largest commercially available bag of charcoal briquettes (20 pounds) cannot self-ignite at a temperature below 250°F. All tested variations—size, different formulations, addition of water or dry wood, aging, and different bag configurations—raised the already high temperature even higher. At normal temperatures (approximately 77°F), Pagni's data showed that a bag of charcoal briquettes would have to exceed the volume of a typical house to self-ignite. Further support comes from no less an authority than the 19th edition of the NFPA's *Fire Protection Handbook*, which states that spontaneous combustion of charcoal sold to consumers is not a possibility because of its "processing, small quantity, and container."

One final question remains: Why do so many people, including many professional firefighters, believe that charcoal can spontaneously combust? The likely answer is that charcoal's "first cousin"—coal—has a well-documented tendency to spontaneously combust when it is damp or stored in large quantities. On coal-powered ships, which were notoriously damp and required "mountains" of coal to fuel their engines, fires were a common problem. The *Titanic*, to cite one well-known example, had assigned twelve men to fight a fire in its coal bin that had been burning from the time the ship left Southampton until it struck an iceberg and sank. ("Good news, Captain, the fire in the coal bin is finally out . . .")

It seems likely then, that since coal and charcoal are similar looking, have similar burning characteristics, and even have similar names, the combustion properties of the two would become confused. Coal and charcoal are not the same, however, and the case for spontaneous combustion by charcoal appears to be nothing more than hot air.

Staying Afloat

YOU DON'T HAVE TO SPEND MUCH TIME on the water before the word "sink" crosses your mind. Could a wave flip the boat over? Could the boat spring a leak? How much chance is there that the boat will slam into a submerged object and start taking on water? Ever since man first devised ways to float on top of the water, he has had to face the disturbing possibility that his fragile craft, whatever it is, could slip beneath the waves. Even a log canoe can eventually soak up water and sink.

Modern boats sink for a variety of reasons. According to the claim files, for every boat that sinks underway, *four* boats sink in their slips. There are two reasons for this discrepancy. One reason is that whenever a boat leaves the dock, someone is aboard, which leaves open the possibility that the leak will be discovered and the problem corrected before it sinks the boat. The second reason is that boats tend to spend the vast majority of their time at the dock.

Why Boats Sink at the Dock

Consider the following BoatU.S. claim. The handsome sportfisherman had been an impressive floating beauty when the owner left the marina barely 13 hours earlier, which is why he was having so much trouble believing that it was his boat on the bottom of the harbor when the call came from the marina manager. There were *five* bilge pumps aboard, all working. How could his boat have sunk so quickly?

The answer was traced to a cracked generator intake hose, which according to the surveyor's report, may have been leaking steadily for weeks or even months. The bilge pumps kept the water out until the batteries (and then the pumps) died, and the boat filled with water.

When a boat sinks at the dock, the question most likely to be asked is: "What happened to the bilge pump?" That's the wrong question. By dutifully emptying the bilge periodically, a bilge pump can

actually *hide* a problem until the pump clogs or the battery goes dead. Water, not a bilge pump, sinks boats. The correct question should be: Where did the water come from? For an answer, BoatU.S. examined 100 claim files of boats that sank in their slips.

Why Boats Sink at the Dock

Reason	Percentage
fitting below waterline failed	50%
rain and snow	32%
fitting above waterline failed	9%
poor docking arrangement	8%
other	1%

Where the Water Came From

Underwater Fittings In 50% of the dockside sinking claims, water found its way into the bilge through leaks at underwater fittings. The majority of the leaks were at stuffing boxes (twelve), followed by outdrive or shift bellows (eleven), failed hoses or hose clamps (eight), sea strainers (four), and drain plugs (four).

There were two sinkings each from air-conditioning fittings, gate valves, transducers, mounting bolts, and mufflers. One boat went to the bottom as a result of a leaking speedometer impeller. It is likely that in some claims more than one fitting had been leaking.

Rain and Snow Water falling from the sky—either rain, snow, or sleet—accounted for a whopping 32% of the sinking claims. Everybody has seen a rowboat or two awash, so this shouldn't be a surprise. What may be startling is that all the claims involved boats with self-bailing cockpits, which should have shed the water overboard. These boats didn't sink in a single deluge; most sank over a period of weeks or even months. The reason most likely to be given was that the bilge pump or float switch failed, but the real reason was often neglect.

Fittings Above the Waterline It is also interesting to note the problem was traced to fittings *above* the waterline in 9% of the sinking claims (see top photo opposite). (Question: How can a fitting that is above the waterline sink a boat? Answer: Fittings that are above the waterline aren't always above the waterline.) More on this later.

Poor Docking Arrangements Boats that sank after getting caught under a dock or banging against a piling accounted for 8% of the claims (see bottom photo). This number *did not* include boats that sank during hurricanes, or the number would have been much higher.

Other

The only claim that didn't fit in any of the first four categories involved a boat that sank after lightning blew a transducer out.

Protecting Your Boat

Outdrive (Sterndrive) Boots Eleven of 100 sterndrive boats sank because the rubber boots on the outdrive had deteriorated. According to experts, outdrive boots should be examined two or three times a year. Rubber that looks dried out and cracked (cracks are most likely to appear in the creases) needs replacing. If possible, store the outdrive down, which eliminates most creases and prolongs the life of the rubber. Finally, for whatever reason, muskrats and other water-swimming vermin like to chew on outdrive boots. Ro-Pel, a malodorous commercial product, is an effective deterrent against such critters (check the Internet for a source).

Seacocks and Gate Valves According to voluntary industry standards, seacocks or gate valves, which can be closed in an emergency or when the skipper is away from the boat for extended periods, must be used on all through-hulls

below the heeled waterline. The valves and fittings must be made of bronze or Marelon, which are not likely to break when struck accidentally with a foot or anchor. (Forespar's Marelon seacocks are the only plastic seacocks that meet UL requirements.)

Seacocks are widely regarded as being more reliable than gate valves. In an emergency, a quick glance at a seacock will tell you whether it is open or closed. With a gate valve, you can't tell. Gate valves also have a reputation for failing internally because the different metals—steel inside, bronze outside—aren't compatible. One sinking claim occurred when a bronze gate valve disintegrated and broke in two. A similar problem occurred with a bronze seacock. In both cases, the failure of the bronze would suggest weakening by stray-current corrosion. Look for a pinkish color on the bronze, which indicates corrosion.

Other through-hulls that need inspecting periodically are transducers and raw-water intake strainers. Ice can bend a strainer that isn't winterized properly. You should either drain the bowl or fill it with antifreeze. Even if the seacock has been closed for the winter, water can enter the boat when the seacock is opened in the spring.

Removable transducers and impellers must be locked in place securely, or they can work loose and sink the boat. One boat sank because the dummy plug for the speedometer had not been locked down properly. Two boats sank because the fittings for the air-conditioner intakes broke. Finally, one boat sank because a stern-drive bolt through the transom was "weeping" a small quantity of water. The boat's owner apparently hadn't been aboard for many weeks or even months.

Three boats in the BoatU.S. claim files sank when a hose slipped off a seacock nipple. To avoid this problem, double-clamp hoses on seacocks using stainless steel hose clamps, keeping in mind that some stainless steel clamps are more stainless than others. Replace rusted clamps. Ridged seacock nipples are preferable because they grip a hose better than smooth nipples. Tapered nipples don't guarantee a firm grip and should be avoided.

Another boat sank because a hose split. Use reinforced hose at through-hulls; it is usually a heavy black hose. Lighter, unreinforced PVC hoses can (and do) rupture and crack. Check the entire length of the hose, as excessive heat from the engine or chemicals (bilge cleaners, battery acid, etc.) can cause isolated failures. A boat in Michigan eventually failed because a hose had been rubbing slightly against the rough edge of a hole cut through the fiberglass. Replace any hoses that are suspect.

Mufflers Backfiring can blow a hole in a plastic muffler. Corrosion can eat a hole in a metal muffler. One boat sank when a plug that was on the bottom of the muffler was removed and not replaced. Inspect both the muffler and the exhaust hose carefully.

How could a 36-foot sailboat with over 3 feet of freeboard be shoved underwater by a few inches of snow? Because a plastic through-hull that was an inch or two above the waterline cracked (inset), and the weight of the snow lowered the damaged fitting to just below the surface. Water then began entering through the crack, and the boat gradually filled with water and sank.

Plastic fittings deteriorate in sunlight and can get brittle in only a few years. How common are cracked fittings? A surveyor in New York estimated recently that of the boats he surveys that have plastic fittings above the waterline, almost half have at least one fitting that is cracked. Why wait until a fitting has deteriorated to replace it? Replace cheap fittings near the waterline with bronze or Marelon; both are much more durable, and the cost difference is negligible.

Through-Hulls Above the Waterline As a general rule, a boat whose gunwale is close to the water (low freeboard) has a greater chance of sinking accidentally. A ski boat, for example, is more likely to be overcome by rainwater, a slow leak, or a following sea than a cruiser whose impressive hull towers far above the water.

But a boat is often much "closer" to the water than its freeboard would indicate. A cracked through-hull at the boot stripe or a cutout in the transom for an outboard motor well that isn't protected by a splash guard means that, as a practical matter, the boat has to sink only an inch or two before it floods and heads to the bottom.

In one claim, holes at the boot stripe were meant to drain the deck of an open boat. Rain lowered the waterline and water began lapping onto the deck, which proved to be less than watertight. In another claim, snow shoved the drain of a 30-foot sailboat underwater. The plastic fitting had deteriorated in the sunlight and cracked, so water was free to enter the boat.

Inspect fittings and hoses above the waterline with the same critical eye that you should use on fittings in the bilge. Double-clamp the through-hulls and consider adding an antisiphon loop or check valve to any that are within 8 to 12 inches of the waterline.

Question: How could a boat sink if the water doesn't come in through the hull (seawater) or fall from the sky (rain or snow)? The answer is that the water comes from the municipal water supply if someone leaves the dockside water hooked up to their boat and a fitting fails!

According to the surveyor's report, a garden hose that was attached to the boat's freshwater supply was left on and a ½-inch screw on the PVC compression fitting parted from the feed line to the galley sink. Water then poured into the boat, and it sank overnight.

Antisiphon Loops and Check Valves When a hose exits the hull above the waterline from a point somewhere below the waterline—at a bilge pump or head (toilet)—installing an antisiphon loop or check valve will prevent water from flowing back into the boat. The high point of the loop must be well above the waterline. Many boats have sunk when they were lowered an inch or two, and water poured through an antisiphon loop that was at or near the waterline.

Dockside Freshwater System Four boats in the BoatU.S. claim files sank because of problems in the boats' dockside freshwater systems. In one case, water entered through a broken fitting in the boat's hot water heater. Another sank after a hose burst (the freshwater system hadn't been properly winterized). The first line of defense against this sort of sinking is to turn off the water at the dock whenever you'll be away from your boat for more than a few hours. (There are devices available at hardware stores that can be preset to shut off the water supply automatically.) Periodically inspect hoses and clamps throughout the system. While you're checking, make sure your system incorporates a pressure-reducer valve, and that all hoses are reinforced hose (look for the crisscross pattern if the hose is made of clear PVC), which accommodates the greatly increased pressure of a city water system.

Cabin, Deck, and Scuppers Even aboard boats with cabins and self-draining cockpits, it isn't unusual to have a leak or two at hatches, ports, chainplates, etc. Caulking these leaks keeps water out of the bilge and may also prevent costly structural repairs later. In colder climates, open boats and boats with especially low freeboard should be hauled in for the winter, as they are prone to being shoved underwater by snow and ice.

Five sinkings were caused by clogged scuppers. When scuppers are clogged with leaves or debris, water backs up and has a tendency to find a way into the bilge. Two other sinkings occurred because scuppers were cracked or broken, and water leaked into the bilge.

Keep the Boat Away from the Dock Ten boats sank because they either got caught under or banged against the dock. Arrange the bow, stern, and spring lines so as to keep your boat in the center of its slip. Be especially aware of swim platforms, which can be bashed against a piling, dock, or seawall and pushed through the hull. Use fenders and fender boards to cushion minor bumps, but keep in mind, they will not compensate for a poor docking arrangement. Double up on lines and use chafe guards if the boat is in an exposed location.

Visiting Your Boat: The First Line of Defense against a Dockside Sinking

If you need a reason to visit your boat more often, consider that the cost of repairing a boat that has been underwater, even briefly, is usually about 40% of its

Boats That Sink on Land

A METAL FITTING that had been fitted to this sailboat's cockpit drains broke, and water began pouring into the bilge whenever it rained. Over time, the bilge pump failed, and water began accumulating. The boat was being stored ashore for the winter. By the time the owner discovered the problem in early March, the water was well over the cabin sole. The total cost to repair the damage was more than $6,000.

The surveyor thought it was possible that the fitting had broken during the season and wasn't discovered because the bilge pump masked the problem. The fitting may also have broken earlier that winter by expanding ice. Either way, there are several lessons that can be learned from this claim.

First, it is critical to visit your boat over the winter, even if it's stored ashore. What works best is to make an arrangement with friends to visit each other's boats. Don't just drive by; go aboard and look around.

Second, every spring, spend an hour or two poking around the hard-to-reach areas of your boat—the engine room, lockers, lazarette, etc. Squeeze hoses. Look at fittings. Open and close seacocks. You may be surprised at the problems you'll avoid later.

Finally, any sinking claim—on land or water—makes a good argument for a bilge pump counter, which alerts you to potential leaks that might otherwise go unnoticed.

value. Besides having to pay the deductible, the skipper typically loses the use of the boat for several weeks while it is being repaired.

At least twice a season, inspect any fittings above or below the waterline that could be letting water into the boat. All too often, skippers rely on bilge pumps to bail them out when they can't visit their boats. The pump fails and the boat sinks. If you can't visit your boat regularly, consider using a buddy system with other boatowners to watch each other's boats. Another alternative is to ask your marina manager to keep an eye on the boat. Many marinas offer routine inspections, but usually at an extra cost.

Why Boats Sink Underway

One reason that fewer boats sink underway is because, unlike most boats at docks, there is someone aboard who may be able to stem the flow of water. When water started pouring over his 25-foot boat's transom 30 miles off the Virginia

This beautiful wooden sailboat sank the old-fashioned way: it struck a reef.

coast, David Van Daalen got on his VHF radio and put out a Mayday that was received by the Coast Guard in Virginia Beach. Though the weather was clear, the Coast Guard had trouble copying his position, David said later, "probably because of the fear in my voice."

Thanks to movies like *Titanic*, most people have at least some idea of the feeling—the fear—that accompanies the realization that a boat is sinking. Unlike the *Titanic*, however, small boats typically sink quickly, often in seconds, and there is little time to find and plug leaks, don life jackets, send out a distress call, or fire flares. David Van Daalen's boat sank after waves poured over the transom and the cockpit filled with water. Other boats lacked bilge alarms and took on water through a broken hose or stuffing box for many minutes before their skippers looked below and saw water rising over the cabin sole.

I've examined fifty BoatU.S. claim files for boats ranging from a 54-foot off-shore sailboat to a tiny personal watercraft that sank underway. None of the fifty sinkings involved fatalities, although that is always a possibility when a boat sinks with passengers aboard. It's no wonder that experts warn boaters to wear life jackets or at least keep them handy—not buried in a locker under the mop, cleaning bucket, and charcoal grill.

Why Boats Sink on Open Water

Reason	Percentage
waves over the gunwales	30%
leaks at through-hulls or hoses	18%
leaks at raw-water cooling system/exhaust	12%
missing drain plug	12%
navigation error (grounding)	10%
boat construction (hull split open)	6%
leaks at outdrive boots	4%
struck submerged object	4%
other	4%

Why They Sank

Any boat has the potential to sink underway for the same reasons that it could sink at the dock—a hose slips off, a packing gland leaks, etc. In the study, 34% of the boats sank because of leaks at through-hulls, outdrive boots, or the raw-water

Flooding from Various Size Holes at Different Depths

SEVERAL YEARS AGO New Jersey surveyors Bob Gibble and John Klose calculated flooding rates for various size holes at several different depths. Gibble needed to convince skeptics that a tiny ¼-inch hole on an outdrive bellows was large enough to sink a boat. Klose was investigating the sinking of an expensive sportfisherman off the coast. Klose and Gibble used Bernoulli's equation, and the chart they authored eventually proved useful to both surveyors' investigations.

Hole Diameter (in.)	Area (sq. in.)	Head[1]				
		6 IN.	1 FT.	1 FT. 6 IN.	2 FT.	3 FT.
⅛	0.01	0.17 gpm[2]	0.3 gpm	0.31 gpm	0.35 gpm	0.43 gpm
¼	0.05	0.88	1.2	1.53	1.8	2.2
⅜	0.11	1.94	2.7	3.4	3.9	4.8
½	0.20	3.46	4.9	6.0	6.9	18.5
¾	0.44	7.77	11.0	13.5	15.6	19.1
1	0.79	13.96	19.6	24.2	27.8	34.0
2	3.14	55.49	78.6	96.1	111.1	136.1
4	12.57	222.1	314.3	384.7	444.5	544.4
6	28.27	499.6	707.2	865.3	1000.2	1225.0

1. *Head* is the vertical distance from the hole to the waterline.
2. GPM = gallons per minute.

Even a tiny hole below the waterline has the potential to sink a boat if it's ignored long enough. According to Bernoulli's equation for fluid mechanics, an ⅛-inch hole that is 6 inches below the waterline will leak 0.17 gallon of water into the boat per minute. Even if the boat has an automatic bilge pump, the constant on/off cycling will eventually wear down the battery and sink the boat. In this case, the hole was in the gearshift bellows, and the boat would have sunk, had it not been for a timely visit by the skipper.

cooling system, all of which are routinely implicated when boats sink at the dock. There are many other reasons that boats sink underway, however, that have nothing to do with loose hose clamps or broken fittings. Boats underway can strike floating debris or stray onto a rocky shoal ("navigation error"). Some claims were from careless skippers who forgot to install drain plugs. And 6% of the boats sank after launching themselves from wave crests, landing hard, and splitting open.

Once a boat starts to sink, the in-rushing water will gain momentum as the boat settles into the water. If a boat has a 2-inch hole that is a foot below the waterline, for example, over 78 gallons of water will pour into the boat per minute. When the same hole is 3 feet below the surface, the flow of water increases to 136 gallons per minute. Keep in mind also that as the boat sinks, through-hulls that were above the waterline will become submerged. If any of these fittings are cracked or missing, the flow of water into the boat will accelerate further.

Stopping the Water

Swamping: Taking Water Over the Gunwales The single most critical reason boats are flooded on open water has to do with transom height. Thirteen of fifteen boats in the sample group that were swamped were outboard powered, with engine cutouts in their transoms that were often only inches above the waves. (Of the two remaining boats, one was an inboard with very low freeboard that took a wave over the bow, and the other was a sailboat that was knocked down and sank when water entered an unsecured cockpit hatch.)

Self-draining motor wells are supposed to be the second line of defense when a wave comes over an outboard's transom, but in some cases the well is too low, too shallow, or not sealed adequately from the cockpit. Scuppers in the motor well and cockpit may also be slow to drain overboard, especially if they're

If a wave comes over the stern, the scuppers should drain water overboard quickly. Unfortunately, scuppers are often blocked with debris. In this case, one of the boat's two scuppers was covered by the mounting bracket for the small auxiliary outboard on the left. A small wave came over the boat's low transom and filled the well with water. The boat's low freeboard was then lowered further by the weight of the water. When a second wave came over the transom and into the cockpit, the boat's fate was sealed. In a matter of seconds, a series of small waves off Jones Inlet in New York flooded the cockpit and swamped the boat.

An ideal transom for an outboard-powered boat offshore. There is ample flotation so the stern will rise in a following sea. The impressively large inner transom sits well *above* the engines, and there is nothing to prevent water in the well from draining overboard. (Compare this transom to the one in the photos opposite and below.)

clogged. And whenever water lingers in the well or cockpit, the chances of another wave coming aboard increase. So too does the risk of being swamped.

Apart from transom height, the other major contributing factor when a boat is swamped is weight distribution—too many people at the stern together with scuba tanks, large coolers, bait wells, etc.—which reduces buoyancy aft. In most cases, the boats were stopped or idling. The one exception was a boat that broached while entering a breaking inlet.

It should be noted that boats under 20 feet are required to have level flotation—that is, to resist sinking even when swamped—so many of the boats in the study remained awash, although several were rolled over by waves or by passengers rushing to one side of the boat.

Especially on outboards with low cutouts, be conscious of weight distribution. Avoid storing heavy objects near the transom. At slow speeds, keep the boat moving toward the waves. Don't anchor a small boat from the stern. Also be aware of a boat's rated capacity for number of passengers (this may be shown on a capacity plate on the stern). If not, a good rule of thumb is to carry only as many passengers as there are seats.

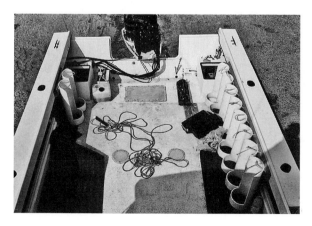

There are at least four reasons why this boat should never have been used as an offshore dive boat: (1) the low cutout at the transom; (2) the lack of any splash guard to prevent water entering the boat; (3) the weight of the scuba tanks (ten tanks, over 40 pounds each) near the transom; and (4) tiny scupper drains.

When the owner and his friends were preparing to go diving, a small wave came over the transom. The additional weight of water lowered the transom even farther so that when a second and then a third wave came aboard, the boat quickly swamped.

Most scuppers are slow to drain anyway, but when they're plugged with leaves and other gunk, water can linger in cockpits and motor wells a dangerously long time. Use a dockside hose with a power spray nozzle to flush out debris.

Leaks at Through-Hulls Any hole below the waterline has the potential to quickly sink a boat. In the BoatU.S. study, leaking through-hulls included stuffing boxes, a bait well discharge, washdown fitting (softened by spilled fuel), knotmeter plug, bow thruster hose, broken scupper, and a failed head discharge. Unlike boats at a dock, which typically sink as a result of relatively slow leaks at through-hull fittings, these failures tended to be sudden, with many gallons of water pouring through the hole every minute. A 35-foot sailboat en route from Maine to Maryland, for example, almost sank when a through-hull knotmeter impeller, which hadn't been secured properly, popped out. The boat had motored many miles before the delivery skipper noticed that the boat seemed sluggish and finally checked below. He managed to save the boat, but water came within inches of sending it to the bottom.

Any "opening" in the hull, whether it's protected by a seacock or stuffing box, needs to be inspected periodically. The same is true for openings that are slightly above the waterline. Seacocks and gate valves should be operable. Inspect all seacocks and hoses periodically and before any offshore passage. See the recommendations on pages 103–4. Should all else fail, it's a good idea to tie a soft wood plug at every through-hull.

Stuffing boxes, where the engine shaft exits the hull, are designed to leak slightly underway but not when the boat is at rest. (The exception is dripless stuffing boxes.) Check not only for leaks, but to make sure the packing material is firmly in place. Once the packing material is gone, water can pour into the boat. While less prone to failure, the stuffing box for the rudder should also be checked periodically.

Leaks at Raw-Water Cooling System/Exhaust A 300 hp engine pumps approximately 30 gallons of water through the cooling system every minute. Depending

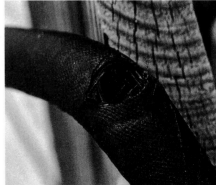

The weak spots in this wire-reinforced raw-water intake hose (left) are clearly indicated by depressions. A hole developed where the wire had corroded away (right), and the sailboat sank.

The owner was several miles off the coast when two exhaust hose clamps failed, and water began to flood in through the exhaust port (covered here temporarily with a board by the Coast Guard). The inferior hose clamps had been corroding for some time, as evident from the rust stains.

on which fitting lets go, you could find yourself with the water pouring into the bilge at the same time the engine overheats, which means you're liable to be greeted by clouds of hot steam when you open the engine hatch.

Which fittings are most vulnerable? Any fitting that is loose or corroded can let go. In one case, a cooling water pump hadn't been adequately tightened. On other boats, hoses slipped off, a raw-water heat exchanger (end cap) burst, and a plastic muffler split open when the engine backfired.

Periodically inspect all fittings in the cooling system for loose connections and brittle or split hoses. Typically, a break in the cooling system will cause the engine to overheat before much water has been pumped overboard. The hatch is opened, the problem is discovered, and the boat can usually be saved. The exception is a break in the exhaust or muffler. Backfiring can blow a hole in a plastic muffler, corrosion can eat a hole in a metal muffler, exhaust hoses can split, and the engine will continue to pump water—a lot of water—aboard.

Even if you don't hear a backfire, you can usually hear the difference in tone and loudness when a muffler or exhaust hose lets go. Stop the boat immediately and check the system for breaks.

Drain Plug Missing Many trailerable boats have drain plugs that are inserted when the boat is launched and removed when it's hauled, but it's difficult to understand how a missing drain plug could sink a boat. Wouldn't the skipper realize that the boat was filling up with water? Typically, the water is in the bilge and out of sight until hundreds of gallons have come aboard. By then, the boat might be floating well below its lines. In some past cases, the source of the leak wasn't discovered until the boat was raised.

How can an absent-minded skipper remember to install a drain plug? Try leaving a drain plug (you should have at least one spare) with the trailer's winch handle or with the ignition key—anywhere it is sure to be seen before launching the boat.

Navigation Error (Grounding) Despite channel markers and buoys, not to mention the electronics available to navigators, boats still go aground, sometimes with catastrophic results. Boats sink after striking underwater jetties, rocks, and, in one claim, a soft bottom. The latter was a boat in California that lost its prop when it struck the bottom near a channel entrance. The boat drifted into the surf before its skipper could set an anchor.

Charts, GPS, loran, compasses, and even radar are all available to help the navigator. Use them! If you're not sure where you are, slow down and keep an eye on the depth sounder.

Boat Construction (Hull Split Open) Three of the boats in the BoatU.S. claim files—6%—sank because their hulls split open. In each claim, the cause of the failure was a lightly built hull slamming into waves or, in one case, another boat's wake.

How can you tell if your boat was intended by the builder to withstand offshore conditions? A boat's weight relative to other boats of the same size and type can give you a clue. So too can the quality of its hardware and finishing work. And if your boat is also sold in Europe, it will have an International Standards Organization (ISO) Category of Use rating of "A" if it is capable of going offshore (winds up to 71 knots and seas over 4 meters). A "D" Category of Use rating means the boat should be used only in a pond.

The best source for finding a boat's reputation, however, is other boatowners, marine surveyors, and repairers. The BoatU.S. website (www.boatus.com) includes message boards that allow you to ask other boatowners about specific makes and models of boats. Other boating sites have similar message boards.

Don't depend solely on a manufacturer's promotional literature. In one lawsuit involving a boat whose hull split open after flying off a large wave, the boat's manufacturer claimed that the boat had been abused. The owner countered with a photo of the same model of boat flying off a wave at high speed. The photo had appeared in the manufacturer's promotional literature. We'll have more on boat construction in the next chapter.

Struck Floating Debris One boat, a 36-foot sailboat, sank as a result of striking a submerged object—the object was never identified—off the coast of Florida. Another boat struck a large log in an inlet on the Potomac River. Submerged or partially submerged boards, logs, etc., are typically swept into rivers and bays after storms and have been responsible for damaging and even sinking many boats.

Things that go bump, part 1. When this boat struck a submerged object, there was little doubt that it had a serious problem. The bone-jarring thud loosened the struts, and the boat immediately began taking on water—a lot of water. Help—either from the Coast Guard or a commercial tower—was too far away to save the boat. The skipper had the presence of mind to quickly turn the wheel and head for shallow water. Given the water temperature in the Pacific Northwest (cold), his quick thinking saved the crew from possible hypothermia (or worse).

Beaching a boat that is taking on water is certainly not a new tactic—skippers have been doing it for centuries because it works. Thanks to his VHF radio, the skipper of the sinking boat was also able to alert a nearby boat, which then stood by in case he didn't make it.

Whenever you see floating debris, slow down. For every log visible on top of the water, there are likely to be two or more bobbing just below the surface. If you do strike something, indicated by an ominous *klunk* somewhere on the hull, open the engine hatch immediately and make sure the boat isn't taking on water. Just to be safe, check at least once later.

Leaks at Outdrive Boots Small holes in outdrive boots are responsible for sinking many boats at docks (as we saw earlier in this chapter) but are less likely to sink a boat on open water. Failures on open water involve large tears and, in one case, the sudden loss of the stainless steel clamp that had been holding the boot to the boat.

Outdrive boots and boots for shift and throttle cables get brittle and must be replaced periodically. Look for cracking, which indicates the boot is drying out and needs replacing. Tears in the rubber are most likely to show up in the creases. Check the stainless steel cable that holds the boot to the boat to make sure it's tight and free of corrosion.

Things that go bump, part 2. The skipper of this boat was cruising in the ocean off Delaware when he heard—and felt—a loud thump from somewhere along the boat's hull. He throttled back and checked the bilge, but it seemed dry so he continued on. Sometime the next day, while the boat was safely tied to the dock, it sank.

The cause was traced to a trim tab, which had been jolted loose by whatever it was that he'd hit the day before. Even though the bilge had been dry when he checked it initially, the trim tab had gradually worked loose, and it took several more hours of bouncing over waves for the hole to open. Lesson #1: Check your bilge when you first strike an object and double-check it later—after the boat has bounced over a few waves—just to be safe. In this case, the boat sank at the dock. Other skippers haven't been so lucky—their boats took on water while they were still aboard on open water. Lesson #2: Installing a bilge alarm—a simple, inexpensive device—will give you an invaluable second set of "eyes" down in the bilge.

Air Vents or Water Vents?

THIS BOAT SANK after water came pouring through the engine's intake air vents at the stern. The owner said he had checked the vents when he first pulled onto the beach, and they were "above the waterline." Given the steep angle of the boat onshore, it's likely he should have said "barely" above the waterline.

Sometime later his wife and a friend were sitting on the transom when they noticed the boat was quickly filling with water. The owner said in less than 30 seconds the stern was completely underwater. The boat's owner blamed a large wake from a passing boat that he said must have pushed water up through the vents.

The ABYC H-2 standard says only that "Ventilation openings should be located with consideration to their potential contribution to water ingress. Ventilation below the shear may lower the effective free-board." On some boats, especially low-pro-file models, vents near the waterline only offer protection from water ingress when the boat is moving forward. These boats have proven to be especially vulnerable when they're stopped or backing down in a follow-ing sea. Owners of these boats should be aware of their boats' precarious vents and not take chances.

Other   One boat was abandoned in a storm at sea and is presumed to have sunk. Another sank as the result of a faulty repair. There are, it seems, many ways to sink.

A Few Words About Pumps and Bilge Alarms

Two BoatU.S. members, Cliff and Sandy Steele, tell a harrowing story about a log that almost sank their boat just before nightfall. After hearing a loud thump, Cliff checked the bilge and, seeing no water, continued on. Sometime later the boat seemed to be losing power and felt sluggish, so he opened the hatch and discov-ered water almost over his engine. Although Cliff had checked the bilge earlier, the damaged hull didn't fail until it had pounded over some waves. Thanks to nearby boaters who responded to Cliff's Mayday by putting extra pumps aboard, the boat was saved.

The sooner a skipper discovers a leak down below, the more likely he or she will be able to find and correct the problem before it's too late. High-capacity bilge pumps and even extra pumps can help in an emergency. So too can using the engine's raw-water intake hose (close the intake seacock before you take off the hose!) for extra pumping capacity in an emergency.

While more and better pumps may be able to keep up with the flow of water, it is critical that you discover the leak quickly, before the electrical system, the engine, or the leak itself is underwater. A bilge alarm is a simple device that warns you when water begins rising in the bilge. This early warning gives you more time to find a leak, get passengers into life vests, deploy extra pumps, and put out a distress call. Bilge alarms are available from most marine chandleries.

Why Fiberglass Boats Sometimes Fail

Several years ago, a man pulled into the parking lot at BoatU.S. headquarters trailering a large boat—a high-performance boat—that looked as if it had dropped off the trailer and bounced along the highway. The man wasn't stopping at BoatU.S. to buy zincs or stove alcohol at the marine center; his mission ultimately was to get a new boat from the manufacturer. Neatly stenciled on the side of the hull, along with a graphic of a large lemon, were the words "It did not hit anything" and "Under normal operation this boat BROKE APART AND SANK." The boat, a rolling testament to his ire, was a boat manufacturer's worst nightmare.

Caroline Ajootian, who heads the Consumer Protection Bureau at BoatU.S., remembers that day well. She recalls that the man told her his boat had been badly damaged—entire sections of fiberglass had been torn away from the hull—by hitting a few waves one afternoon.

Are some boats "lemons"? As noted earlier, 6% of the BoatU.S.-insured boats that sank underway did so because their hulls split apart. One well-documented reason that hulls split is because reckless boatowners slam into boat wakes and waves at high speeds. Another reason, according to Dave Gerr, a naval architect and director of the ABYC's Westlawn Institute of Marine Technology, is the boats themselves. Gerr, who has written several books on boatbuilding, blames stiff competition among boatbuilders: "A designer used to be able to tell the front office what would or wouldn't work,

but that doesn't happen anymore. The last word in building a boat goes to the people who sell the boats."

Gerr notes that most boatbuilders do an excellent job. He cites as an example a sailboat manufacturer on the West Coast that builds boats that are both strong and lightweight. The key he says is quality control. Another naval architect, Mike Kaufman of Annapolis, Maryland, who also works as a marine surveyor, notes that boats today, though lighter, tend to be built better than the heavier boats that were the norm in years past. He says that there have been improvements in most systems, including fuel tanks, through-hulls, wiring, and, most important, the quality of the layup. The latter has to do with how resin is applied to the fiberglass to build a hull. In the early years of fiberglass boat building, a lot of mistakes were made because builders didn't know any better. These days, Kaufman says, failures are more likely to be the result of poor quality control.

Bruce Pfund, a highly respected consultant on composite fiberglass construction, agrees that quality control can be a problem, but he has also found that some builders deliberately use cheaper materials and take shortcuts to save money. So while boats may look alike—shiny gelcoat with lots of bright chrome—beneath the gelcoat can be significant differences.

A Primer on Fiberglass Boat Construction

To understand why fiberglass components can sometimes fail, you have to understand something about how a fiberglass boat is built. Typical production building techniques haven't changed much since the early days of fiberglass: a mold is used to build up layers of chopped strand mat and woven roving that are bonded together with resin. How many layers are used depends on a boat's scantlings—the dimensions of its structural parts. A boat with heavy scantlings is said to be better able to cope with heavy stresses such as weather and seas.

Polyester resin, the most basic resin type, remains the most widely used resin for boatbuilding. It's easy to work with, inexpensive, and reasonably strong. More recently, vinylester resin has been used by some boatbuilders to prevent blistering below the waterline. Vinylester laminates are typically tougher and more resilient than polyester and can be used with polyester application equipment. Epoxy resins are tougher still, more resilient, and even more resistant to blistering. They are not, however, compatible with gelcoats—the shiny polyester surface finishes—and cost roughly four times as much as polyester resin. Epoxy tends to be used mostly on expensive custom boats (typically built for racing) and in special situations, although recently there have been exceptions. Tartan Marine, for example, began using epoxy on its production boats starting in the late nineties.

Laminates One of the most crucial jobs in boatbuilding is the even distribution of resin over the various layers (plies) of fiberglass cloth to form a solid bond that is free of voids and puddles. The plies are typically made of layers of woven roving—long strands of glass fibers woven together—alternating with layers of fiberglass mat—short strands of glass fibers randomly bound in a thin "blanket" that absorbs resin. Because it is made up of longer fibers, woven roving is much stronger than chopped strand mat (CSM). The latter is used to absorb resin and bind the various layers of woven roving together. Without the mat, woven roving would be filled with unreinforced puddles of resin.

You might think that gooping a lot of resin would make the various plies stronger, but in fact the opposite is true. Puddles of resin mean a *weaker* laminate. According to Dave Gerr, "The sole way to get a strong, light laminate is to use just enough resin to get a thorough wet-out and a good bond—not one whit more. The more fiberglass used in proportion to the resin, the stronger the laminate." This sounds easier than it is. Applying too little resin means the laminate will be "resin starved," which can cause the various plies to separate. Pfund adds that resin starvation is easier for manufacturers to spot, so excess resin tends to be the more common manufacturing problem.

There are several techniques to aid in mating resin with glass. The least expensive is to use a chopper gun to spray a combination of chopped glass fibers and resin into a mold. This method is quick and inexpensive. The drawback is that chopper gun construction is imprecise and can result in thicker, heavier hulls (which translates to reduced performance). Since the proportion of resin to glass fiber is high, and since the glass fibers are short, chopper gun hulls, though heavy, are not especially strong.

The industry standard, the one used by most boatbuilders, is to apply resins just as was done in the earliest days of fiberglass—using a spray gun. To build a strong hull, just the right amount of resin needs to be sprayed evenly over the layers of glass fiber cloth with no bare or thick spots. In the hands of an experienced employee, the resulting laminate will be sound and relatively light.

Another technique, one that is used to build strong, lightweight hulls, is vacuum bagging. With this technique, resin-impregnated wet laminates are covered with a plastic film, which is then sealed to the edges of the mold. Using a vacuum pump, air under the plastic is sucked out, compressing the resin onto the laminate and removing any excess resin. Although it isn't foolproof, the result of vacuum bagging can be less resin in proportion to glass fiber than is typically found in laminates sprayed by hand.

By itself, a fiberglass hull will be flexible, so bulkheads, stringers, and interiors are added later to give it rigidity. These are (or should be) "tabbed" to the inside of the hull with several layers of fiberglass. Adding wet layers of laminate over previously cured dry layers is called secondary bonding, a mechanical bond that is not as strong as the primary bond. The latter is a chemical bond that results when layers are added while they are still wet.

If tabbing isn't done correctly, a slightly weaker secondary bond could become even weaker. Whatever is being tabbed to the primary laminate for structural support, typically wood or foam, must be tapered to eliminate sharp angles. Sharp angles are not as strong as tapered angles. This is also true of adding cores, typically foam or balsa, which are used on most boats to makes decks stiffer and to reduce weight up high. Cores are sometimes used in the hull, more often above the waterline, for the same reason—to reduce weight and add stiffness. Plywood cores, which are stronger and heavier than cores made with balsa or foam, are used in areas that must accommodate a lot of weight or compressive loads, such as transoms on outboard powerboats.

Whenever a wood core or stringer is added, it must be well soaked with several applications of resin before the laminates are added. A single application of resin would be absorbed into the wood, with little or no resin remaining to be absorbed by the glass cloth. Core material, either balsa or foam, sometimes has notches and grooves called kerfs to accommodate compound curves in the boat's deck and hull. To maximize strength as well as to prevent water from filling the voids, the kerfs should be filled with resin or putty before the laminate is applied.

Note that if stringers, bulkheads, cores, and interiors are not sufficiently strong to stiffen the hull, or if they fail (i.e., the fiberglass bond breaks or separates), tiny cracks will develop in the flexing laminate. The tendency will be for these to deepen, which can ultimately lead to a catastrophic failure of the laminate.

Inspecting Your Boat

Several years ago, Mike Kaufman invested a considerable amount of money in a device that would gauge the thickness of the fiberglass in a used boat. He was surprised that most of his clients could have cared less. For the average boatowner, who lacks a degree in naval architecture, the thickness of the laminate in various areas means little. So how can a boatowner know if a boat is going to wind up looking like the boat with the lemon painted on the side?

A boat's weight relative to other boats of the same size and type is one clue. The quality of its hardware and finishing work is another. But with any boat, new or used, the best guide is its manufacturer's reputation. According to Caroline Ajootian, price is not necessarily an indication of quality. Some high-volume builders, for example, build consistently sound hulls at a reasonable price. They're also good with warranty repairs. Other builders, even builders of expensive boats, can hide shoddy fiberglass work behind expensive cabinetry. If you're not familiar with a manufacturer, ask your surveyor and do some research online. The Coast Guard's recall information is available at the BoatU.S. web page (www.boatus.com/recall). You can also contact BoatU.S. Consumer Affairs at con sumeraffairs@BoatUS.com to learn of problems that have been reported by other BoatU.S. members. Finally, the BoatU.S. website (www.boatus.com) includes a

"Boater to Boater Directory" that allows you to ask over 1,100 boatowners about specific makes and models of boats.

If you already own a boat, the best defense against unpleasant surprises is to spend time occasionally examining its structure. (Some boatowners hire a marine surveyor periodically to get a more professional examination.) Any problems, if noticed early, can usually be corrected before expensive damage occurs.

First, examine the bonds at bulkheads, stringers, engine beds, and any other parts that add support to the hull. Look for deep cracks that presage separation. Look also for spiderweb cracks on the outside of the hull. Superficial cracks are fairly common and may only be in the gelcoat, but longer, deeper cracks at the stringers, bow, and transom could mean trouble. Discoloration of woodwork is a sign of leaks that need to be corrected. Soft spots in the deck are also a strong indication of water penetration. You can "hear" delamination and other fiberglass problems as well as wood rot by tapping various areas with a plastic hammer. Tapping over a wide area gives you a good sense of what a healthy fiberglass or wood surface is supposed to sound like. A sharp—thwack, thwack—sound is good; a duller—thump, thump—may indicate a problem. It's important to note, however, that built-in tanks, core terminations, and core density can affect sound. Should you have any doubts, contact a marine surveyor or repairer.

Building Fiberglass Boats: What Can Go Wrong?

Phil Cappel, Chief of the Coast Guard's Recreational Boating Product Assurance Division, said the Coast Guard issues about 300 manufacturer identification codes (MICs) each year to aspiring boat manufacturers. Obtaining a MIC code is necessary before a company can build and sell boats. Cappel said the Coast Guard has a video it sends to these aspiring boatbuilders to make them aware, among other things, that building and selling boats is a complex and difficult business.

Building a fiberglass boat requires a series of steps, some simple and some

Laminate problems— what to look for. Thin, shallow cracks in the gelcoat are fairly common and usually don't indicate anything more than a cosmetic problem. Deeper, wider cracks, however, that run along the chines, stringers, or bulkheads may be indicative of a more serious problem. Cracks at the stem or keel and transom are especially worrisome; these areas are supposed to be heavily built and should not be prone to cracking.

The bow in the left photo is a good example of stress cracks that indicate a laminate failure. Dye was used to highlight a series of deep stress cracks at the bow. Farther aft (right photo) the hull laminates have already begun to separate. Jack Hornor, a naval architect who investigated the damage, said the problem appeared to have been caused by a combination of hard use and a weak hull.

The photo at right shows what can happen when water seeps into the core, typically at a fitting. Unlike the builder of the boat shown on page 121, some builders remove the core at areas surrounding through-hulls below the waterline and build it back up with fiberglass. Since the fitting is then installed through solid fiberglass, any leaking will seep into the boat and not the core.

The photo above shows a section of deck above a stanchion that has been leaking and letting water penetrate the core (a wood block). In this case, the caulk used to keep water out of the screw holes had dried over time and cracked. Water then seeped into the core, froze, and lifted the fiberglass off the core.

complicated, that must be done correctly to assure that a boat's structure will be sound. As with most endeavors, a good job requires skill and patience. A lot of people are usually involved, and it's the better builders who maintain tight quality control to assure that each job is done correctly. Not all builders are careful.

What can go wrong? The very first step in building any fiberglass boat is to thoroughly stir the resin that will be used to give the fiberglass its rigidity. It's a seemingly simple job that distributes thickeners evenly throughout the resin before the catalyst (hardener) is added. Bruce Pfund watched a worker in one boatbuilding facility roll a drum to agitate the resin, a technique resin manufacturers specifically warn against since the slug of resin thickener in the middle of

Water penetrated the plywood core on the transom of this fiberglass boat via a transducer fitting that was added by the boatowner. Whenever a hole is drilled through a core below the waterline, it should be tightly sealed with an epoxy paste and caulked to prevent water penetration. Considering what's at stake, it's one job that you may want to leave to a skilled professional.

the drum stays put. Pfund notes that the warning is clearly printed on the drum! Naval architect Dave Gerr has been in shops where the resin was *never* stirred. And when it isn't agitated sufficiently, the resin will be too thick in some areas to wet the fiberglass effectively, and too runny in others. The result is a weaker laminate. To learn more, read *The Elements of Boat Strength: For Builders, Designers, and Owners*, by Dave Gerr.

Sailboat Stability

Aside from breaking up, boats have been swamped or sunk because they lacked the stability necessary to cope with sea conditions. While the sea has always had the power to overcome even the stoutest ships, there have been instances at sea when the boat itself—its design—was clearly lacking. One of the most dramatic examples occurred in 1979, when a Force 10 gale (48 to 55 knots) battered a fleet of 303 boats racing around Fastnet Rock in the Irish Sea. During the 12 hours or so that the storm raged, more than 100 boats—a third of the fleet—were knocked down, at least until their masts touched the water, and 70 of them were knocked down even further. Eighteen boats were rolled completely over, and fifteen of the fleet's sailors died in what has become known as the Fastnet disaster.

Twenty-two years earlier, a similar gale swept the 1957 Fastnet Race fleet, but with strikingly different results. One boat had its deck ports stove in, one was dismasted, and a crew member on one of the boats climbed out of the companionway and was knocked overboard. None of the boats, however, was rolled over or lost.

The destruction of so many boats in a race was unthinkable in the 1950s, when boats were built with the rounder, narrower design typical of commercial sailing vessels—unlike the boats that were rolled over in the 1979 Fastnet Race. The rounder bottom meant that the older boats, whatever their limitations on the racecourse, would also right themselves quickly after a knockdown.

For reasons that had much to do with racing rules and speed and nothing to do with seaworthiness, many boats built after the early 1970s had wider beams

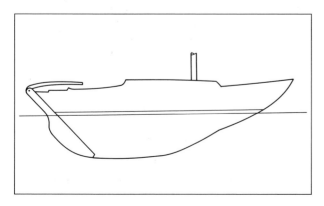

The same traditional designs that grip the water in a blow will also grip the water in a race. While this sort of design may be slow, it will be more stable and quick to right after a knockdown.

The more modern design has a flatter bottom with less wetted surface, which helps it zip around a race course but makes it less stable and slower to right after a knockdown.

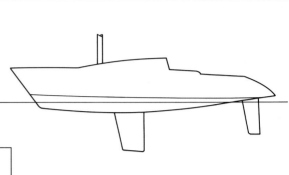

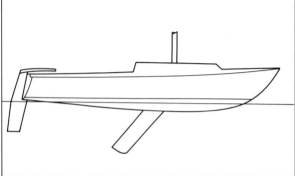

Another popular design that won't do well in heavy weather is a swing-keel sailboat. These boats are designed for trailering and gunkholing, not offshore sailing.

and flatter bottoms. These boats, which are also far lighter than their older predecessors, are steady initially but can be agonizingly slow to right after a knockdown.

A boat on its beam ends is obviously vulnerable to sinking, and the longer it remains over, the more vulnerable it becomes. In one BoatU.S. Marine Insurance claim, a 24-foot sailboat on the normally docile Chesapeake Bay was knocked down in a sudden squall just as the crew was preparing to lower the sails. In a similar claim, a sailboat went out of control during a spinnaker jibe and rolled onto its beam ends. Both boats sank after hundreds of gallons of water poured through open cockpit lockers.

Racing designs aren't the only potential capsize victims in heavy winds and seas. Shallow-draft boats with swing keels designed for trailering and/or gunkholing are also vulnerable in a knockdown. Like modern racing sailboats, these trailerable boats tend to be light, with relatively flat bottoms. One boat that capsized on the Great Lakes weighed 2,100 pounds and had a 575-pound swing keel, which was locked in place like a fixed keel. The boat's owner reported that his boat was heeled sharply by a wave, then capsized by a combination of the steep angle near the wave's apex and the 40-knot wind pushing against the exposed bottom of the boat.

Think Defensively

Skippers, especially skippers of smaller sailboats, should make it a practice to keep hatches, ports, and especially cockpit lockers closed and latched in a blow. The latch should be secured so that it won't flip open accidentally. And needless to say, when the wind strengthens, the crew should put on life jackets and remain on deck.

The first line of defense, however, is to be aware of a boat's capabilities and avoid inclement weather if the boat is vulnerable to capsize. Knowing whether your boat will be vulnerable in a knockdown, however, is another matter.

How Safe Is Your Boat in a Blow?

In *Seaworthiness: The Forgotten Factor*, C. A. Marchaj notes that racing designs can "contaminate" yacht design in general. Older racing boats also tend to find a niche in the market as fast (and often inexpensive) cruising boats. As a result, he says, "many boat buyers nowadays . . . cannot distinguish an honest, sturdy, and long lasting cruising boat from a flimsy, unseaworthy, and short-lived racer."

Not knowing the difference can be dangerous. A woman was drowned when a sailboat, a popular one-design racer, capsized on a small lake in Arkansas. Far from being a racer, the skipper had merely taken a group of friends out for an afternoon cruise. Winds had begun to strengthen, and a gust knocked the boat onto its beam ends. (Crew weight was mostly to leeward, which almost certainly wouldn't have been the case if the boat had been racing in those conditions.) Two of the crew were thrown overboard, and the woman was drowned while the skipper struggled to recover and turn the boat around.

One measure of how a boat will behave in a blow is its range of positive stability (RPS). This number indicates how a boat's shape and ballasting will influence its ability to resist capsizing. A boat with an RPS of 110° can be knocked down 110°—its mast in the water—before it will cease to resist capsize and roll completely over. The higher the RPS, the more resistant a boat will be to capsizing, and the quicker it will spring back up after a knockdown.

More to the point for small-boat skippers, a low RPS means that the boat will have to struggle to right itself after a knockdown. The boats in the BoatU.S. Marine Insurance claim files that have been knocked down and sunk all had an RPS of 105° or lower. A good offshore boat, according to experts, should have an RPS of at least 120°.

The range of positive stability involves a complicated formula that is all but impossible to calculate without a degree in naval architecture and a sophisticated computer program. You may be able to learn your boat's RPS number from the builder, but this is difficult. Several builders we contacted said they could get an RPS number for some of their boats but not for others. None of the builders had the RPS number available immediately, however, and anyone interested in learning the number from a builder will have to be persistent, assuming the number is available at all. Another possible source, at least for some racing boats, is the US Sailing Association (USSA) in Newport, Rhode Island, which keeps stability numbers on all boats in the International Measurement System (IMS) fleet.

Karl Kirkman, a naval architect and the former chair of the Small Craft Committee of the Society of Naval Architects and Engineers, has done a lot of valuable research on stability since the Fastnet disaster. Kirkman, together with Olin Stephens, Jim McCurdy, and Richard McCurdy, published a capsize screening formula (CSF) that uses readily available numbers to give at least a general indication of a sailboat's resistance to capsize. To use the formula, convert the gross weight of your boat in pounds into the equivalent volume of displaced seawater by dividing by 64. (The gross weight includes the weight of a boat plus the estimated weight of water, fuel, gear, etc.) Divide the cube root of this number into the boat's maximum beam in feet. A number greater than 2 indicates the boat may have a capsize problem.

$$CSF = Beam\ (A)/\sqrt[3]{Displacement\ (lbs.)/64}$$

Applying this formula, the boat that flipped over on the Great Lakes had an unacceptable screening number of 2.3, and the boat in Arkansas an even higher 2.4. By contrast, a 25-foot fiberglass Folkboat, an older design with a full keel, had an acceptable screening number of 1.7. Kirkman warns that the formula is not infallible and says a number greater than 2 is intended to be a red flag for potential capsize problems and not a final measure. Conversely, a number of less than two is certainly no guarantee of stability under all conditions.

Powerboat Stability

Here's an excerpt from a BoatU.S. claim: "After we anchored, we were relaxing and looking around when all of a sudden we were struck by a huge wave. The impact threw us out of the boat along with all of our equipment. When I came to the surface, I could see that the boat had been swamped and was sinking."

The skipper had chosen to ride out some rough weather at anchor, a tactic that proved to be a dangerous, almost fatal, mistake. Sailboat skippers can shorten sail to reduce windage or heave-to. Powerboats, on the other hand, don't have deep, heavy keels and are more stable when they are moving.

Movement through the water creates lift (dynamic stability), which has a stabilizing effect on planing hulls and to a lesser extent on semidisplacement and displacement hulls. The faster the better, although there are safety limitations. A lightly built boat crashing into heavy seas is extremely rough on the boat as well as the crew. Also, higher speeds will mean added pressure on the helmsman to react quickly. If the strength of the hull is suspect, or if the skipper finds he or she cannot cope with the helm, the best choice is to slow down.

Aside from speed, how a powerboat behaves in rough water has a lot to do with its shape underwater, which—depending on the size, shape, and direction of the waves—is itself constantly changing. When seas are on the bow, a helmsman must stay away from breaking crests and steer toward the flatter ends of waves. When waves are met, the throttle should be used to keep the bow up. A bow that is down when it meets a steep wave can be buried.

Some skippers claim that their boats tend to be easiest to operate when seas are on the beam, although the rest of the crew might complain about the awkward motion. To turn when seas are on the beam, a helmsman should turn *into* breaking or steep waves. Turning *away* from a breaking wave (a natural reaction) could cause the boat to *broach*—suddenly turn sideways to the wave.

By far the most difficult sea to contend with is a following sea. Boats are designed to move toward a breaking sea. Unlike a boat's bow, which is typically higher, flared outward, and more buoyant the deeper it is immersed, a boat's stern is low and flat-sided.

A boat with a low outboard cutout in its transom can be particularly vulnerable in a following sea, especially if the motor well is only marginally deep. A boat in New Jersey, to use one of many possible examples, was trolling when a wave came over the transom and swamped the boat. The surprised skipper reported the wave "wasn't even very big—a few feet, maybe."

Another problem in following seas involves a lack of stability when boats are on the tops of wave crests. The longer the boat is perched on the wave, the more vulnerable it becomes. As a general rule, a boat should either be moving much faster or slower than the waves. There are two exceptions. With smaller outboard boats, which are vulnerable to being pooped, the best tactic when large seas are astern is to move faster than the waves. And in an inlet, where waves tend to be steeper and come in regular sets, the skipper should keep the boat between crests and move at the same speed as the waves.

The absence of sails on a powerboat means less windage aloft, although there have been instances where powerboats have been blown over. A flybridge trawler with a displacement hull, for example, was blown over during an especially violent thunderstorm on the Chesapeake Bay. Stability tests performed afterward indicated that the boat was no less stable than similar designs. Any boat, it seems, can be rolled over if the wind is strong enough or the right combination of wind and wave hits at just the right moment. Boats with flybridges or tuna towers are that much more vulnerable.

Keep the Boat Dry

A boat that is partially swamped in heavy seas is almost certain to take more water aboard, with predictably glum results. For one thing,

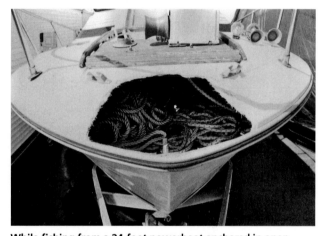

While fishing from a 24-foot powerboat anchored in open water off California's Catalina Island, three men noticed that clouds were building and the wind was freshening. They continued to fish, and the weather continued to deteriorate. Sometime later a series of 6-foot waves came over the transom, flooding the scuppers and overwhelming the bilge pump. They grabbed buckets and began bailing. A larger wave came aboard and flooded the engine, which after several desperate attempts, wouldn't start. Fortunately, they were able to call for a tow over the radio. However, while help was on the way, the water-soaked boat was being tossed high into the air by the waves, with the result that the anchor roller and part of the foredeck were yanked overboard. The men were rescued but had to endure a 13-hour tow back to the mainland.

If sea conditions become severe in open water, it is usually safer to keep the boat moving, making slow headway through the waves. If it remains anchored to the bottom, the boat's natural tendency to rise over the waves will be thwarted. One other point: This boat clearly wasn't designed or constructed to go offshore.

the freeboard will be much lower. The boat will also be much more unstable. Karl Kirkman compares operating an open boat that is partially filled with water to carrying water in an ice cube tray without the cube dividers; the water will slosh freely from one end to the other. With an ice cube tray, this means spilled water. With an open boat, this sloshing water can quickly roll the boat over, even in moderate seas. As one skipper whose boat rolled over after taking water over the transom said, "Things just got out of hand so fast; one minute it was a little water and all of a sudden the boat rolled to one side. There was all kinds of water, I barely had time to get a Mayday out."

How does water come aboard? One way, as mentioned previously, is over a low-cut transom. Another is from rain and spray. Lesser amounts of water should drain overboard through the scuppers. In one claim, however, a skipper who had been concentrating on maneuvering through steep seas discovered that water was accumulating on deck because the scuppers were blocked with leaves. When he slowed the boat to clean out the scuppers, the boat rolled, and a wave came over the stern.

A Powerboat's Secret Weapon: Speed

Sailboats have keels, which gives them a certain advantage in heavy weather, while powerboats have the advantage of being faster and able to seek shelter quickly when storms are forecast. This is a huge advantage, but only if a skipper listens to weather forecasts and takes their predictions seriously.

Should you get caught in rough weather and lack the experience to power through building seas, you might want to look around for a larger boat that's headed back to port. A BoatU.S. employee, who used to operate a large charter boat on weekends, says that every time he came in from fishing in rough weather, one or two smaller boats followed along in his boat's flattened wake. This is an excellent tactic for smaller boats, providing the larger boat is going toward the nearest port.

Six Rules for Operating Powerboats Offshore in Heavy Weather

1. If possible, keep the boat moving. Water passing beneath the hull, especially a planing hull, stabilizes the boat.

2. Make sure everyone aboard is wearing a life jacket.

3. Never overload a boat. On boats built after 1982, federal law requires a capacity plate to indicate the maximum number of people who can be aboard. A good rule of thumb for any boat is to limit the number of passengers aboard to the number of seats on the boat. (Keeping people seated will go a long way toward remedying another cause of boating accidents—passengers who fall overboard because they were seated on gunwales.)

4. Always be aware of the number of people on the flybridge, especially on boats under 30 feet. In heavy weather, keep the weight off the flybridge.

5. Keep cockpit drains free of debris. If a wave finds its way aboard, you'll need all the help you can get.

6. Keep the crew seated and secure. If you have to move around, use handholds.

The Art of Securing Your Boat

As one BoatU.S. surveyor found: "There are multiple abrasions and impact damages to the hull side where the vessel rubbed against the dock. The lifeline stanchion on the port side near the abrasion is also bent. . . . The vessel appears too large for the slip it is moored in; the width is not wide enough to be able to tie off the vessel without rubbing against both finger piers. We also noted that several other piers had carpet installed on them where the vessels rubbed against them."

Every year there are many claims for boats that are damaged because docklines were too slack, and the boat came in contact with a dock or piling. In some cases, boats have sunk as a result; in fact, 8% of boats that sink at the dock do so because of poor docking arrangements. Typically, the boat drifts under the dock at low tide, the tide comes in, and the boat is forced underwater.

What's the best way to secure a boat at a dock? Wallace Venable, a boatowner and professor of engineering mechanics, recommends leading docklines (preferably nylon, which stretches yet is strong) in the direction of the loads as much as possible for the best mechanical advantage. In the top illustration on page 130, the lines will accommodate winds on the bow or stern but not the beam. In contrast, lines led perpendicular to the boat, as shown in the middle illustration, will stretch less and stand up well to crosswinds, but won't offer much resistance when winds are on the bow or stern. The solution, shown in the bottom illustra-

tion, is to use spring lines, which will contain fore-and-aft as well as lateral movement. This is the classic docking arrangement because it works, provided the lines are adequately sized for the boat and the dock.

In a tight slip, tide is the major consideration. Nylon line stretches, but still in tidal areas there must be adequate slack in the line. Too little slack, and the line will be stressed at low tide. Too much slack, and the boat will bang against the dock and pilings at high tide. Fenders, fender boards, and rubber dock guards on pilings can help. So too can the gizmos on pilings that allow lines to move up and down with the tide. Lines to floating docks are the ultimate solution, since the boat and dock can move up and down in tandem with the tides. In hurricane-prone areas, however, the pilings for floating docks should be tall enough—18 feet above mean high water is ideal—to accommodate storm surge.

Other tricks include crossing stern lines behind the transom to add to their overall length, while still providing maximum resistance to crosswinds. Also place chafe protection at critical areas, and remove or cover any nails, bolt heads, etc.

When you are confident that the lines are properly adjusted to the dimensions and tidal range of the slip, mark the rope where it should be tied off on board. *Leave the docklines permanently at the slip.* This allows the boat to be secured exactly the same way every time. When using lines with spliced loops (preferable) on freestanding pilings, provide a wooden hook or some other means (besides a sharp nail) to assure that the loop always remains at the same height on the piling. You can also hang the coiled line from the hook whenever you leave the slip.

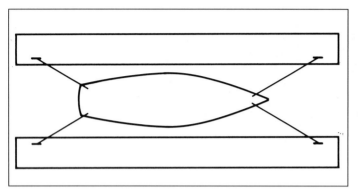

This docking arrangement is resistant to winds on the bow or stern, but less resistant to crosswinds.

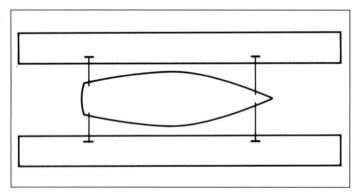

This arrangement is resistant to crosswinds but less resistant to winds on the bow or stern.

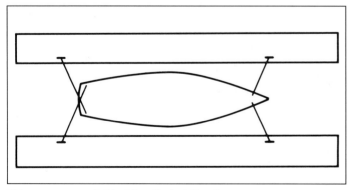

This arrangement is ideal for all wind directions.

High winds precipitated a chain of events that sank this 37-foot sailboat. First, one of the bow lines chafed through—there was no chafe protection—and the bow swung around and began bumping into a piling. The wind continued blowing and blew much of the water out of the harbor. The boat's keel then got stuck in the mud, and its stern became wedged against a piling. When the displaced water returned, the stuck boat stayed put—on the bottom.

Suggestions for Securing a Boat at a Dock

- Check your boat regularly. If you can't, make sure someone else does. It's a good idea to have an agreement with other boatowners to keep an eye on each other's boats. You can also ask the marina to check on your boat occasionally, although there may be a charge for the service.

- Use only one line for one function, and dead-end the line on the pier or cleat so marina personnel can more easily make adjustments from cleats on the boat in high winds.

- Make extra lines readily available to marina personnel if needed.

- Reduce windage by removing biminis, dodgers, sails, etc., if you plan to leave the boat a long time.

- Hang large fenders or fender boards opposite pilings that may come in contact with the boat.

- Remove exposed nailheads from pilings and piers.

- Dock defensively. Keep an eye on your neighbor's boat and report any mooring concerns you have to the marina office.

- Provide chafe guards where needed.

Boats on Lifts

Several years ago, a retired gentleman in Fort Myers, Florida, got some really bad news from his neighbor: "Your boat is sinking." Fortunately, the boat was next to its lift, so rather than hassle with emergency pumps, all the owner had to do was press the lift's "Up" button and wait; the boat's salvation was at hand, or so he thought. The lift's motor whirred away and the boat, with thousands of pounds of

As with many similar claims, the surveyor's report on this incident noted that the cables were badly corroded (inset). A cable may show signs of wear and need replacing in as little as two years. Since a cable costs only about $40, trying to squeeze another season out of an iffy cable is a poor way to economize.

water still trapped in the hull, rose oh-so-slowly out of the water. Then, just when the owner was reaching to shut off the lift's motor, there was a loud snapping noise, and in an instant the lift and boat were plunged back into the water. The boat landed on the twisted metal stump—that only seconds before had been supporting the boat—punching a hole in the hull. Before he could find an emergency pump, the boat sank.

The owner learned a tough lesson about his boat's lift: the rated capacity (usually on a label) is its lifting capacity. A lift rated for 6,000 pounds, for example, is not designed to lift boats that weigh 6,100 pounds; there have been claims for lifts that failed when snow added additional weight to a boat.

Besides the lift itself, there are several other ways a boat hoist can fail. The most common, according to the BoatU.S. Marine Insurance claim files, involves cables that fatigue and break, either because of misalignment, chafe, corrosion, or a combination of all three. Excessive chafe on the cable is typically caused by faulty sheave alignment, incorrect sheave groove diameter, or improper drum winding. Sheave alignment can be inspected easily by sighting down the cable to make sure it's centered and fits neatly in the groove. Anything less than dead-on puts pressure where it isn't designed to be and will hasten the cable's—and the sheave's—demise. Misalignment may also cause the cable to jump out of the sheave.

Improper drum winding occurs most often when the cable is momentarily slackened, which can cause excessive wraps around the drum to backlash like line on a fishing reel. The cable becomes crisscrossed as soon as pressure is reapplied. The result is uneven wear and damaged strands as well as a loss of cable "memory." The latter is what helps the cable pay out neatly onto the drum. Excessive turns encourage a tangled mess; to reduce backlashes, leave at least two turns (but not many more) on the drum when the cable is fully unwound.

Note: Whenever a cable comes off the sheave or becomes jammed, or there is an overrun on the drum, DO NOT use your hands to repair the problem. There have been several claims filed for people who lost fingers when a cable suddenly snapped back onto a turning sheave or drum. If possible, lower the boat back into the water to eliminate pressure—load on the cable. Tools, not fingers, should then be used to work the cable. *If you can't easily remedy the problem, call the installer.*

Lift Maintenance Nothing lasts forever. Even if the cable glides smoothly over the sheaves and drum, it still needs to be replaced periodically. Internal abrasion occurs whenever strands work against each other under load. External abrasion occurs when the cable bends around winch drums or spindles. Just how long a cable lasts depends on how often it's used. It also depends on where it is used—salt or fresh water—and the amount of care it receives.

First, take care to rinse salt water off the cable every time you launch the boat. Especially in salt water, cables should not be left overboard while you're out on the boat. Aside from keeping salt crystals out, galvanized cable requires a squirt or two of penetrating oil occasionally to preserve the galvanized coating and minimize abrasion between strands. Do not use grease, as it traps moisture inside the strands. Stainless steel cable, which is more expensive but holds up better in salt water, also benefits from a few squirts of penetrating oil between strands. (*Note:* Don't be tempted to replace galvanized cable with stainless steel; the two cables require different sheave and drum sizes.)

Assuming cable is well cared for, how long should it last? Some experts say that to be safe, you should replace galvanized cable every two years. All things being equal, stainless cable will last longer—up to twice as long. However there are no hard and fast rules; expectations on a freshwater lake in Vermont will be far different than those in the Florida Keys. Strong indicators that the cable needs replacing include broken strands, kinks, deformities, and areas of heavy abrasion. In the BoatU.S. Marine Insurance claim files, the galvanized cables that broke tended to show signs of corrosion (e.g., rust). Look for a slight discoloration, which indicates the protective galvanized coating has been worn away. Concentrations of heavy rust indicate that the steel cable itself has lost considerable strength. Be aware, however, that internal abrasion and rust are hidden; a cable can sometimes fail without prior warning. When in doubt, replace the cable; trying to get another year out of a $40 cable isn't worth the risk of dropping your boat.

The Boat You can't hoist just any boat out of the water. Aside from making sure the boat and gear aren't too heavy for the lift, the bow and stern eyes on the boat must be capable of supporting the vertical loads. A cleat is intended to withstand horizontal loads and should not be used to lift a boat. Eyes at the transom may or may not be adequate; some are intended for water-skiers. If you're not sure, contact your boat's manufacturer. You can also contact a marine surveyor or go to the BoatUS.com message boards and ask other owners.

There are several other considerations. Stern eyes, which support the boat's engine(s), must be especially stout and slanted so that the angle of pull will be *directly* in line with the cable. If stern eyes are set vertically, you must use a spreader bar so that the cables line up with the eyes. If eyes are slanted inward, lead the cables to a single bridle or, depending on the angle, separate the cables with a shorter spreader bar.

When lifting a boat on slings or a cradle, typically two I-beams, position it according to the boat's weight, not its length. Because the engine, batteries, fuel tanks etc., tend to be aft, most of a boat's weight is near its stern. Providing adequate support for the hull usually means positioning the cradle nearer the stern with the bow sometimes jutting well out beyond the forward I-beam.

Limit Switches Depending on whom you ask, limit switches are a convenient safety feature that stops a boat's ascent at a predetermined height, or—the contrary view—limit switches are prone to failure and unreliable. The latter says limit switches have a history of failure from corrosion and can unexpectedly fail and lift a boat into the top of a boathouse. Supporters counter that the technology has become more reliable.

Whatever view you have, if your lift has a limit switch, it is important to remain nearby to monitor the boat's ascent, making sure that the cable is winding on the drum properly and the hoist stops when it should. A master switch should be in view at the electric panel.

Boat Hoist Dos and Don'ts

- *Do* take the plug out of the drain while the boat is on the hoist. If the plug is left in, rainwater collects and can wreck wiring and machinery. The additional weight can also collapse the hoist.

- *Do* put the plug back into the drain when the boat is being placed into the water. Without the plug, the boat will sink. (You should leave the drain plug—or a duplicate—on the lift switch as a reminder.)

- *Do* use penetrating oil (not grease!) to lubricate cable strands and reduce internal abrasion.

- *Do* rinse off the cable and lift with fresh water whenever they've been dunked in salt water.

- *Don't* leave cables dangling in salt water while you're out on the boat.

- *Don't* use the hoist to raise more weight than it's designed for.

- *Don't* replace galvanized cable with stainless steel or vice versa; they require different sheave and drum sizes.

- *Don't* carry people up or down on a boat. A boat lift is not an elevator. People jumping in and out of a boat create shock loads that strain the cable and hoist motor. The effect is multiplied with davits, which are cantilevered 5 or more feet away from the lift's vertical support.

Boats on Moorings

Keeping a boat safely at a mooring is altogether more demanding than keeping a boat at a dock. For one thing, a boat on a mooring is typically more exposed to open water and secured with one or maybe two lines while boats in slips have at least four lines and probably more. Fewer lines means more strain and wear on each line. And unlike docks, which last for years or even decades without much maintenance, moorings are held in place by chains, swivels, and anchors, all of which deteriorate steadily and require annual inspections.

The boat on the rocks (top) came to rest (as in RIP) as a result of badly corroded—and neglected—chain. In a similar claim, the chafed line on the bow rubbed against an anchor (middle), setting the boat free to drift around the harbor and bash into other boats. Either the anchor should have been stowed elsewhere or the mooring pendant should have been secured to a bow eye farther down on the hull (bottom).

In the top photo, a badly corroded chain broke in high winds, and the boat came to rest (as in RIP) on rocks. The lines in the middle photo chafed against an anchor at the boat's bow, setting the boat free to float around the harbor and bash into other boats.

Not one single component in a mooring can be ignored. Line must be protected against chafe. And even when it's protected, a line should not be allowed to chafe, day in and day out, against something as sharp as an anchor. Either stow the anchor elsewhere or secure the mooring pendant at a bow eye farther down on the hull (bottom photo).

Chains and swivels must also be inspected at the beginning of every season. Replace the chain when any link is more than a third worn (remember the old adage about the weakest link . . .). Avoid using components that are far apart on the galvanic scale. For example, don't use a stainless steel shackle with galvanic chain.

Also inspect the mooring's anchor periodically, either via a diver or by pulling it out of the water.

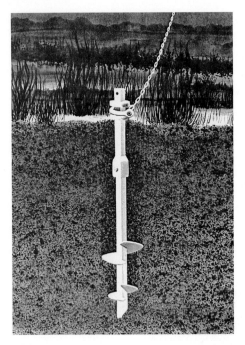

Tests have consistently shown that helix anchors, which are screwed down into the bottom using a device that measures torque, have tremendous holding power compared to traditional mushroom and dead-weight anchors.

Mooring Anchors The destruction of thousands of moored boats after Hurricane Bob swept through New England in 1991 prompted a lot of harbormasters to take a critical look at the traditional mooring anchors. Depending on the harbor bottom, traditional mooring anchors, both mushroom and dead weight, had tended to sit on top of or just below the sediment surface. Theoretically, the holding power of a mushroom anchor is increased up to tenfold once it becomes buried sufficiently in mud. In most harbors, though, a mushroom anchor might be buried a foot or two in a mud bottom and is usually canted to the prevailing winds. If a storm comes out of a different quadrant, it can easily pop out the mushroom. Mushrooms also don't do well in silt bottoms or in denser bottoms such as sand or clay. In the latter, the mushroom tends to sit on or near the surface and must rely solely on its weight to anchor the boat. A dead-weight anchor may gain some advantage from suction in a mud bottom, otherwise its holding power depends completely on its weight, or more exactly on its *submerged* weight, which in the case of a concrete anchor is about half its dry weight.

Another factor has to do with *scope*, the ratio of rode length to water depth. Scope has as much to do with holding power of a mooring as the anchor itself. Studies have found that when the angle of pull increases to 25°, a mooring's holding power begins to weaken considerably. So in shallow harbors, where boats are squeezed together with a scope of 3:1, the advantage of scope is all but eliminated in a storm by a combination of tidal surge and the high, pumping motion of waves.

Advantages of the Helix Mooring Probably the best innovation to come out of Hurricane Bob was the helical or helix anchor, which is screwed down into the bottom. Comparing the holding power of a helix anchor with a traditional mushroom or dead-weight anchor is like comparing a wood screw to a thumbtack or paperweight. A study by the BoatU.S. Foundation, *Cruising World* magazine, and the Massachusetts Institute of Technology (MIT) found that a 500-pound buried mushroom could be pulled out with 1,200 pounds of pull (supplied by a 900 hp tug); an 8,000-pound dead-weight (concrete) anchor could be pulled out with 4,000 pounds of pull. The helix, however, could not be pulled out by the tug, and the strain gauge recorded 12,000 pounds of pull—its maximum—before a shackle burst from the strain. Scope in each case was slightly less than 3:1. (In an earlier test, a strain gauge had registered 20,800 pounds before the hawser snapped.)

Installing a helix mooring, unlike a traditional mooring, requires expertise and special hydraulic equipment. The anchors are made by A. B. Chance, a subsidiary of Hubbell, from hot-dipped galvanized steel with 1¾-inch shafts and either 8-, 10-, 12-, or 14-inch-diameter helices. Extenders can be used to drive the mooring farther into the seabed for additional holding power. Royce Randlett Jr., president of Helix Mooring Systems, says the company has installed several thousand helix anchors plus a similar number of a smaller (5 feet 6 inches with a round shaft) "lighter load" helix anchors with a single helix. The latter is installed by a diver and suitable only for smaller boats.

The helix isn't infallible; in several cases, they have been pulled out. In one case, a helix was being used to secure a 72-foot sailboat in Marion, Massachusetts, during an especially fierce northeaster. While a helix requires less scope than a conventional mooring, this helix had almost no scope because of the storm's surge, according to George Jennings who was then the harbormaster in Marion. It was pumped out of the bottom by the boat's fore-and-aft rocking motion.

In another case, a helix let go because it was installed by an inexperienced individual, who drove it only partway into the bottom. One problem has been the limited number of people who are qualified to install helix anchors; there are about two dozen installers, mostly in the Northeast, with a handful in other states—Maryland, Florida, and Washington.

Ham Gale, who installs helix anchors in the area around Annapolis, Maryland, uses a specially designed platform—a raft—for the hydraulic installation equipment, which can be towed to the spot where the mooring will be installed. Two long metal pipes—called spades—at the ends of the platform are then lowered into the harbor bottom to anchor the platform and prevent it from twisting while the helix is being screwed into the bottom. The holding power of a helix is ultimately based on the density of the bottom and the depth of penetration into the bottom. Using a pressure gauge, an installer can estimate a helix's holding power by translating pounds per square inch to torque. If a helix goes into the bottom too easily, the installer can add an extender to take it down further to firmer soil. Most installations take about an hour. The cost for a large helix with installation is comparable to a mushroom anchor.

14 Seamanship

IN THE PAST FEW DECADES, the introduction of affordable fiberglass boats, GPS, single-sideband (SSB) radio, radar, weatherfax, and the comfort of knowing that help can be summoned with an EPIRB has had the effect of luring more and more small-boat sailors offshore. These innovations have forever changed recreational boating, but what can't be changed is the sea itself. In the span of a few minutes, it can go from sparkling, deep blue with limitless, bright skies to gray and dangerous. "The sea," Joseph Conrad said, "has never been friendly to man," and it is still true.

This chapter looks at some offshore claims that involved seamanship, both good and bad. And since seamanship isn't limited to boats offshore, there are sections on man-overboard recovery, grounding, salvage, and seamanship in "smaller waves" (boat wakes).

Going Offshore

At first glance, the sailboat being abandoned by its crew in the photo opposite looks like it's been out for a Sunday sail. The boat is floating comfortably on its lines, the seas seem only moderately choppy, and the crew perched on top of the cabin looks comfortable, even relaxed. But when you look carefully, you notice that both spreaders are gone, swept away by a 30-foot wave that rolled the boat over 110°, broke the companionway boards, flooded the cabin, stopped the engine, and wrecked the electrical system. The two crew on watch were only kept aboard by their safety harnesses. Later that night the sailboat was knocked down a second time before the decision was made to call for help.

The crew had been enticed offshore—300 miles offshore—by a favorable weather forecast that promised to make the early April passage from Charleston, South Carolina, to Annapolis, Maryland, swift and uneventful. A weak cold front was supposed to come through followed by a pleasant, high-pressure system that extended all the way to California. So instead of heading in at Morehead City and plodding up the Intracoastal Waterway, the crew sailed out beyond the Gulf Stream and around Cape Hatteras.

It's tempting to complain about the erroneous forecast. With all the expensive technology forecasters have at their disposal—Doppler radar, weather satellites, and computerized weather models—you'd think somebody would have noticed a Force 9 gale creeping up the coast. According to Dave Feit, chief of the Marine Forecast Branch at the National Center for Environmental Prediction, a typical weather forecast may be based on as many as twelve different weather models, each of which handles the data slightly differently. These models represent the best science available, not just in this country but worldwide. Sometimes the models will point toward slightly different forecasts, so the forecaster's job is to pick the right one, based on his or her knowledge of how the various models perform. On most days, a majority of the models will be pointing toward the same forecast. Usually the models are correct, but not always. There have been days, Feit notes, when all the models had confidently predicted the same weather pattern, and *all* of them were wrong.

Incidents involving weather forecasts and boats offshore occasionally make the news, including the Caribbean 1500 and the 1998 Sidney–Hobart Race. Almost three decades ago, a gale that hadn't been predicted swept across the Fastnet Race fleet in the Irish Sea with devastating results. Instead of pointing fingers at weather forecasters, however, the official committee report afterward concluded, "In the 1979 race the sea showed that it can be a deadly enemy and that those who go to sea for pleasure must do so in full knowledge that they may encounter danger of the highest order." That's true even if the forecast is for sunny skies and fair winds.

So don't go far offshore unless you're prepared for the worst.

The Loss of *Morning Dew*

On March 17, 1998, a representative of the Coast Guard met with the wife of the owner of *Morning Dew*, a sailboat that had struck a jetty on the morning of December 29 in Charleston, South Carolina, with the loss of all aboard. The wife lost not only her husband but her two young sons and a nephew as well. The group commander had come to play a tape recording of a distress call so that the family could help him determine whether it was related to the loss of that *Morning Dew*. He warned that listening to the tape might be painful.

When the tape was played, the woman immediately recognized the voice of her younger son. She was shocked; the accident had occurred almost three months before, and this was the first she had heard of the distress call.

Morning Dew.

She wasn't the only one who was upset. Local investigators, who had been stymied by the scarcity of information on the accident, contacted South Carolina's Senator Fritz Hollings. Eventually, the National Transportation Safety Board (NTSB) was asked to investigate the loss. The result was an extensive, almost two-year investigation that culminated in a 68-page report. It was one of the most comprehensive investigations that has ever been conducted into a small-boat accident. BoatU.S insured *Morning Dew*.

According to the NTSB report, the 49-year-old owner of *Morning Dew* planned a trip to move his newly purchased, 1978, 34-foot sailboat from its berth at a marina at Little River, near Myrtle Beach, South Carolina, to Jacksonville, Florida. He was accompanied on the trip by his two sons, ages 16 and 13, and his 14-year-old nephew. The owner's brother had been planning to go on the trip and accompanied the group to the boat in Little River, but he left at the last minute because their father had fallen ill.

The two brothers were still together on the morning of December 26 when they bought charts covering the Intracoastal Waterway (ICW) between Little River and Jacksonville. The skipper then penciled in the intended route, which, according to his brother, followed the ICW.

The skipper's brother said they returned to the boat and tried to start the diesel engine, but the battery was dead, and it took quite awhile to get it started. The VHF and navigation lights were checked and found to be working. The brother recalled that before he left, they had gotten a weather report.

The owner and the three boys got underway at about 1230 on December 27, then stopped for fuel at a nearby marina. They made about 20 miles that day and tied up at a marina in Georgetown, South Carolina. The owner called his sister-in-law from a motel, according to the report, and again stated his intention to stay in the ICW all the way to Jacksonville.

On December 28, a salvage master who had seen *Morning Dew* earlier at the marina saw the boat again at 1430 near buoy 26, heading east in the shipping channel of Winyah Bay. This was past the point where the ICW turns south, and the salvage master said that the boat was heading toward the ocean. He reported seeing the boys on the bow dressed in windbreakers and an adult dressed in foul-weather gear at the helm. Thinking that they might have missed the turn to the ICW, the salvage master tried to raise *Morning Dew* to warn that they were headed for the ocean. He said he also heard a sportfishing vessel trying unsuccessfully to raise *Morning Dew*.

After passing the point where the channel for the ICW turned south, it was necessary for *Morning Dew* to pass twelve channel markers, all indicated on the chart, before reaching the ocean. The weather at the time was sunny, but the forecast called for winds to increase that night to 15 to 20 knots from the east, with rain developing.

At 0217 the following morning, December 29, Coast Guard Group Charleston received a VHF radio call on Channel 16. The watch stander was at the coffee machine in an adjoining room and thought he heard the words "Coast Guard" repeated twice. The watch stander responded twice, "Vessel calling the Coast Guard, this is Coast Guard Group Charleston, over." There was no answer, and the watch stander did not feel the call was anything other than a routine message, perhaps a radio check. He did not play back the message.

Four minutes later, another call was received that sounded like a brief burst of static. Although unintelligible, it seemed to have been transmitted by the same person. The watch stander again responded twice, but received no response. He did not log either call.

About 0620, the boatswain on an incoming automobile carrier, *Pearl Ace*, said he heard cries for help coming from the water near buoy 22 on the starboard—north—side of the entrance to Charleston Harbor. He immediately alerted the bridge, which then informed the pilot who was in charge of bringing the ship into port. The pilot, the ship's captain, and the ship's chief officer went outside with a small searchlight but saw nothing. At about 0625 they notified the pilot boat *Palmetto State*, which was in front of the ship. The pilot boat's dispatcher also notified the Coast Guard at 0628, but the watch duty officer decided not to send a boat, since the pilot boat was already at the jetty.

It was still dark, the wind was blowing 25 knots from the northeast, and it was raining. *Palmetto State* took 10 minutes to reach the area where the voice had been reported. Using floodlights and stopping every 50 feet to go on deck and listen, the operator said he searched from buoy 22 to buoy 2. The operator contacted *Pearl Ace* and reported that he had not seen or heard anything. The pilot requested that *Palmetto* remain in the area until morning light. Another search was conducted from buoy 2 to buoy 22 and then to buoy 130, which was near the entrance to the ICW. At 0648, the pilot boat dispatcher again notified the Coast Guard, which took no further action. *Palmetto State* had been in the area for about 30 minutes.

Shortly before 1100, a couple walking along the beach on Sullivans Island spotted a body, dressed in boxer shorts and a pullover shirt, floating in the surf. They described sea conditions as rough, with extremely strong winds. A short time later, a second body, also lightly dressed, was spotted in the water near Sullivans Island.

At 1115, the Coast Guard operations duty officer received a call from an Isle of Palms police officer to report the discovery of the bodies and to request a Coast Guard boat to search the area. The duty officer then told the group operations officer about the 0628 call from the harbor pilot dispatcher, he said, because he was concerned that the 0628 call and the 1115 call might be connected. It would be another five hours before the watch stander would mention the possibility that the 0217 call might also be related to the accident.

At 1144, the operator of the pilot boat *Sis*, which was escorting *Pearl Ace* back out to sea, called the Coast Guard duty officer to report a mast sticking out of the water between buoys 16 and 20 near the north jetty. At 1146, a Coast Guard helicopter took off, and a few minutes later, a 41-foot utility boat was heading to the area. At 1246, the helicopter crew spotted a third body floating in the water. The fourth body, that of the owner, would not be found until January 23, when it was discovered by a passerby near the lighthouse on Sullivans Island.

Some Key Questions

Given his intention to follow the ICW to Jacksonville, is it possible that *Morning Dew*'s skipper missed the turn at the ICW and inadvertently followed the shipping channel to the ocean? Realizing his mistake later, he may then have opted to proceed to Charleston in the open ocean rather than going back 8 miles to the ICW. According to investigators, witnesses stated that southbound boaters following the ICW through Winyah Bay sometimes lose track of the ICW and inadvertently follow the main shipping channel toward the ocean.

The NTSB concluded that a navigational error was unlikely. According to NTSB investigators, *Morning Dew*'s skipper was an experienced sailor, having sailed extensively in Florida and the Bahamas in the 1970s. He had owned several boats and had lived aboard a 33-foot sailboat in the late 1970s and early 1980s. He had taken Coast Guard–sponsored safety courses and read and studied nautical reference books.

The skipper knew how to read charts and follow a marked channel. The report concluded that the appearance of a buoy or other marker without the yellow ICW symbols would have indicated that the vessel had left the ICW. Even if the first marker had been missed, continuing in the shipping channel and entering the Atlantic Ocean would have required passing sixteen buoys, any one of which, by referring to the chart, would have shown the vessel's position.

If he hadn't missed the turn on the ICW, why would an experienced skipper, fully aware of the dangers involved, make the decision to go to sea when his intention had been to follow the ICW? The NTSB concluded that he might have been frustrated at his lack of progress. When the skipper called his sister-in-law on the evening of December 27, he remarked that they had only made 20 miles because of a late start (the dead battery). The following day, for unknown reasons, they again started late and did not begin the transit through Winyah Bay until noon or later.

The report outlines the dangers they faced in the ocean: there was only one adult aboard; the weather was marginal; the seaworthiness of the vessel was unknown; much of the trip would be at night; and the boat was not equipped to sail offshore. With regard to the equipment aboard, *Morning Dew* had only the standard Coast Guard–required equipment plus a compass, a strobe, and a VHF radio. There was no GPS, life raft, survival suits, cell phone, handheld VHF, or EPIRB. (The report did not mention whether binoculars were aboard.) In what seems like an understatement, the NTSB concluded that "neither *Morning Dew*, its operator, nor its passengers were adequately prepared or equipped for a trip into the open ocean, and the voyage should not have been attempted."

Why did *Morning Dew* hit the jetty? The ICW chart book that was aboard included a chart of the jetty, and the report notes that, by referring to the chart, it would have been possible for *Morning Dew* to have sailed around the jetty and into the harbor. The accident occurred at low tide, which meant that the jetty would have been about 7 feet above the water. (Scrape marks on the rocks indicated that *Morning Dew* went up and over the jetty sometime later, when the tide had risen.) Seas were about 4 feet, the wind was out of the northeast at 25 knots, which, if they were following a compass course to the entrance, would have tended to push them toward shore. There was no moon, and it was either raining or about to start raining when the sailboat struck the jetty. The boat had been under power, and damage to the prop indicated that it was still turning when it struck the rocks.

One clue as to what went wrong was that, based on the lack of clothes the teenagers were wearing, it is likely the skipper was the only one on deck. Assuming that he woke up at 0900 the previous morning, the skipper would have been awake for 17 hours at the time of the accident, which, according to the report, would have meant that he was at the nadir of his biological rhythm. The wind, spray, constant pounding, vibration, and stress of constantly steering with a quartering sea would all have added to his considerable fatigue. The report also notes that the clothing the skipper brought for the trip did not adequately insulate him against the cold and wet conditions he encountered. The NTSB concluded that the skipper was "probably severely fatigued and hypothermic to such a degree that his judgment and ability to keep track of his position may have been severely impaired."

The report concluded: "The National Transportation Safety Board determines that the probable cause of the sinking of the recreational sailing vessel *Morning Dew* was the operator's failure to adequately assess, prepare for, and respond to the known risks of the journey into the open ocean that culminated in the vessel's collision with the jetty at the entrance to Charleston Harbor. Contributing to the loss of life in this accident was the substandard performance of the U.S. Coast Guard Group Charleston in initiating a search-and-rescue response to the accident."

The Coast Guard's Role

One of the key points made in the report is that the Coast Guard search-and-rescue mission is largely a function of the readiness of its operations and communications centers: "These centers are the primary links between mariners in distress and people who have the assets and skills to render assistance." If a message was sent by the crew of *Morning Dew*, why didn't Coast Guard Group Charleston respond? According to the Safety Board, there were several reasons, involving both mistakes in judgment by Coast Guard personnel and by the Coast Guard's antiquated communications equipment.

Mistakes in Judgment Since the watch stander was at the coffee machine instead of by the radio, he did not hear the Mayday clearly. What he understood to be "Coast Guard, Coast Guard" was actually an excited adolescent voice saying, "May . . ., Mayday, U.S. Coast Guard, come in."

Based on the NTSB's replaying of the tape recording, if the watch stander had replayed the 0217 call, the report concludes that he would have "recognized immediately" that it was a distress call. According to investigators, the watch stander was not guided by any formal procedures that could have helped him deal with the situation. He had not been trained to use "all available means to aggressively follow up on uncertain calls—especially those received under unusual circumstances [late at night when weather conditions were deteriorating]—in an attempt to determine their nature."

Given the nature of the work, the NTSB concluded that staffing policy should require having two persons on watch at all times. The NTSB also questioned the efficacy of requiring personnel to stand 12-hour watches. The report noted, "Sleep loss has immense potential to exacerbate the problems of excessive shift length, monotony, and boredom." Would standing 8-hour watches or 4-hour watches improve watch stander vigilance and overall performance? The NTSB recommended that the Coast Guard should study the problem.

Investigators listened to tapes that were recorded around the time of the *Morning Dew* accident and discovered a large number of personal telephone calls made by watch standers, which, the investigators said, could conflict with the levels of attentiveness. The investigation also revealed that the Coast Guard has no program to periodically evaluate the proficiency of its subordinate districts—a practice that is common with watchstanding in the military. Without the possibility of periodic inspections, the NTSB concluded that the readiness of Coast Guard personnel can be expected to gradually decline. The NTSB said that the Coast Guard should immediately institute procedures to provide improved management oversight of communications and operations center performance, including instituting a program to periodically review the tapes of recorded radio transmissions and telephone calls.

Equipment   The NTSB concluded that the tape recorder may have contributed to the Coast Guard's lack of response. Investigators found that the tape recorder being used by Coast Guard Group Charleston (and other stations) was difficult to operate when searching for a specific message. The report noted that the Canadian Coast Guard used a recorder model that allowed a watch stander to easily press a button to play back the most recent message. "The emphasis," the NTSB said, "should be on 'easily,' because the easier the task, the more likely it will be performed."

Had the 0217 message been replayed by the watch stander, at a minimum, the report noted that he could have broadcast an urgent marine information broadcast that would have alerted other mariners of the distress call. It was also likely, the report said, that the watch duty officer would have responded much differently to the 0628 call from *Pearl Ace*, had he been aware of the 0217 call.

What the Coast Guard watch stander wouldn't have been able to do was ascertain where the Mayday call was coming from. According to the NTSB's report, Coast Guard Group Charleston's direction finder (DF) had limited range and was "inaccurate, unreliable, and obsolete." Tests of the equipment found bearing errors of as much as 101°. (Charleston's DF could only give a line-of-sight bearing and could not fix a vessel's position.) Investigators found, not surprisingly, that watch stander records indicated that the Charleston's DF was usually turned off.

Furthermore, the DF in Charleston was located *behind* the watch stander's station, and a bearing could only be taken while a signal was being broadcast. The NTSB recommended locating all equipment that must be viewed during the handling of a call at an appropriate distance and angle for concurrent, effective viewing.

The Coast Guard spent more than 400,000 hours on search-and-rescue sorties in 1997, the year *Morning Dew* struck the jetty in Charleston. But even in cases where the Coast Guard was notified, records indicate that 287 lives were lost. The report concluded that if Coast Guard stations had more effective direction-finding capabilities, at least some of the 287 lives might have been saved.

A Coast Guard briefing in April 1999 noted, "Most recreational boaters would be alarmed to learn how fragile this weak link is in our search-and-rescue system. As matters now stand, there is a vast disparity between the communications capability that the public thinks we have and the communications system that we do have."

Thanks to a modernization project spurred by the *Morning Dew* hearings, the Coast Guard has since deployed a state-of-the-art digital recording capability that allows watch standers to play back messages easily and with less bleed-through between channels. It will also continue to record incoming messages whenever an earlier recording is being played back.

The new system's premier feature allows a watch stander to track, within 2°, incoming VHF-FM transmissions so that rescuers will have a dramatically smaller area to search. Dubbed the "Rescue 21" system, the new equipment goes a long way toward taking the "search" out of search and rescue, according to a Coast Guard spokesperson. *Morning Dew*'s original Mayday could have come from anywhere. That same brief Mayday, were it to be received by the new system, would give a line of bearing that would take a rescue pilot directly over the Charleston jetty. The 330-foot towers used with the system will be able to hear a 1-watt signal for 20 miles. A 5-watt or 25-watt signal could be received from boats as far as 50 miles away.

Lessons

In its summary, the NTSB recommended that the Coast Guard Auxiliary, the U.S. Power Squadrons, BoatU.S., and other boating organizations "use in your recreational boat programs the circumstances and lessons learned from the accident involving the sailing vessel *Morning Dew* as a means of educating boaters about the relationship of good judgment and decision-making to boating safety."

The following are a few of the more important lessons from the loss of *Morning Dew:*

- Pay attention to weather forecasts. The NTSB report noted that even in daylight, the weather was not favorable for taking a boat offshore.

- Don't go offshore without experienced crew. Operator fatigue and hypothermia, according to the report, may have severely impaired the owner's judgment and his ability to keep track of his position. Since the boat lacked an autopilot, there should have been enough experienced crew aboard for at least two two-person watches. Each of the watches should also have included someone with considerable offshore experience to act as watch captain.

- Even boats going a few miles offshore need to carry adequate electronics and safety equipment. *Morning Dew* should have carried a GPS (and maybe a handheld backup GPS), an EPIRB, strobe lights for each of the crew, safety harnesses, man-overboard equipment, and detailed charts. There should also have been a backup means of communication, either a cell phone or a handheld VHF radio (or both), as well as at least a coastal life raft.

- Carry suitable clothing. Even in the summer, nighttime temperatures can be chilly offshore. In winter, heavy clothing and foul-weather gear are essential. And the farther north you venture, the more necessary it is to carry survival suits for the crew.

- Know your boat. Not every boat is capable of cruising offshore. If you're not sure how suitable your boat is in the open ocean, don't go offshore.

- File a float plan. Give a copy to your spouse or friend—anyone you check in with periodically who can let the Coast Guard know when you're overdue.

The Loss and Recovery of *Grey Girl*

On May 30, 2000, Brian Warwicker was headed from Florida to Boston to rendezvous with the tall ships of OpSail 2000 when he made the decision to abandon *Grey Girl*, his 43-foot Oyster sloop, 150 miles off Cape Hatteras. The decision wasn't made lightly, and it wasn't made by frightened, inexperienced sailors who got caught offshore in a summer squall. Warwicker, who is British, had logged over 40,000 miles offshore, most of it in the inhospitable waters of the North Sea and English Channel. He'd crossed the Atlantic once, when he sailed the newly built *Grey Girl* to his winter home in Florida. Another member of his crew had also logged over 40,000 miles offshore, and the third member of the crew, a retired naval officer, had sailed across the Atlantic three times, including a solo passage when he was 17.

But the boat was caught in an altogether different set of circumstances than any of the crew had ever encountered offshore before. In the Gulf Stream, 150 miles off Cape Hatteras, they found themselves in seas that were monstrously large and confused. The wind was blowing 50 mph, a Force 10 gale but in itself unusual by offshore standards. What made it especially dangerous was that it was blowing from the north, against the strong northerly flow of the Gulf Stream. Normally, Warwicker would have run before the wind or maybe put out a sea anchor, but not in these confused conditions. The wind pushing against the current produced waves that were large, about 40 feet high, and dangerously steep.

The waves were 8 seconds apart, which meant that the time it took for *Grey Girl*—under bare poles with the engine driving the boat slowly southward—to pass from the crest of one wave to the next wave took a scant 8 seconds. Brian had been in a Force 10 gale before, but then the waves had been much farther apart, with 20 or 30 seconds between crests, and not nearly as steep or dangerous.

The boat was designed and built for extreme offshore conditions—it weighed 20 tons—and was able to handle the giant seas for over 24 hours with a minimum of discomfort. Then, at about 1400 on the second day of the storm, *Grey Girl* was rolled almost 180° by a gigantic wave that the watch on deck said was taller than the boat's 63-foot mast. Warwicker and another member of the crew had been below and were thrown against the side of the cabin, but apart from some bad bruises and cuts, both were OK. The man on deck was dragged over the side of the boat and wound up dangling from his safety harness over the boom when the boat finally righted itself. With the exception of a deep gash in his hand, he too escaped without serious injury.

The boat remained inverted for what seemed like an eternity, according to an account given by one of the crew, and when it finally righted, the hatch boards were missing and a considerable amount of water had been shipped below. Food and equipment that had burst out of lockers were scattered over the bunks and cabin sole.

After everyone was accounted for, the first order of business was to bail out the water. The job went fairly quickly, although water continued to drain slowly from the lockers and cabinets. At 1500, Brian broadcast a Pan-Pan urgency alert message on the SSB radio—the VHF radio was no longer working—and raised the Coast Guard station in Elizabeth City, North Carolina. During the course of the conversation, the radio broadcast became weaker and the reception almost inaudible. The Coast Guard advised them to turn on their EPIRB, which they did, so that *Grey Girl* could be located should the SSB fail completely. A short time later the SSB did fail—the Coast Guard could still hear them, but they could no longer hear the Coast Guard.

Not long after the EPIRB was activated, a Lear jet appeared and circled for almost a half hour. Warwicker tried to raise its pilot but was unsuccessful. He learned later that the pilot had reported the sea state and the condition of *Grey Girl* to the Coast Guard.

At 1700, a Coast Guard helicopter appeared. Using a handheld VHF, Brian was able to talk to the pilot, who asked how he could assist. After talking with the other crew, Brian asked that he and the crew be taken off the boat. "The decision to abandon the boat," he said later, "was not easy."

The press hasn't been kind to sailors who abandon their boats. In his book *Fastnet, Force 10*, about the storm in the Irish Sea that killed seven people in a 1979 sailboat race, John Rousmaniere notes that the strongest criticism after the race was reserved for the twenty-four crews who abandoned their boats: "the survivors and the press could come up with no explanation for the abandonments other than the crews had panicked. There was simply no logical explanation for leaving one's ship."

The reason for the criticism is that, in most cases, the boats themselves will usually survive after they've been abandoned. In the Fastnet Race, only five of the twenty-four lightly built racing boats that were abandoned eventually sank. Heavily built cruising boats, not surprisingly, fare even better. *Satori*, a Westsail 32 cutter, became famous, or perhaps infamous, in a more recent book about offshore disasters, *The Perfect Storm. Satori* (*Mistral* in the movie) was abandoned off Rhode Island at night in a rescue that endangered the lives of the Coast Guard helicopter crew as well as the crew of the boat. Two weeks later, the sturdy cutter was found intact, washed up on Assateague Island, Virginia.

A *Washington Post* article commenting on the incident in the movie noted that, "Every rule of the ocean says . . . stay with the vessel until it sinks out from under you. Your chance of survival is almost always greater with your boat than in the perilous process of rescue."

Brian Warwicker, however, makes no apologies for their decision to abandon *Grey Girl*. Although he was well aware of the maxim about staying with the boat, he said the decision to leave was more practical than emotional. The storm showed no sign of abating, and there was a strong possibility that the boat would be rolled again. What if the boat was rolled again and one of the crew was injured and had to be airlifted off in the dark? A rescue during the day was one thing, but the same rescue at night, especially with an injured man, would be much riskier for both the boat's and the helicopter's crews. Would they even be able to reach the Coast Guard? Two of the three radios aboard were now inoperable, and the one that remained had a broadcast range of maybe a mile or two.

The rescue, despite the waning daylight, went smoothly, thanks to the professionalism of the Coast Guard pilot and crew. The helicopter hovered just above the wave tops, while a member of its crew was lowered into the water and swam over to the boat. One by one, the men aboard *Grey Girl* jumped into the sea and swam over with the Coast Guardsman, who strapped them into a harness and then rode with each of them up to the helicopter.

For all of his experience, Warwicker is hard-pressed to say what he could have done differently. He would carry an extra set of hatch boards (the ones he thought had been lost were found later in the pile of rubble on the cabin sole) and maybe put drains in the lockers. As for tactics, Warwicker says the seas were far too confused for a sea anchor or drogue to be effective.

There will be skippers who will want to second-guess Brian Warwicker's decision to abandon his boat. The boat, after all, survived. In the conclusion to his classic book *Heavy Weather Sailing*, K. Adlard Coles quotes John F. Wilson, master of the SS *Pioneer*: "Whatever decision you may make, if you get into trouble you may be sure that someone who was not there will come up with something you should have done."

Warwicker, however, says he has no doubt that his decision was the correct one. The sudden knockdown—the *violence* of the knockdown—when the boat was rolled by the giant wave completely changed his perspective on abandoning a boat at sea. *Grey Girl* was caught in the wrong place at the wrong time. "In the end," he says, "it came down to the safety of the crew. If we had encountered another giant wave, we might not have been so lucky."

Coping with Monster Waves

In the movie version of *The Perfect Storm*, the fishing boat *Andrea Gail* met her fate trying to climb the face of a gigantic wave. As the wave started breaking, the boat slipped backward, stern first, and then rolled over and sank. Even if you didn't see the movie, you may have seen the wave swallowing the boat on promotional posters.

Nobody really knows how *Andrea Gail* went down, but the Hollywood version isn't a bad guess. Waves in storms can be big, very big, but the occasional monster wave—a rogue wave—will coalesce from a conjunction of forces to tower far above the others. One example involved the 963-foot *Queen Elizabeth II*, which in September 1995 was in heavy seas caused by a hurricane to the south. The crew saw a wave—they said it looked like the White Cliffs of Dover—approaching at eye level with the bridge, which is 98 feet above the water. According to the captain, a tremendous shudder went through the ship, followed seconds later by a smaller shudder as the giant ship "fell into a hole" behind the wave. No one was injured, but the encounter carried away the forward whistle mast.

A boat doesn't have to be in a storm or hundreds of miles offshore to encounter a rogue wave. One BoatU.S. insured, Roy Hope, was with his family and several friends aboard his 23-foot cruiser watching a whale in Bodega Bay, California, when a rogue wave—he called it a "sneaker"—crept silently out of a light fog.

The wave, which Hope estimated was 10 to 12 feet high, crested over the boat, filling the cockpit with water and sweeping a 6-year-old boy over the side. The child was soon rescued, but several of the crew were injured, including one who fractured a cheekbone and broke several ribs.

There are several theories about how these waves are formed, but from a practical standpoint, what can you do to protect yourself? Adlard Coles, in *Heavy Weather Sailing*, says, "The skipper of a small yacht cruising for pleasure in coastal waters should keep as alert an eye for the unusual as the skipper of a racer in mid-ocean and the master of a liner in a storm." Depending on your boat, you may be able to maneuver around the wave or outrun it. If not, head into the wave (slowly) and hang on. If there's time, have everyone aboard put on a life jacket.

The Last Few Hours of *Proteus*

Gabriella Gyyulka, a spunky 27-year-old, was sailing alone across the Pacific Ocean when she came upon a 54-foot sailboat, its masts dangling over the side, wallowing in a gentle swell about 1,000 miles off the coast of Hawaii. She brought her 38-foot ketch alongside and yelled hello. Silence. The only sounds Gabriella heard coming from the ghostly sailboat were the rhythmic gurgling of its scuppers and an occasional slap of a wave against its hull. Its name, PROTEUS, and home port, SEATTLE WA, were painted in dark blue letters on the transom.

Going aboard *Proteus*, a modern-day *Flying Dutchman*, she said, "was spooky—the scariest experience of my whole trip." She climbed down below; the cabin was a mess. Gabriella looked for a logbook, a note, or anything that might explain the crew's fate. Nothing. There seemed to be plenty of food aboard, as well as up-to-date charts, clothing, and navigation equipment. What could have compelled the crew to abandon a $200,000 sailboat in the middle of the Pacific Ocean? Pirates? Some strange disease? Gabriella said she kept thinking that whatever happened to the crew of *Proteus* might happen to her. She climbed back up the companionway ladder and made a hasty departure.

The ill-fated voyage had begun well enough, according to *Proteus'* skipper, Wayne Garton, and the events that compelled him and his crew of three men and three women, all experienced sailors, to abandon ship hadn't involved pirates or strange diseases, unless you consider seasickness a disease. The boat, a 54-foot Skookum, had been en route from Seattle to San Francisco, a sometimes inhospitable stretch of coast that is marked by rocky shoreline, fickle weather, cold water, steep seas, and very few harbors of refuge.

Perhaps the first night at sea after leaving Cape Flattery on July 1 should have been a warning. Most of the crew became seasick, and Garton said he stayed up all night sailing the boat. But seasickness isn't unusual the first day or two at sea, as crew members work to get their sea legs, and by the morning of July 4, everything was looking up: the crew were healthy, the sky was deep blue, and a brisk, 20-knot northwest wind was at their backs. Commenting later, Garton said there had been no hint of what was about to happen.

Everyone had finished lunch and was out on deck blowing bubbles to celebrate Independence Day when the wind jumped dramatically to 35 knots in the span of a few minutes. The crew scrambled to drop the sails and raise a small staysail, but by 1500 even the staysail had to be lowered. *Proteus* was sailing downwind under bare poles, caught between two high-pressure systems in a storm that hadn't been predicted. By nightfall, the wind was blowing a steady 40 mph with occasional gusts to over 65 mph—the maximum on the wind-speed indicator. Garton said the boat handled the seas beautifully, and only one of the crew was slightly seasick.

Later that evening Garton made a mistake of sorts. While he was refueling the generator to charge the batteries, some fuel, not much, spilled. And although it was mopped up quickly, the odor found its way into the cabin. Moments later, when the generator was restarted, a few whiffs of exhaust also found their way below. The combined smells of spilled diesel fuel and exhaust made three more of the crew seasick. That left only two healthy crew members, one of the male crew members and Garton, to stand watch that night.

Conditions on deck grew steadily worse. The 45-knot northwest wind was blowing over the 50°F water, making the air unusually cold for early July. Even down below, one woman reported shivering uncontrollably despite wearing seven layers of clothes, and one of the men said he couldn't get warm even in his sleeping bag.

Seas had built to 25 feet and were getting increasingly large and steep. Several buckets were lashed to lines and trailed astern to slow the boat, a technique that Garton found worked reasonably well. Under bare poles and with the makeshift drogue, *Proteus* was "slowed" to maybe 6 or 7 knots. Even though they were only 45 miles off the coast, near Cape Mendocino, Garton never considered putting in at one of the few small ports between the Strait of Juan de Fuca and San Francisco Bay. The huge swells would have made those tricky inlets far too dangerous. If anything, Garton said, he wished he had been farther away from the rocky coast.

Another option Garton never considered was deploying the boat's life raft. With the cold water and wind, hypothermia would have been inevitable, even if the crew hadn't been physically exhausted. And if they did somehow manage to survive the cold, there were precious few places along the rocky coast where they could have landed safely. Better to stay at sea with the boat.

Both men were desperately fatigued. Garton, as skipper, hadn't been able to get much sleep on the trip, none the first night when everyone else was feeling queasy and only brief naps since then. On the night of July 4, sleep was out of the question; the intensity of the boat's motion made it impossible to rest for even a few moments. Once when Garton was below, he was slammed into a hanging locker so violently that he thought for a while he had broken his arm. As the long night wore on, the lack of sleep, the numbing cold, and the constant physical struggle to control the boat took its toll on both men. Garton said that several times in the darkness he found himself dreaming with his eyes open—hallucinating—a tendency he fought hard to overcome.

Everybody aboard was praying that the weather would abate the next morning, but when the sun peeked over the horizon it seemed to get worse. The treacherous seas were looming high overhead, well up on the mast, and the wind gusts were pegging the wind-speed indicator at 65 mph for longer, frustratingly longer, intervals.

Maybe the sun was only letting them see what had been there all along, or maybe the waves did get bigger and steeper, but shortly after dawn a monstrous wave came crashing into the cockpit. *Proteus* had been pooped. One woman in the cockpit got thrown down onto the sole and was badly shaken, but otherwise everyone was OK. Garton thought the wave had been a warning; it was only a matter of time before they would broach and be rolled completely over, and whoever was on deck would be swept overboard despite wearing a safety harness and life vest.

At about 0700, *Proteus* entered the shipping lanes, and then, as if on cue, a tiny speck appeared on the horizon—a ship. Moments later Garton went below and quietly announced that he was going to radio for help. One of the women was stunned: "Leave *Proteus?* It's your whole life!" Most of the crew, however, seemed relieved. As for Garton, he said the decision to abandon his boat wasn't difficult; the crew's safety came first.

After a lifetime on the sea, including a stint in the navy, five years working aboard a survey ship off the coast of Alaska, and thousands of miles sailing offshore, Garton took the loss of his boat very hard. He had spent twelve years building *Proteus*, and looking down from the deck of the freighter at his abandoned boat, Garton said, was as painful as anything he had ever experienced.

Several weeks after he last saw *Proteus* disappearing in the ship's wake, Garton heard that it had been sighted, not once but three times. The masts were dangling overboard, but it was otherwise intact. He quickly booked a flight to Hawaii and hired a small airplane to look for his boat, but a week into the search he gave up. Garton had been naive; it's a big ocean, and there was little chance that one plane would be able to find *Proteus*.

What could he have done differently? You might expect that Garton would have a lot to say about seasickness, about the need to find crew with iron stomachs when you're planning to sail offshore. Instead he says that while it is important for a skipper to ask questions about seasickness when selecting crew, he notes that his crew had a lot of experience and for most of them seasickness, debilitating seasickness anyway, had never been a problem. Some of them were wearing antiseasickness ear patches, but when the weather turned fierce they hadn't helped. How can you tell until you're in rough weather—the kind of horrific weather that most offshore crews never experience—how someone will react?

As for tactics, Garton was never enthusiastic about heaving-to, a tactic he says didn't work well for *Proteus* even in calm weather. The boat tended to fall off and then begin sailing, which would have been dangerous in the steep seas and fierce winds.

The seas off Cape Mendocino, the area where *Proteus* was abandoned, are noted on charts as frequently having waves over 10 feet, and the seas there on July 5 seemed much larger and steeper than the wind strength warranted. Garton said he had sailed through the same area several times before without difficulty, but he wonders if the seas farther offshore might have been smaller and less treacherous. The one tactic Garton is emphatic about, however, is sea anchors: he wishes he had had one aboard. Before the ill-fated voyage, he had always believed that sea anchors didn't work, but after reading numerous first-person accounts of skippers who have used them successfully, he has since changed his mind. The drogue these skippers rigged off the stern using buckets had slowed the boat. But a sea anchor, a large parachute type, rigged with 250 to 300 feet of line, would have slowed the boat to maybe a half knot or less and kept the bow toward the breaking seas. This would have eliminated the chance of the boat broaching and being rolled, as well as kept it well away from the rocky coast.

Deploying a sea anchor would also have allowed everyone to go below and hunker down until the storm had passed. A sea anchor, he says, would have saved *Proteus*, and he recommends that anyone going offshore should read up on the subject to learn what to carry aboard and how and when it should be deployed.

Coastal Cruising: Abandoning Ship

The 34-foot sportfisherman shown sinking in the photo opposite had been cruising at 20 knots about 40 miles off Virginia Beach, Virginia, in heavy seas when everybody aboard felt a jolt. Immediately afterward, the starboard engine stopped. Rather than checking the bilges and investigating the stalled engine, the skipper decided to first raise another boat on the VHF. Several sportfishing boats were in the area that day, and using a sort of buddy system for just this sort of emergency, the skipper wisely had made radio contact whenever one came into view.

The skipper was able to raise another boat immediately. He said calmly that he might have a "potential problem" and gave the other skipper his boat's loran position.

Contacting another boat before dealing with a potential leak was smart. Had

he jumped below and checked the bilges first, which must have been tempting, the boat's electrical system—and the VHF—might have been inoperable by the time he returned to the bridge to call for help.

Once another boat had been properly alerted, the skipper opened the hatches and discovered the worst: the engine apparently had been torn completely off its mounts, and water was swirling into the bilge, probably through the shaft log. Nothing was certain because the enormous amount of steam billowing through the hatch made a close inspection all but impossible. Everyone aboard was instructed to don life jackets.

The skipper could not even be certain that the bilge pumps were operating. Within 15 minutes after the initial jolt, the vessel was listing badly. The boat that had been contacted earlier, as well as a second vessel that overheard the conversation, was now standing by, and the skipper decided to transfer his passengers to safety.

Abandoning ship went fairly smoothly, although one of the passengers, a young boy, was frightened and required considerable coaxing before he would swim to the other boat. Once they were all safe, the skipper tried raising the Coast Guard to request a pump, but static from an approaching storm prevented his making contact with the station in Virginia Beach. He raised a second station farther away at Cape Hatteras and managed to briefly describe his situation before being cut off by static. He did not have time to give his boat's position. The skipper briefly resumed his efforts to save the boat but was soon forced by rising water to scramble over the hull to safety. Once aboard the other boat, he contacted the Coast Guard at Cape Hatteras to report that everyone aboard had been rescued and was safe.

About 40 minutes after striking the submerged object, the sportfisherman rolled completely over but did not sink immediately. Buoyed by an air pocket, the partially submerged hull continued to drift out to sea at about 4 knots. Shortly afterward, a thunderstorm struck with 50 mph winds and 10-foot seas, forcing the rescue boats to return home. The partially submerged hull is believed to have sunk but was never located.

Although the skipper lost his boat, he followed correct—and safe—abandon-ship procedure, and saved everyone aboard.

Entering Inlets

"On the afternoon of January 14 at approximately 3:30, the insured was operating in the Boca Raton [Florida] inlet when the loss occurred. When he got to the mouth of the inlet, he decided the conditions were 'excessive' and decided to turn his vessel around. As he turned, he became caught between two sets of breaking waves and the vessel flipped over in the middle of the inlet. He was able to swim free of the vessel and climb onto the jetty. His vessel was pulled out by the outgoing tide and was eventually deposited on the beach next to the jetty."

Welcome to an inlet, one of those inhospitable places where big, big oceans and bays squeeze through tiny little openings to quiet harbors. This relationship between wide open and narrow, and between deep and shallow, often results in breaking waves, tricky currents, meandering channels, and dangerous rock jetties.

For a skipper, entering an inlet shouldn't be business as usual. Especially when boats are headed toward the quiet safety of a harbor a few hundred yards away, there may be a tendency to relax and maybe talk about going ashore, meeting friends, or preparing a hot meal. In one claim, for example, the boat's skipper was standing in the companionway, without a life jacket, talking quietly to the helmsman just before dawn, when, according to the helmsman, "his eyes looked behind me and well above my head. I turned just enough to see this monster

Entering an inlet, even in seemingly calm conditions, demands your full attention.

wave already lifting the boat rapidly into an almost vertical position and then everything went black."

According to the claim files, there are four things that a skipper and crew should be wary of when they're entering an inlet: breaking waves, shifting channels, crowds, and darkness. Any one of these conditions can make an inlet dangerous; more than one could make it so treacherous that the inlet should be considered impassable.

Breaking Waves

Consider it a maxim: unless you have prior experience, you should enter an inlet that has breaking waves in the channel only as a last resort. Consult your cruising guide or Coast Pilot, check the fuel gauge, get a weather report, and if possible, head for a safer inlet. You can also drop an anchor or heave-to and wait until the channel is calmer. *Most accidents at inlets could have been avoided by simply waiting for conditions to improve.* While you're waiting, consult your *Tidal Current Tables*. (You can also check the *Tide Tables*, but the times of high and low water do not always correspond with slack water.) The optimum time to enter an inlet is during slack high water when the channel is deepest and waves are least likely to be breaking. (Slack high water is when the tide is high and current is weak or nonexistent.) Conversely, waves are most likely to break when tidal currents are ebbing. Strong flood tidal currents can also create problems for a helmsman, especially if waves continue to break.

Next, study the appropriate chart. Note the locations and characteristics of lights and markers, and calculate the courses between them. Note these courses for quick reference. It is also wise to keep a hand-bearing compass nearby to note the bearings to charted towers, spires, lighthouses, etc., that could be used to ascertain your position should a charted buoy be missing or have shifted. If waves are breaking, everyone aboard should be on deck and wearing life jackets. Contact the Coast Guard, let them know you are about to enter the inlet, and arrange to contact them once you are safely through.

Waves generally travel in sets, or groups, of three or more, with the largest being the last. Note the distance between waves as well as the interval between sets. Planing boats may be able to slip through the inlet between wave sets or even between waves by maintaining a comparable speed. If the boat is going too fast, it can climb over the back of a breaking wave. If the boat is going too slow, it can be pooped. One of the crew should be looking aft so the helmsman can concentrate on the channel ahead.

Slower, displacement-hull boats stand a greater chance of being overtaken by waves. To avoid broaching—being turned sideways by the wave—a skipper must keep the stern square to the incoming waves. When a wave passes under the hull, the water will rush past the stern toward the bow as though the boat were backing down. To move the stern to port, the rudder has to be moved to port. On

Check and Double-Check

ADMIRAL CHESTER W. NIMITZ'S famous observation is worth pondering, even if you're only a weekend boater: "Nothing is more dangerous for a seaman to be grudging in taking precautions lest they turn out to have been unnecessary. Safety at sea for a thousand years has depended on exactly the opposite philosophy."

This photo shows the results of ignoring Nimitz's advice. A dinghy that hadn't been well secured broke loose in heavy seas and began alternately bashing into the side of the boat's cabin and then swinging way out over the water. After repeatedly hitting the boat, the dinghy destroyed the horns, spotlight, antennas, mast, handrails, and windscreen; it also damaged the wheelhouse and bridge. When swung out over the water, however, the real damage was done. The owner reported the boat would heel over almost onto its side, causing it to swing perpendicular to the steep waves. He wasn't able to even try to secure the dinghy because the only other person aboard was terrified and refused to take the wheel.

As the owner struggled to make it back into the harbor, the floundering boat fetched up on a jetty. The two men spent some time clinging to the rocks and were lucky not to have been seriously injured.

At first glance, it appears that the grounded boat is salvageable. If you look closely, however, you'll see that the entire aft section is missing. It was a total loss.

boats with twin screws, increasing power on one engine and backing down with the other will also turn the boat. Another technique is to use a drogue to keep the boat's stern to the sea, then run the engine as fast as possible to maintain steerage. In any case, you can see why handling a boat in a breaking inlet takes experience and should only be attempted when all other possibilities have been eliminated.

Shifting Channels

Inlets are often subject to strong tides, waves, and currents that can sometimes change the contours of the bottom overnight. This is especially true in heavy weather when jetties and bridge abutments interrupt the normal flow of water and create silting.

One case that received a lot of publicity involved a brand-new 66-foot sportfisherman that ran aground in the middle of the channel at Rudy Inlet in Virginia Beach, Virginia. It was winter, and the $1.6 million yacht (not insured by BoatU.S.) was en route from New Jersey to Florida for the Miami Boat Show. Several winter storms had moved sand into the inlet, and the boat ran aground in the middle of the channel. Before the yacht could be freed, it was broken up by waves and sank.

A few months earlier, a 58-foot motoryacht almost suffered the same fate when it ran aground farther south at Oregon Inlet, North Carolina. Again, the large yacht had been in the middle of the channel when it struck the bottom. The skipper and his 6-year-old son had to be rescued by helicopter. Their boat was eventually freed by a salvor, but not before it had been badly damaged by many hours of pounding on the bottom. The skipper learned later that the channel had shifted during Hurricane Bertha, and the new channel had not yet been marked.

Both of these incidents could have been avoided had the skippers read the Coast Guard's *Local Notice to Mariners* or consulted the regional *Coast Pilot* (see the Government Publications section below). If that isn't possible, and you're faced with an unfamiliar inlet, you can try calling the Coast Guard (on VHF Channel 16 or 22) or a local tower. TowBoatU.S./Sebastian, for example, gets contacted routinely by boaters who are approaching Sebastian

These photos were taken at Jupiter Inlet, Florida, in January 2005. The tide was low and getting lower, which is the worst time to negotiate a breaking inlet (the flow of outgoing water meets the incoming waves, causing them to build and become larger, steeper, and more dangerous). In this case, 4- to 8-foot waves had been breaking across the inlet. All four people aboard—two men, a woman, and a 10-year-old boy—were rescued. None had been wearing life jackets.

An inlet is most likely to be passable at slack high water, when the tide is high and the current is negligible.

Inlet on Florida's Atlantic coast. Towers know local inlets as well as anyone and are glad to help. As an alternative, try contacting a nearby marina. If all else fails, following a local boat (with comparable or greater draft) through an inlet is probably OK, provided you're *sure* it's a local boat. Contact the boat's skipper on your VHF before proceeding.

Crowds

Many inlets attract crowds of boats heading through the narrow channel to get to open water. At some inlets, such as Port Everglades, Florida, small boats share the narrow inlet with giant, oceangoing ships. Weekends, according to one of the ship pilots in Port Everglades, can be "unbelievable."

Good seamanship and common sense are critical in these inlets. *Most* skippers know to stay to the right and proceed slowly through the channel to open water. But there are always a few boats that go blasting through the inlet with throttles wide open, despite being surrounded by other boats, creating huge wakes. There may also be one or two boats on the wrong side of the channel, or the occasional skipper who decides to go fishing, raise the sails, pull a water-skier, or as in the claim below, even "play" in the inlet.

The skipper of a 20-foot center console was entering Jupiter Inlet in Florida, going less than 10 mph, when he was startled to see a small PWC turn immediately in front of his boat. Waves that day were large, so the skipper had been carefully staying between two swells to avoid being broached. The skipper of the incoming boat was peering straight ahead at the wave when he suddenly saw the PWC. The PWC operator, he said, appeared to be playing in the waves and was even more startled by the encounter than he was. To avoid the PWC, the skipper made a hard turn, which caused his boat to broach in the wave, and his two kids (not wearing life jackets) wound up in the water and had to be rescued by another boat.

Whenever you're in a narrow fairway, stay to the right, watch your speed (and wake), and be aware that other skippers may not be as conscientious as you are.

Darkness

Whenever possible, plan to arrive at an unfamiliar inlet during daylight. The more experience a skipper has, the more likely he or she will avoid unfamiliar inlets after dark. Vito Dumas, a legendary sailor and author who spent most of his life at sea in small boats, was especially wary of entering an unfamiliar inlet at night. In his book *Alone Through the Roaring Forties*, Dumas wrote that even when sea and wind conditions seemed ideal, he would wait until daylight rather than enter a harbor in the darkness. The reason, he said, was that it was often difficult to distinguish lighted buoys from lights onshore.

The loss of *Morning Dew* is a dramatic example of what can go wrong when

This boat was rolled by a rogue wave while entering Humboldt Inlet shortly before dawn. The tide was ebbing and would have been low at 6:08 A.M. Conditions had been deceptively calm at sea, but the description in the California *Coast Pilot* advises mariners to use extreme caution and warns that the entrance is often impassable when water is ebbing. There was one fatality.

entrance lights either aren't found or are misidentified. No one knows for sure what happened, but when the father tried to enter the inlet, his sailboat was on the wrong side of the jetty, perhaps because he was heading for lighted buoys—the wrong buoys—farther inside the harbor.

Aside from the considerable problem of identifying lights, another hazard in an inlet at night is breaking waves. A 45-foot sailboat entering California's Humboldt Inlet before dawn on an outgoing tide was between the breakwaters when a "rogue wave" pitchpoled the boat and swept one of the crew overboard. (He wasn't wearing a life jacket or safety harness.) The other crew said they could hear him, but in the dark they couldn't see him, and he drowned.

The rogue wave was caused when a swell met the outgoing tide, but in the darkness the crew couldn't see the size of the waves that were forming inside the inlet. Had the skipper only waited another hour, there would have been sufficient light to see the waves. He should also have called the Coast Guard before proceeding through the inlet. Finally, the skipper should have insisted that everyone on deck wear a life jacket.

Government Publications: Reading Your Way Through an Inlet

Besides charts, two reference books that should be carried aboard any coastal cruiser are the appropriate regional editions of the *Tidal Current Tables* and the *Coast Pilot*. Consult these books while your trip is still in its planning stages. Using the *Tidal Current Tables*, you can plan your departure so that you arrive at an inlet during optimum slack high water. *Tidal Current Tables* also give the time and velocity of maximum current.

A *Coast Pilot* provides a brief description of the various inlets along the coast and can warn a skipper of an inlet that is not suitable for inexperienced skippers. For example, the skipper of the large yacht that grounded at Oregon Inlet would have been forewarned that it was dangerous by reading the *Atlantic Coast Pilot: Cape Henry, Virginia to Key West, Florida:* "Oregon Inlet, about 2.5 miles southward of Bodie Light, is entered over a shifting bar. A lighted whistle buoy marks the approach; other buoys, not charted, are frequently shifted in position to mark the best water. A fish haven is about 5 miles southeast of the lighted whistle buoy. The inlet, used by local fishing vessels but not recommended to strangers, requires continuous dredging; it deepens with northwest winds and fills in with northeast winds. Tidal currents in the inlet are reported to be as much as five knots, but with southwesterly winds as much as 6 to 8 knots."

In addition, *Coast Pilots* cover a lot of other useful information important to navigators, including anchorages, bridge and cable clearances, currents, tide and water levels, prominent features, weather, ice conditions, wharf descriptions, dangers, routes, traffic separation schemes, small-craft facilities, and federal regulations applicable to navigation.

There are nine *Coast Pilots* available, which you can purchase at bookstores and on-line for $26. They also can be downloaded for free at http://nauticalcharts.noaa.gov. Each volume is broken into chapters, so you won't have to download hundreds of pages, for example, if you're only interested in the St. Clair River or Lake Champlain. The site includes information on charts, electronic charts, and updates to the *Local Notices to Mariners*.

Local Notices to Mariners contain notices and changes in the status and capabilities of aids to navigation (buoys, radio beacons, loran, etc.), chart updates, information on drawbridge operations, and warnings of a variety of events and activities that could affect safe navigation in your area. You can access *Local Notices to Mariners* on the Internet at www.navcen.uscg.gov/lmn.

Light Lists are a series of seven volumes published by the USCG that provide information on aids to navigation that aren't shown on a chart. Like the *Coast Pilots*, *Light Lists* cover all coastal and inland waters. You can access them at www.navcen.uscg.gov/pubs/LightLists/LightLists.htm.

The *Eldridge Tide and Pilot Book* (www.robertwhite.com) has tables giving the time and height of high and low tide, and the time and strength of the current on the East Coast. The price is about $12. *Reed's Nautical Almanac* (www.reedsalmanac.com) covers tides and currents, lights, beacons and buoys, and celestial navigation tables. The North American East Coast edition covers Nova Scotia, the Atlantic and Gulf coasts, plus Bermuda and the Bahamas. The West Coast edition covers from Mansanillo, Mexico, to Kodiak, Alaska, including Puget Sound, the British Columbia inside passage, and the Hawaiian Islands. There is also a Caribbean edition that covers southeastern Florida, all the Caribbean islands, and the coast from Venezuela north through Mexico. The price of any *Reed's* edition is about $30.

All About Boat Wakes

For anyone planning to go offshore, there are many excellent books that have been written (and should be read) on boat handling in waves offshore. The advice is usually helpful. In *Heavy Weather Sailing*, for example, K. Adlard Coles and Peter Bruce describe a good offshore boat and give no fewer than twenty recommendations for preparing the boat for heavy seas: "don safety harness; secure cockpit lockers; stow loose gear; put stopper on hawse pipe," etc.

Good advice. But what about boat wakes? For most people, an errant boat wake can be no less daunting than growlers offshore. True, they are much smaller, but they are also steeper, closer together, and in many respects equally dangerous.

There are two kinds of wake-related claims in the BoatU.S. Marine Insurance files: skippers whose wakes rocked other boats ("I was barely moving!") and skippers who were thrown topsy-turvy by another boat's wake ("**!@*%

$&*@!!"). Without exception, skippers in the latter category didn't take it very well. An elderly gentleman in Alabama, a retired minister, became a local "celebrity," according to the claim file, when he had the skipper of a transient motoryacht arrested for rocking his boat in a no-wake zone. In another claim, a skipper working on his boat in Florida got so angry at the owner of a passing boat that he hopped in his car, drove to the next bridge, parked in the center of the span, and refused to move until the startled bridge tender agreed to call the Marine Police. And in Texas, where discouraging words aren't supposed to be heard, a man whose boat had just been rocked grabbed the VHF mike and yelled, "When I catch you I will unleash my German shepherd and have it rip off your face!"

Eight Rules for Coping with Wakes

Claim files that involve confrontations are the exception, however; most skippers barely manage a glimpse of the other boat's transom because they are too busy coping with its wake. Done correctly, lessening the impact with an oncoming wake can reduce damage and avoid injuries—as well as calm frayed tempers. Here are a few rules.

1. *Seat passengers aft or amidships, away from the bow.* By far, the most serious injuries in the BoatU.S. Marine Insurance files have been to passengers who were seated near the bow. It is especially important that older passengers be seated aft. Dr. Gordon Smith, assistant professor at Johns Hopkins Center for Injury Research and Policy, says that in a severe trauma, such as being tossed in the air by another boat's wake, anybody can be injured, but the older you are the more likely you are to suffer a back fracture. Generally, Dr. Smith says, serious back injuries are more of a problem when someone is over 55.

    While the bow is most vulnerable, there is no place on a boat that isn't going to be rocked when a boat collides with a wake at high speed. Injuries in the BoatU.S. insurance program include several passengers who were thrown into windshields or instrument panels. Falls on deck are also common, and a few passengers were thrown out of a boat (which supports the case for wearing life jackets). All of these passengers were standing, and courts have tended to find skippers liable when passengers are not instructed to sit down when a large wake is approaching. While being seated is no guarantee of safety, especially when someone is seated near the bow, sitting on a cushion (to absorb the impact) with a firm grip on the boat reduces the chances that a passenger will lose his or her balance and be injured.

2. *Don't wait until you're in the middle of a wake to throttle back.* Slow the boat before the wake arrives. The larger the wake (and the smaller your boat), the more important it is to lessen the impact with an oncoming wake.

3. *Don't come to a complete stop.* With an especially large wake, you may be tempted to stop the boat to minimize the impact. Don't. Without adequate headway—at least 3 or 4 knots—a wave could shove the bow to the side, and you wouldn't be able to continue maneuvering toward the wake. Small boats especially could be rocked violently or even swamped.

4. *Warn passengers when you're about to cross another boat's wake.* "Sit down and hold on! Boat wake!" is usually sufficient. A warning is especially important when crew are below and can't see the approaching wake. On larger boats, and boats with flybridges, the most practical way to warn passengers in the cabin is with an intercom system.

5. *Don't hit waves head-on.* Rather than crossing an oncoming wake at a perpendicular (90°) angle, try bearing off a few degrees so that you cross the wake at a slight angle. This allows your boat's bow to grip the wave longer and helps to prevent the bow from being thrown high in the air.

6. *When overtaking another boat, cross its wake quickly rather than riding the waves.* Keep both hands firmly on the wheel and stay well away from the other boat's stern. Remember to signal the other boat before passing, and be aware of the wake created by your own boat.

7. *Avoid taking a steep wake on the beam.* Especially in smaller boats, which are prone to being rocked violently, it is better to turn back into a wake briefly and then come back on course.

8. *Anchor away from busy channels.* A woman on a boat anchored near Long Island Sound was scalded by a pot of boiling water when her boat was rocked suddenly by a wake. Similar accidents have been caused by irresponsible skippers, but in this case the boat was anchored in a busy area near open water.

Overloaded Boats

Six passengers were spilled into the water when a 16-foot boat in Tennessee went through—not over—a wake, filled with water, and rolled over. There were no fatalities, but two people were injured.

In that case, keeping passengers aft to raise the bow might have prevented the mishap. A better solution, however, would have been to limit the number of passengers aboard. By law, a boat's capacity (both number of persons and total weight) must be posted on all boats 20 feet and under. If the boat doesn't have a capacity plate, the best rule of thumb is to limit the number of passengers to the number of seats onboard. Never let passengers sit on the side of the boat.

Minding Your Own Boat's Wake

Many of the same skippers who hate being rocked by other boats have been guilty, perhaps unknowingly, of rocking other boats themselves. I say unknowingly because the most common type of boat wake claim involves skippers who say that they had "slowed" and could not have created such a large wake. Almost always, their boats had planing hulls.

Although some displacement hulls—larger commercial ships and tugs—create large wakes, sailboats and smaller displacement powerboats, like trawlers, don't. They can't. When a displacement hull attempts to go faster than its hull speed (1.34 x the square root of its waterline length), it digs a "hole" in the water behind the boat, and the stern squats lower and lower as more power is applied. The engine must work harder and harder, wasting an enormous amount of fuel, to make the boat go even a fraction of a knot faster. That's why boatbuilders don't put large, turbocharged engines on displacement hulls.

A planing hull, on the other hand, has V-shaped bottom sections at the bow and relatively flat sections aft, which allow the boat to lift itself out of the hole and get on plane, traveling much faster than its hull speed. Depending on the boat's size, the size of its props, and the efficiency of its design, a planing hull may create a fairly large wake when it reaches cruising speeds, but not nearly as large as the wake it creates when its stern sinks into the water just before coming on plane or just after falling off plane.

All too often the skipper of a boat will come off plane in a no-wake zone and plow through the anchorage with the boat's bow way up in the air and the stern dug down deep in the water. Instead of reducing the size of the boat's wake, this token reduction in speed *increases* the size of the wake. Even a small boat in the stern-down position can throw up a huge wake. A center console off the coast of San Diego, California, to cite one example, inched past a 34-foot trawler, then crossed its bow and ran down the other side. "Having experienced this type of 'courtesy' before," the trawler skipper recalled, "I called to my wife to hang on because we were about to get rocked from three sides. She grabbed the bimini but couldn't hold on. She landed on the steering console, knocking out three of her front teeth." The boat that caused the dangerous wake was only 22 feet long.

Overtaking Boats

If you're overtaking a boat in open water, give it a lot of room. Passing as far away as possible reduces the wake's impact (not to mention ill feelings). Conversely, in a narrow channel, overtaking a boat without regard for your boat's wake can have serious consequences. The skipper of a 42-foot motoryacht in North Carolina, for example, slowed down only slightly and sent a 25-foot sailboat surfing wildly onto a sandbar. (Talk about ill feelings!)

Aside from risking serious injuries to passengers, this sort of thing can quickly wreck a boat.

When you are the overtaking boat, use VHF Channel 16 and/or your horn to signal your intentions (one short blast if you're overtaking the other boat on its starboard side, two blasts if you're planning to pass on its port side). Cross the wake quickly (don't ride the waves), but be aware of your own boat's wake. If you're being overtaken, come completely off plane so that your stern is level. Slowing your boat will allow the overtaking skipper to slow his boat as well. Let's hope the other skipper is as courteous as you are.

Besides risking the ire of other boaters left rocking astern, skippers who fail to slow sufficiently are liable for damages caused by their boat's wake. A large cruiser went blasting close by a much smaller boat on a lake in New York without so much as a horn signal. A woman who was below on the smaller boat was thrown against a bulkhead, breaking her glasses and severely injuring her right eye. Although she regained much of her vision, the jury awarded her $750,000. The skipper, it is worth noting, only had $100,000 in liability coverage.

Other Suggestions

- Always be aware of your boat's wake at various speeds and hull trim. Glance backward whenever you increase or decrease speed. Also, keep an eye on your depth; shallow water increases the size of a boat's wake.

- Position passengers to keep the boat level. Too much weight aft lowers the stern and increases the size of the boat's wake. If available, use trim tabs to come on plane quickly and keep the boat level.

- Use horn signals and/or your VHF when you are overtaking another boat. This alerts the other skipper, who may then choose to reduce speed so that you will be able to pass at a slower speed.

- Slow down before you are abeam of another boat, marina, etc. Your wake moves at right angles to the path of the boat.

What About Your Own Boat?

According to Rob Schofield, a naval architect and expert on fiberglass construction, the average family cruiser in the United States is designed to withstand an impact of 3 g (g is the acceleration due to gravity); the average sportfisherman, 4.5 g; and the average high-performance boat about 6 g. The message is simple: If you drive your average family cruiser like a high-performance boat—leaping and pounding over waves—something is bound to give.

What gives is sometimes the crew, but more often the boat itself. While boats

Wakes and G Forces

BACK IN THE EARLY SEVENTIES, Hatteras Yachts wanted to verify proposed BIA (Boating Industry Association) design specifications for g forces on fuel tanks. Instead of getting out their calculators and pencils, the folks at Hatteras decided the only foolproof way to test g forces on a boat was to don their football helmets and crash into a few waves. And crash into waves they did.

Using a 45-foot convertible loaded with instruments to measure the impact, they sped through 8- to 12-foot waves at 25 mph on a blustery day in January off Morehead City, North Carolina. (The results should interest anyone contemplating charging into an approaching wave or boat wake at full throttle.)

They discovered that one of the worst places to be on the boat was at the flybridge helm, where an impact with a wave produced forces up to twelve times the force of gravity. To put this in layman's terms, a 200-pound crew member might float like a butterfly at zero gravity when the boat flew off a wave, but he would weigh the equivalent of 2,400 pounds as the boat plunged into the next wave. Remember, this test was performed at 25 mph; imagine the impact at 40 mph! Fortunately, the extreme forces lasted only 0.15 of a second.

Where was the safest place to be? As you might expect, the g forces were much smaller when the rider was lower in the boat and amidships, where the impact with waves didn't exceed 6 g (half the impact felt by crew on the flybridge).

generally don't break in two or even split open (although some have), pounding into boat wakes takes its toll in more subtle ways. Looking for cracks can give you an indication of how hard a boat has been used. Cracks in the laminate—the fiberglass structure—are far more serious than cracks in the gelcoat.

It isn't unusual to see tiny, spiderweb cracks in gelcoat; chemistry doesn't allow boatbuilders to make a gelcoat that is tough and flexible as well as glossy. Schofield says it's the deeper, wider cracks that run in long lines along chines, stringers, or bulkheads that you need to worry about. If you find cracks at the stem or keel, you should be especially concerned; these are the areas that are supposed to be heavily built and *not* prone to cracking. The chines, keel, and transom edges are all supposed to be double-lap laminated, which makes them very rigid. If you find a crack in these areas, something is wrong. Cracks under the stringer are not so definitive; they may indicate a problem that is structural or merely a problem with the gelcoat.

Decks aren't supposed to have cracks, although cracks on decks are fairly common. Gelcoat experiences built-in stress from the curing process so is more brittle to begin with, and gelcoat that is too thick will flex and crack. Gelcoat that was cured too hot is also more brittle.

What to do if you suspect a problem? If you own a boat that is still under warranty, Schofield notes wryly that the guy with the nicest personality is always the customer service manager. Give him a call. With older boats, consult a marine surveyor to see if the suspect area should be repaired.

Grounding and Ungrounding

Elliot Hammerman wrote to BoatU.S about a brand-new, 65-foot Viking that had run hard aground on submerged rocks in an area known as Lower Middle in Boston Harbor. Elliot noted that this navigational "oversight" (by a professional captain, no less) resulted in a staggering $98,000 bill to repair the bottom and replace the struts, rudders, shafts, and props.

This wasn't the first time a skipper had misread the markers and come to grief on Lower Middle. Hammerman said boats have been grounding on the rocks for years. As a kid almost fifty years ago, he and his enterprising buddies would row out and search the shoal for boat parts—props, rudders, struts, and shafts—which they then sold to a local junkyard.

Like a lot of other boatowners who write letters expressing concerns about various local shoals, Hammerman thought the area should be better marked. But because of huge budget cutbacks at the Coast Guard, the chance of getting more and better markers is remote. Another BoatU.S. member, Captain John Shepard, wrote twenty-seven letters and made 103 phone calls before a lighted marker was placed at the entrance to Cuckold Creek on Maryland's Patuxent River. Captain Shepard's tenacity is the exception; unmarked or poorly marked shoals remain all too common on many waterways. The only tried-and-true way to avoid having the bottom of your boat ripped off is to use your charts and compass.

One important note: anyone, even the best skippers, can occasionally bump the bottom. On some bodies of water (the Chesapeake Bay comes to mind), an occasional bump or even a grounding is almost inevitable. The difference between someone who studies charts and someone who uses the "look for a marker and go" approach is that the former can quickly recognize a risky situation and slow down. Whenever something is amiss—a marker isn't where it's supposed to be or has

After running 50 feet up into this marsh, the skipper reported the accident to the Coast Guard and had to assure them that the boat was in no danger of sinking. He theorized later that he had mistakenly been heading toward the port running light of another boat.

the wrong blinking pattern, etc.—to shove the throttle forward and continue plowing ahead as though everything is fine invites a nasty grounding.

As one skipper claimed, "Upon observing the flashing marker, I altered course slightly and at the same time began looking for the chart to find a place to anchor for the night. As I resumed my scan of the marker, it appeared slightly dimmer, nothing more unusual than that. I did not notice that the magnetic course was now due east.

"Within minutes, [one of the crew] said he saw land. I stood up and looked around and a few seconds later we went hard aground. The boat had been going 28 mph and we wound up about 50 feet up into the marsh. I believe now that the 'marker' I saw was actually the port light of another vessel. I contacted the Coast Guard to inform them of the location of my vessel. I assured them that we were in no danger of sinking."

This skipper's use of a chart and compass was much too casual, especially considering his boat's speed and the reduced visibility at night. Even in daylight (and even if you're using a state-of-the-art GPS), it is critical to use a chart and compass to confirm your position. If a marker isn't where it's supposed to be, either you're off course or you're looking at the wrong marker. In the meantime, slow down! Or, if something you're seeing doesn't seem right—the "dim" marker (that wasn't flashing) or the land

It's not unusual for a boat to run aground in unfamiliar waters, especially when the skipper doesn't bother to consult a chart. The odd thing about this grounding is that the boat's skipper was familiar with the channel and had passed through it many times. So what caused him to run so far aground?

The answer likely has to do with confidence, or more to the point, overconfidence. Even in familiar waters, overconfidence can lead to a momentary lapse in attention. And when you're working your way through a tricky channel (in this case, in the dark), that may be all it takes to send a boat astray.

As this boat was approaching a bridge late on a hazy summer afternoon, the skipper must have thought everything was lining up just as it should; there was a red marker on the right, a green marker to port, and a tall bridge span looming in the background. Perfect. Had the skipper even glanced at a chart, however, it would have been immediately apparent that he was making a huge mistake: there were two other markers farther out from the bridge that had to be honored. His boat hit the jetty at peak high tide, doing considerable ($16,000) damage. It's yet another example of why it's necessary for even smaller boats to carry *and use* charts.

that was spotted by the crew—stop the boat immediately until you confirm your position.

The Problem with Depth Sounders

"We were leaving Harbor Island Marina [in Solomons Island, Maryland] at 0600 and decided to cut across the gap between the lighted marker and the one further out at the entrance. It's less than 200 yards between the two markers and would save us considerable time. I had seen dozens of boats take that exact same route. My boat doesn't draw very much water, so I didn't think it would be a problem.

"Just when [my wife] was coming up the companionway, the depth alarm started beeping followed immediately by a bump and then another bump as the boat came to a complete stop. The rudder must have hit something hard because the wheel yanked hard to the right and wouldn't budge."

Depth alarms can be handy, but if you don't slow down, they're just as likely to tell you that you've gone aground (past tense) as to warn you that you might go aground. As a general rule, set the alarm as deeply as practical to maximize the chance of an early warning. The exception is when you're already in shoal water, in which case you can lower the alarm depth and proceed cautiously at a greatly reduced speed.

Depth sounders typically can be adjusted to indicate depth beneath the keel, the actual depth (from the waterline), or the depth beneath the transducer. Adjusting the readout to display the water beneath the keel saves having to constantly do the calculations, simple though they may be (depth on the display minus the boat's draft), to know how close you are to the bottom. On the other hand, setting the readout from the boat's waterline (the actual depth) gives you the advantage of instantly matching the depth sounder to the chart. This can be especially useful when you're using the depth sounder to navigate (see the Following Contour Lines section). The important thing, whichever you choose, is to know how your depth sounder is set.

Note, however, that the depths indicated on a chart are referenced to mean low water, and there are situations that can lower water levels further, such as sustained offshore winds or spring tides. River and lake levels can also fall dramatically, making areas that are ordinarily navigable too shallow for navigation. There have been many claims for groundings on the Great Lakes, for example, when water levels have been unusually low.

One other comment: The skipper who grounded after coming out of Harbor Island said he had seen dozens of other boats take the same shortcut. The skipper was by every definition "a local," which is a good example of why you have to be careful when you rely on someone else's local knowledge. The skipper learned later that the other, somewhat savvier skippers in his area only cut the marker at high tide. In a similar example, a hard grounding occurred because a Connecticut skipper relied on a friend in Miami for advice before he headed south to the Florida Keys. The Miami friend assured the skipper that he wouldn't have any problems in Florida Bay, despite his sailboat's deep draft. As it turned out, the sailboat ran aground three times trying to make its way across the bay.

Guests: Something Else to Keep an Eye On

Another frequent cause of groundings in the claim files is the inexperienced guest who is left alone at the helm. (Unattended guests are also the cause of many collisions with other boats.) In one well-documented claim, the skipper turned the helm over to a guest, and several minutes later, the boat struck a shoal, breaking several of the skipper's ribs as well as the boat's skeg. The skipper had instructed the guest to "Keep her in the middle of the channel" before going below. Not being fluent in nautical terminology, the guest interpreted the "middle of the channel" to mean the "middle of the river."

There are many reasons why boats go aground: inattention, shifting channels, and poor navigation are a few that come to mind. In this case, the skipper turned the helm over to a guest, and several minutes later the boat stopped abruptly on a sandbar. The tide was dropping, and soon the trawler was high and dry, requiring considerable effort by a salvage crew and crane before it was refloated. (No mention was made in the claim file of what was said between skipper and guest, either before or after the boat grounded.)

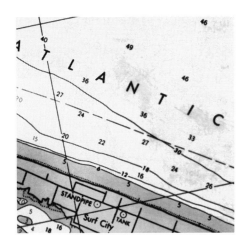

Contour lines.

Guests, and alas even a few experienced skippers, tend to equate distance from shore with deeper water. When you give instructions, go over the route with the crew, noting on the chart any tricky or dangerous areas you'll be encountering. It's also a good time to make sure everyone is familiar with the boat's controls and navigational equipment as well as its safety equipment. Nothing is more helpful to a skipper than a crew who knows what they're doing.

Following Contour Lines

You may encounter a situation when visibility is severely restricted because of fog or heavy rain, and you can't confirm your position as you approach a harbor. Even in good visibility (especially at night), there will be times when navigational marks or shore features aren't easily recognized, which can be especially worrisome if there's a reef or other underwater obstruction lying close to the shore near the approach to a harbor entrance. GPS can help. So too can radar. But if these electronic conveniences aren't available—or if they let you down at a critical moment—you can use your depth sounder, compass, and the contour lines on a chart to find your way into a harbor. It's a nifty trick that's worth practicing in clear weather.

Similar to the lines on a weather map linking areas of equal barometric pressure, a good chart also has contour lines that link soundings of equal depth—say 30 feet and 20 feet—which outline the underwater profile of the seabed off the adjacent shoreline. If you're uncertain of your position as you approach land, simply look at the chart and take note of the depth of a contour line and the compass course along it that follows the coastline to the entrance of the harbor. Then head slowly toward the shore—purposely well off to one side of the harbor—while keeping a close eye on the depth sounder.

When the depth sounder indicates that you've reached the chosen contour, turn onto the predetermined compass course and continue to monitor the depth, "feeling" your way along the contour line by making small course alterations to maintain the required depth until you reach the harbor entrance.

What to Do If You Find Yourself Aground

It doesn't matter whether you've been boating fifty years or fifty minutes; whether you own a powerboat or sailboat; whether your boat draws 2 feet or 6 feet; or whether the tide—if there is a tide—is rising or falling: the first thought that pops into your head the instant your boat unexpectedly touches bottom is always the same—"Oh *&#@* !!*@!"

If you're lucky, it's just a momentary scare—the boat bumps, and you continue safely on your way. But the boat could also be hard aground—stuck fast—with many hours of frustration ahead before it's freed.

The Initial Bump: Maybe You'll Be Lucky If you're going to get off lightly, with maybe just a brief bump to let you know you've strayed off course, you'll have to react quickly. A little luck helps too. Just how you react depends on circumstances as well as the design of your boat.

Sailboats If a boat sailing upwind is to be freed quickly, the helm should be thrown over immediately and the boat tacked. The crew should move to leeward to reduce draft, and then with a little luck, the wind will nudge the boat back to deeper water. If the boat is sailing downwind, the chances of getting free immediately are slim unless you happen to have bumped a very short shoal. The temptation will be to try and spin the boat 180° so that it's heading back toward open water. It could work, but then again, spinning the boat around could damage the boat's rudder, especially if it's a deep, spade rudder, and the boat has a shoal-draft keel. If the boat remains on the shoal, drop the sails immediately so that it won't be blown farther aground.

If you use your engine, make sure it's pumping water. When a boat is heeled, the intake could be out of the water or, equally as serious, sucking up sand, mud, or gunk from the bottom. Check periodically to make sure water is flowing freely from the exhaust, and keep an eye on the temperature gauge.

Powerboats A powerboat skipper's initial reaction should never be to increase throttle, either in forward or reverse, and hope for the best. The boat's engine gets its cooling water from somewhere under the boat, and if it sucks up enough mud or sand the engine could be wrecked. Shut down the engine until you've ascertained how far the intake is from the bottom. A light-displacement boat with a shoal draft can probably be walked or pushed to deeper water by the crew (preferably wearing shoes).

Check props and rudders to make sure they haven't been damaged. On most

There is a tendency for some owners with outdrives to raise them higher and higher to pass through shallow water. This is a bad—and expensive—practice. While it's acceptable to run with the outdrive raised up to the trim-level limit, raising it higher by using the trailering switch puts excessive strain on the spline teeth and can lead to costly repairs.

As the outdrive is raised beyond the limit (with the prop just below the water surface), the steel input shaft pulls slightly out of the aluminum coupler. This results in a sloppy fit and excessive wear between their respective spline teeth at slow speeds (the softer aluminum teeth tend to wear more). Worn spline teeth will make noise at slower speeds and be even louder when the sterndrive is turned hard over to either side. If you hear such a noise, have the sterndrive pulled for inspection; wear and tear is not covered by insurance.

powerboats, underwater machinery is vulnerable and must be considered as you work to free the boat. Raising an outdrive or outboard slightly will reduce draft. If you decide to use the engine, keep one eye on the temperature gauge to make sure it's pumping water and not sand or mud.

A Few Considerations Whether you're freed quickly or not, anytime your boat bumps bottom check the bilge for rising water. Inspect rudder and shaft stuffing boxes, and on sailboats, check the keelbolts. If the boat is leaking badly, man the pumps and call for assistance immediately. Even if the bilge seems to be dry initially, keep checking periodically to make certain it remains dry.

If wind and current are in danger of putting you farther onto the shoal, you'll need to get an anchor astern to prevent the boat from going harder aground. You can also use the anchor as a kedge to free the boat (see Set a Kedge in the Techniques section opposite). If a dinghy is available, hang the anchor on its stern and flake the line in the boat so it will pay out smoothly as you row. If you don't carry a dinghy, float the anchor out using fenders, life vests, or seat cushions. Whatever way you get the anchor set, you'll want at least a 3:1 scope.

Your next step is to take soundings of the surrounding bottom so you'll know what you're up against. Use a lead line or boathook to measure water depth around the boat, and if possible, get in the dinghy and take additional soundings farther away from the boat. While you're probing, find out what type of bottom the boat is stuck in. Boats aground in mud can be rocked from side to side to break the suction (see Rock the Boat in the Techniques section). Presumably there's deeper water astern, and it's probably deeper to one side or the other.

Whenever you go aground, tide, if any, is an important consideration. If you're lucky (there's that word again), the tide will be low and rising. If the tide is anywhere near high, however, you'll have to work quickly. Consult the tide tables, or jam your boathook into the bottom next to the boat and mark the water level with a piece of tape. When the water has risen an inch or two above the tape, you can start working in earnest to free the boat.

The tidal range in some areas is such that a falling tide can leave a sailboat with a deep keel high and dry. Should this be a possibility, you'll want to put seat cushions, fenders, life jackets, etc, against the hull to protect it from gouges. Things to check if the boat will be lying at an awkward angle include the battery, fuel vents, engine oil dipstick, and gas bottles. Shut off the latter to prevent pressure from building up in hoses.

Techniques *Lighten the boat.* If the boat is really stuck, empty the water tanks—water weighs 8.3 pounds per gallon. Shift heavy objects—anchors, spare batteries, etc.—either to the deep-water side of the boat or put them into the dinghy temporarily. If you're anywhere near land, you may opt to use the dinghy to carry heavy gear ashore.

Rock the boat. Depending on the type of bottom (both the bottom of the boat and the seabed itself), rocking the boat back and forth while also twisting the wheel can be very effective. Start with the engine in reverse, but if the boat isn't pulling free after a few seconds, stop, as the wash from the prop can shoot more silt up under the boat. You can then try going forward and turning the wheel back and forth. Going from forward to reverse and turning the wheel from side to side will often free the boat. Then again, you may need to try something else.

Shift weight. With powerboats, try moving the crew to the section of the boat that seems to be in deeper water. This may lift the section that's aground off the bottom slightly.

A sailboat with a full keel and a cutaway forefoot can sometimes be refloated by moving the crew forward. Fin-keel boats, on the other hand, are most likely to be refloated when crew weight is moved to the rail. Which rail depends on where the water is deepest; the keel should be pointing *toward* deeper water. To gain another degree or two of heel, try swinging the boom out with one or two volunteers clinging to the end.

Boat wakes. A passing boat can send up a wake that can give your efforts a momentary boost, literally. Using the engine, time your bursts on the throttle with each passing wake. As noted before, make sure the engine is pumping water and keep an eye on the temperature gauge.

Set a kedge. If you've shifted weight, gunned the engine, etc., and the boat remains stuck, you've got some work to do before resuming your quest (and by now it will have become a quest) to get the boat free. Setting a kedge (anchor) out in deeper water can help free the boat and will also prevent it from being nudged farther up onto the shoal.

A manual windlass gives you a terrific mechanical advantage pulling the boat out to deeper water. An electric windlass, however, is not designed to operate under heavy loads and should not be used.

On sailboats, you can use snatch blocks to lead the anchor line from the bow to the largest winch aboard, which is usually at the cockpit. One proven trick involves running the halyard over to the anchor line and using the halyard winch to heel the boat. When and if the keel floats off, use the engine to work the boat out to deeper water.

If you can't pull the boat off, at least try and get the bow headed back toward deeper water. You may then be able to use the kedge together with wave action, the occasional wake, and even your engine to free the boat.

Call for professional assistance. It may be that after the tide has come and gone, you'll still be stuck. You've tried everything from heeling the boat to setting out a kedge, and the boat won't budge. More than one skipper has gone a little bonkers and started randomly tossing things overboard. This is not advised. Sometime later, in a moment of quiet reflection, you'll wish you hadn't.

A better option, when all else has failed, is to use your VHF or cell phone to call for commercial assistance. You can call directly or have the Coast Guard contact a professional tower.

And next time remember to pay more attention to your charts.

The Question of Salvage

Let's say a boat, in this case a sailboat, is hard aground on rocks (an actual claim). The skipper has tried every trick he knows to get free. Seas are maybe 2 to 4 feet, and his boat is bouncing up and down on the rocks. He gives up and calls a professional tower. Twenty minutes later, a towboat arrives. Using the sailboat's spinnaker halyard, the towboat's captain deftly heels the sailboat, and in a few minutes, the sailboat is refloated. Damage is limited to a few scrapes and a slight gouge on the keel.

Now here's the question: was the sailboat *towed* or *salvaged?*

The question is important, not just for the skipper of the sailboat, but for any skipper who finds him- or herself aground and in need of professional assistance. A salvage bill can often be greater—sometimes by tens of thousands of dollars—than a bill for towing or ungrounding. Towing plans (including the TowBoatU.S. plan) typically only pay for towing and ungrounding and *do not* pay for salvage. Instead, the bill must be presented to your boat's insurer, which, at the very least, means that you will be paying the policy's deductible.

For centuries, courts have allowed for "excessive compensation" when a salvor risks his life and equipment to save a vessel that is in peril. In this case, "excessive" means something more than the usual posted hourly rates. So whenever the question of towing versus salvage is raised, the answer always will ultimately depend on two highly subjective words—risk and peril. An ungrounding that involves risk and peril is considered salvage. In the case above, to the tower, the sailboat was in peril—on the rocks and in danger of breaking up in the 2- to 4-foot seas. Since the tide was almost high and would soon begin falling, he reasoned that his quick response prevented an already bad situation from getting much worse. The tower later presented a bill to the boatowner's insurance company for $16,000.

The owner of the sailboat that was stuck in the rocks considered that his boat had been towed. The seas, he said, were a wind-driven chop that wasn't powerful enough to endanger his boat. The full operation, from the time the tower arrived until the time the boat was freed from the jetty, took 15 minutes.

If you think $16,000 is a lot of money for 15 minutes' work to save a boat in moderate seas, you're not alone. Salvage companies historically—this also goes back hundreds of years—have submitted initial demands for salvage that appear to be extraordinarily high.

BoatU.S. Marine Insurance routinely receives, negotiates, and pays salvage bills. Because marine insurance adjusters investigate the incident and negotiate with the salvor, the final payment is typically less—sometimes significantly less— than the initial demand. The final payment can still be a healthy sum; in the claim above, the bill was eventually negotiated to a much more reasonable $2,900. Peril to the vessel, in this case, was considered to be only slight—a low-order salvage—and the risk to the salvor and his equipment was negligible.

Four Things You Should Know Before You Call for Help

1. *Check your insurance policy before you need assistance.* Ideally, the policy should cover the entire cost of salvaging your boat, not just a percentage of its value.

2. *Find out whom to contact when something goes wrong.* If the situation is life threatening, contact the Coast Guard on VHF Channel 16 or 22. With salvage, you'll have to contact your insurance company. In a towing situation, you'll want to contact your towing service. When in doubt, contact the Coast Guard. By remaining calm and contacting more experienced hands, you'll avoid unpleasant surprises later.

3. *Ask how much the service is going to cost.* As with any service, this avoids unpleasant surprises later. TowBoatU.S. and Vessel Assist towers are required (if physically possible) to inform a boatowner that a job is salvage before proceeding. The exception might be if time is especially critical, or conditions are so fierce that the tower either doesn't have time to communicate or can't communicate with the boatowner.

4. *You don't have to sign anything!* A contract that has prices and terms that are agreeable to both parties is fine, but you should never sign a Lloyd's Open Form Salvage Contract or a form with blanks that the tower/salvor says he'll fill in later. A signed contract is not necessary in order for the salvor to have permission to salvage your boat. If in doubt, call your insurer.

Overboard Rescues from Sailboats

Martin Taylor and a friend were sailing on a beam reach in gusty 20-knot winds on Chesapeake Bay when a freak wave suddenly spun Taylor's 35-foot sailboat around. In an instant, the boom whipped across the deck, slammed his friend under the eye with the force of a baseball bat, and knocked him into the water.

If ever there is a moment on a boat where a skipper has to know what he's doing, it is the terrifying instant a person falls overboard. Considering that Taylor was now by himself on a boat moving away at 6 knots, the seas were covered with whitecaps, and the overboard crew was unconscious, the decisions Martin had to

The Quick-Stop and Encirclement Maneuver

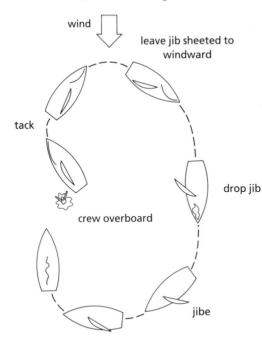

wind

leave jib sheeted to windward

tack

crew overboard

drop jib

jibe

FOR A BOAT SAILING UPWIND: immediately tack with the jib left sheeted to windward. Drop the jib while the boat is sailing downwind.

For a boat sailing off the wind: jibe back immediately before circling back to the victim.

In both cases, designate a spotter (or spotters) to keep an eye on the victim. If possible, punch the Save button on your GPS to record an accurate position should a search be necessary.

When practicing the maneuver using a cushion as "victim," make sure everyone is able to do each job, including managing the helm.

The quick-stop method.

make in the next few seconds were especially critical. Adding to his sense of urgency were the late autumn temperatures: the water was 60° and the air was only 50°, which meant that hypothermia was a possibility.

One decision—an important one—had already been made. His friend had been wearing a bright red float coat (a foul-weather jacket with a built-in life vest), which was keeping him afloat. The coat stood out like a lighted target against the churning water.

Taylor had also practiced the quick-stop and encirclement maneuver (see the sidebar) on different points of sail using float cushions for victims. Without even a second's hesitation, he turned the wheel and circled back toward the victim. As he was starting the turn, he threw a Lifesling, a flotation collar with a tethered line that was attached to the boat, and "littered" the area with cushions to guide himself back to the general area, just in case he became disoriented or blown off his intended course.

Taylor deftly turned the boat again, dropped the sails, and glided slowly toward the victim. His friend had finally been able to respond, albeit weakly, to Taylor's instructions and had pulled the collar of the Lifesling over his shoulders. Taylor was then able to use the boat's stepped transom and boarding ladder to bring the victim, who was still extremely groggy, back aboard. His friend's first words were "How did I get here?"

Seven Rules for Man-Overboard Situations

Any fall overboard should be taken very seriously, even in calm weather. There have been several cases of accidental drownings in the BoatU.S. claim files that involved victims who fell overboard while a boat was at anchor. When someone on a sailboat falls overboard you should:

1. *Stop the boat.* Stopping the boat is your first priority. A boat traveling at 6 knots will be moving away from a victim at about 10 feet per second. A 30-second hesitation will leave you the length of a football field from the victim—too far to see someone in heavy seas.

   The advantage of the quick-stop method (see the sidebar opposite) is, as the name implies, that it stops the boat quickly. The disadvantage is that it requires practice, preferably in a variety of conditions. You won't become comfortable with a complicated sailing technique simply by reading about it. You and the rest of your crew should practice the maneuver from several points of sail on a calm day, using a cushion as the "victim." Once everyone has mastered a "rescue" or two in light air, practice again later in heavier air.

   Ideally, you should approach from dead downwind and coast to a stop just as you're reaching the victim. You may find that this isn't always possible, especially when someone falls overboard while the boat is sailing downwind, so you should also practice approaching the victim (in this case, a cushion) from leeward and windward. Both approaches have advantages and disadvantages, and you should decide which feels most comfortable. Victims to leeward will be sheltered by the boat and easier to bring aboard. On the other hand, they could also be run over by the boat, and the rescue could be further complicated by billowing sails. Victims to windward won't be overrun but it might be harder to keep them next to the boat. Larger seas also create problems when someone is to windward.

   If you have to use the engine, make sure lines are not trailing overboard. Several years ago, a crewman aboard an ocean racer off Florida drowned after falling overboard because lines fouled the prop when the engine was started. If you are under power, NEVER back down toward the victim. Claims involving props and severed limbs are numerous and dreadful.

2. *Use a spotter.* Designate a spotter whose sole job is to point toward the victim and keep the helm informed of his or her whereabouts. The larger the waves, the more difficult it will be to keep the victim in sight. If several crew are available, it would be advisable to designate more than one spotter.

3. *Remain calm and shout encouragement to the victim.* Anyone who suddenly finds himself overboard is likely to panic. Tell him everything will be OK, even if you're on the verge of panic yourself.

4. *Throw flotation overboard.* Throw anything handy that floats, such as seat cushions or life vests—the more the better. Not only will it give the victim something to hold onto, the "debris" leaves a trail back, should you become separated.

   If you're sailing in an area where waves can be large, a man-overboard pole is essential. These poles float high out of the water to give the victim, as well as the onboard spotter, a more visible target. Poles are attached to a flotation device to give the victim something to grab onto while the boat works its way back. Most poles also have a drogue that will slow drift, as well as a light to make it visible at night.

   The best throwing devices, such as the Lifesling, are attached to the boat via a long line. Trailing a flotation device with a line as you circle the victim is an excellent way to bring them up to the boat. Keep an eye on your boat's speed, however, as you could drown someone if you're moving too quickly. In the case of the Lifesling, the flotation collar can also be tucked under victims' armpits to hoist them back aboard.

5. *Get the victim back aboard.* Even when there's plenty of pulling strength available, the awkward angle and daunting weight make it almost impossible to muscle a soaking wet victim back aboard. Several years ago, an overboard sailor in the Pacific Northwest died of hypothermia while the crew desperately sought a way to get him out of the water.

   Don't wait until the victim is alongside to deal with the problem. A stepped transom and/or a ladder that extends a foot or so beneath the transom is an ideal way to bring a victim aboard. Transom ladders are standard equipment on many boats, especially newer models, or they can be added.

   If your boat doesn't have a ladder, or the victim is unconscious or disabled, someone can be brought aboard by rigging either a Lifesling, a boatswain's chair, a sail, or a line with a loop in it to the end of a halyard. You may be able to use a winch to hoist the victim directly out of the water, but this is difficult. Lifesling makes an optional block and tackle that can be used at the end of the halyard to significantly increase mechanical advantage. You could also improvise using the boom vang or mainsheet. If someone has to go over the side to assist, make sure they're tethered to the boat.

6. *Take precautions beforehand!* If there's one foolproof method of preventing an overboard disaster, it is to take precautions beforehand. Martin Taylor, despite his quick reaction, could probably not have found and recovered his friend if the friend had not been wearing a life vest. Not only did the float coat's vest help keep the victim's head above water, its bright red color made it easier for Taylor to keep him in sight. Several years ago, when white foulweather gear was in vogue, a well-known British sailor fell overboard in sim-

ilar circumstances and was lost because his white foul-weather jacket was camouflaged amid the numerous whitecaps. At night, a man-overboard light and reflective tape should be worn on a life jacket.

7. *Don't rely on lifelines.* While a stanchion, or for that matter a shroud or stay, may appear to be sturdy, all have been known to give way unexpectedly. Inspect fittings regularly, but don't rely on them for support in critical situations.

In heavy weather and at night, wear a safety harness. Rig a jackline from bow to stern and hook on whenever you go forward. If a harness isn't available, stay seated inside the cockpit. If you have to go forward, keep a low center of gravity and use the grab rails. Don't be overconfident; nobody plans to fall overboard.

Overboard Rescues from Powerboats

If you were to fall overboard from a powerboat, there couldn't be a more qualified person to bring you back aboard than Bart Ehman. For starters, Bart's boat-handling skills are second to none: He's been boating for over forty years and works as a commercial fisherman in Alaska during the summer. Bart has spent hundreds of hours, in fair weather and foul, deftly maneuvering his boat next to crab pots. He's also a big man: 6 feet 3 inches tall and 230 pounds. That much "beef" would come in handy if you needed help climbing back aboard.

But despite his size and considerable skills, Bart had a lot of problems rescuing two men who had been thrown into the water when their 20-foot boat capsized at the entrance to Tomales Bay in Northern California. When Bart first spotted the two men, he thought they were divers and altered course to keep his distance; one of the men seemed to be waving his arm to warn him away. But why would divers be so far offshore? He again altered course and went closer to investigate. What he saw next startled him; not only were the two men not divers, one appeared to be unconscious. Bart, who was alone, immediately called the Coast Guard and explained the situation, giving them a brief description of his boat as well as its exact position.

Winds were blowing 15 to 20 knots and seas were heavy. Despite his impressive boat-handling skills, Bart had to make three passes before he was able to bring his boat directly alongside the two victims. Being alone made it difficult to keep the victims in view while also maneuvering the boat, and Bart knew from his years of crabbing that even a slight miscalculation could lead to disaster.

Once he was alongside, he set to work trying to pull the unconscious man aboard, but he couldn't get a firm grip on either his clothing or the Type III life vest he was wearing. Bart then turned his attention to the semiconscious victim. He was able to grab the man's belt and haul him onto the deck. After removing the wet vest and placing the man under warm blankets down in the cabin, Bart returned to the remaining victim.

This time, probably because of fatigue, it took Bart seven passes to bring the boat alongside. The unconscious man appeared to be dead but Bart couldn't be sure, and he wouldn't allow himself to give up. He later compared the rescue attempt to trying to grab a slippery, 170-pound log that just kept rolling over and over. Bart said the frustration was overwhelming.

Finally, a Coast Guard helicopter arrived, and divers were able to get both victims into baskets so that they could be airlifted to a hospital. The first victim eventually recovered. The second victim was already dead, having had a heart attack, probably brought on by hypothermia, before Bart arrived on the scene. The men were wearing life vests and had been in the 55°F water for about three hours when Bart saw them.

Even months after the rescue, Bart was still having difficulty talking about his experiences, especially the frustration of trying to hoist the unconscious man out of the water. It was, he said, the hardest thing he had ever tried to do in his life.

As a result of the ordeal, Bart has spent a lot of time thinking about how to outfit his boat for any future overboard rescues. This rescue is a good example of why skippers of powerboats need to be prepared for a man-overboard rescue and what equipment they need aboard to make sure the rescue goes smoothly. How much chance, Bart wondered, would his wife have if she had to lift his 230-pound bulk out of the water?

He now carries a 150-foot rope with several small floats to make the rope more visible to both the victim and the onboard crew. The rope would be extremely useful in bringing the victim alongside the boat.

Preparing for the Worst

If a victim is conscious and healthy and seas are calm, a swim platform or ladder is obviously the best way to bring him or her back aboard. If you have a choice, the ladder should be rigged at the side of the hull, away from the prop. Other alternatives include an inflatable dinghy, if one is available, or a "stirrup" rigged over the side using a bowline tied in a dockline. The latter functions as a step but can be difficult to use, especially in rough weather. An overboard victim off the coast of New Jersey reported that it was "impossible" to use this step due to the boat's pitching, which caused the line (and him) to twist and swing wildly.

Victims, however, aren't always conscious and healthy and seas aren't always calm. It isn't unusual for someone to be incapacitated by the fall overboard or by exposure to cold water. The claim files include instances of people who were injured by props or from being slammed against the hull or lifelines on their way over the side. And in choppy seas, a swim platform could come down hard and seriously injure the victim.

If the victim is unconscious, it will be much more difficult to lift him or her out of the water, even using a ladder. A windlass, if one is available, gives you tremendous extra muscle in an overboard emergency. Using a block to lead the line aft, away from the higher sheer at the bow, will make retrieval with the windlass less awkward. If the boat lacks a windlass, attach a block and tackle with at least a 4:1 purchase and ½-inch line (preferably polyester, which won't stretch) to the cabin roof or horizontally across the cockpit to hoist the victim back aboard. The key to using any retrieval procedure is *practice*.

The best guarantee that you won't have trouble retrieving overboard crew, however, is to keep them aboard. Never let people sit on the gunwales or the transom while underway. In rough conditions, keep people in the cockpit or down below. If they must be on deck, make sure they wear life jackets and use the handrails. And make sure they're sober. Not only is a drinker more likely to fall overboard, he or she is also more susceptible to the effects of hypothermia and will be more difficult to bring back aboard.

Getting Back to an Overboard Victim

Trying to get a powerboat alongside a victim can be difficult, especially in rough seas. Rescuing a crew member who has fallen overboard from a powerboat is similar to the sailboat rescue described above. In both cases, slow the boat immediately and circle back toward the victim. Alert the crew and throw flotation to the victim. Appoint one of the crew to act as a spotter. Finally, shout encouragement to the victim, which will help calm both of you.

There is a chance that the victim will have fallen overboard sometime earlier, without being noticed. If you discover a crew member is missing while the boat is underway, make a note of your current position as a starting point (if possible, punch the Save button on your GPS to record an accurate position) and use the compass to get a reciprocal bearing before turning the boat around to begin searching. Then circle back and retrace your course, following the boat's wake as a "trail." Broadcast a Pan-Pan alert message over VHF Channel 16 to alert other boaters in the area as well as the Coast Guard.

Boat Handling in Thunderstorms

Thunderstorms are much more than bolts of lightning (for more on lightning, see Chapter 6). In many parts of the country, a lazy afternoon of seagoing bliss can, in the span of a few minutes, give way to hurricane-force winds, torrential rain, hail, and even waterspouts. After a request for stories, several dozen BoatU.S. members sent along detailed accounts of thunderstorms they had encountered on the water. There's no better teacher than experience, and these accounts contain a lot of hard-earned wisdom.

Several members mentioned that they had been caught in thunderstorms on numerous occasions and submitted accounts of storms that were especially ferocious. Sometimes the storm stuck in their minds because something happened—they were caught unaware with the sails up, for example—but often it was because of the storm itself. According to *Weather for the Mariner*, by William J. Kotsch, there is a vast difference between an isolated thunderstorm that typically forms on a steamy summer afternoon and a line of thunderstorms, called a squall line, which is more likely to form in the spring or fall. The latter can stretch for hundreds of miles and produce much more violent weather. Cliff Moore, in Keyport, New Jersey, was once caught in an "extreme storm" with horizontal rain, hail, lightning, and winds that reached 90 knots briefly before dropping off to 60 knots for 5 to 10 minutes. He says he spends a lot of time on the water and expects to be whacked at least once a season by a thunderstorm, but this storm was different. Even at full power, he could not keep his boat's bow headed into the wind during the storm's peak.

One thing that the following stories make clear is that there is no single strategy to help you cope with a thunderstorm's high winds and blinding rain. Whether you decide to seek the security of a marina, beach the boat, head for open water, or drop the anchor, your strategy must be flexible and take into account your boat's immediate location, as well as your crew's and your boat's capabilities.

Lessons Learned: A Few Strategies

Monitor the Weather Band The most violent storms, the ones that accompany the arrival of a cold front, can arrive at any time of the day or night, and the only way to get an early warning is to listen to the weather band. Whenever an approaching front and violent weather are predicted, stay in port. If you're on the water, head for shelter.

The typical summer thunderstorm, however, is another matter. These storms usually build during the heat of the day and reach a boiling point later in the afternoon. In many areas, they're mentioned so often in summer forecasts that they tend to be ignored. Whenever they're predicted, the simplest plan is to get in early.

Several skippers noted, some less delicately than others, that the weather forecasts aren't always accurate. You can often get some warning from the high clouds, and by counting the seconds between a lightning strike and the sound of thunder (5 seconds equals 1 mile). But don't be lulled into thinking that a storm that's still a few miles off is a safe distance away; thunderstorms can travel at speeds over 50 mph. Several skippers mentioned the value of radar at spotting storms, measuring distance, predicting their path, and even estimating the storm's severity. (The thicker the clutter on the screen, the heavier the rain that is falling.) Robert Schrader has used his radar (24-mile range) to track many storms and says storms make very distinctive targets and won't be confused with anything else.

Have a Contingency Plan   After surviving an especially fierce storm on Long Island Sound, Jerry Palmiotti, who now does his boating on Lake Lanier in Georgia, says he never leaves the dock without a thunderstorm contingency plan. He constantly makes mental notes of where he will go and what he will do should a thunderstorm rear its ugly head.

However, contingency plans must be tailored to the immediate area. Jerry says he prefers to beach his boat, which in some areas (and with boats that can be beached safely) is a possibility. L. J. Wallace says he has used this tactic many times in storms in Charleston, South Carolina, and beaches his 50-foot catamaran on any island that is protected from the west. A beach on a lee shore, especially downwind of an open expanse of water, would be too exposed to wind and waves.

Dan Arsenault was moving his boat from its winter storage in Michigan to his marina via a narrow, unmarked channel. It was April, and the Coast Guard had not yet put out the mid-channel buoy. The weather forecast had mentioned the chance of a thunderstorm, and when it hit, Dan was caught in the narrow channel. He had carefully noted his loran position and had also taken bearings, but he did not account sufficiently for leeway. The boat was bounced off the bottom but got through, pushed by the storm's fierce winds. Next time, he said he would take the longer, offshore route. As one of his Power Squadrons instructors told him, "It's not the water but the hard stuff around it that causes the problems."

Remain in Open Water   Dan Arsenault wasn't the only skipper to mention the desirability of remaining in open water. Even though the safety of a harbor in Naples, Florida, must have been tempting, Robert Schrader opted to remain offshore: "It was obviously a large thunderstorm and would soon obscure the inlet. I planned to stay offshore about 2 miles, slow down, and let the storm pass. I didn't want to get caught in the narrow pass or winding river."

Don Ross, who has a 100-ton Coast Guard license, says he has encountered many storms on Chesapeake Bay and always uses the same tactic: "I head for open water and pick a spot on the horizon [preferably upwind] that gives me a clear course. I then note the compass course as well as the reciprocal course. On my first pass I note the time and then turn around and proceed back on the reciprocal course for the same period of time. I keep doing this over and over until the storm passes."

By taking the wind and seas on the bow, the boat should be easier to control. Remember, however, that the downwind leg will be significantly faster than the upwind leg. Cliff Moore notes that many skippers head downwind, because visibility is better without rain in your eyes, but then wind up on the beach. The message: keep one eye on the compass and the other on the depth sounder.

Anchoring Is an Option With rain or hail blasting you in the face, throwing the anchor overboard and going below to dry off is certainly a temptation. Anchors don't always hold, however, and for every skipper who said dropping the hook is a good idea, another would have a horror story. Skippers who voted to drop the hook invariably mentioned that they carry large anchors and extra chain. Carla Coutts-Miners and her husband use a 55-pound CQR to anchor their 41-foot Morgan sailboat. Russ Campbell says he uses a 25-pound CQR with 80 feet of ⅜-inch chain and 200 feet of ½-inch nylon rode on his 28-foot Cape Dory sloop. He has used the system successfully in several thunderstorms, including one that had 70 mph winds.

Cliff Moore says he'll only anchor if he can find a spot that is well away from boats trying to find their way in. He said he would rather risk bouncing over a shoal than be anchored near a channel filled with "panicky, scared boaters all headed back to their marinas at full speed in zero visibility." Anchoring too close to a lee shore is also a bad idea, even in moderate conditions. Stephen Desaro, who weathered a storm on a Jet Ski (he had numerous welts from hail hitting his body), noted that several boats that had been anchored near a lee shore wound up on the beach.

While boats often drag their anchors in storms, it is also possible, even in a relatively short thunderstorm, to break an anchor line. Don Arsenault anchored his Hunter 37.5 with 40 feet of chain and ½-inch braided nylon rope on Lake Michigan. Minutes later he heard a loud bang, which was the sound of his anchor line parting suddenly.

Finally, never underestimate the value of luck in an emergency. Ken Reim was anchored, or trying to anchor, near the mouth of the Chesapeake and Delaware Canal using two anchors. The boat was dragging ever closer to a rocky breakwater when the anchors mysteriously held. He discovered later that they had snagged an abandoned cable.

Wear Your Life Jacket Put on life jackets and other safety equipment *before* the storm; safety equipment can't save you if you're not wearing it. Tom Buell, a skipper on Long Island Sound, reported: "After the storm we learned that a 40-footer had sunk to the bottom and an unfortunate man had died right outside our canal after falling overboard." The man had not been wearing a life jacket.

Many skippers said the storms taught them the need to don life jackets at the first hint of foul weather. One admitted sheepishly that he'd never taken the life jackets out of their wrappers until the storm hit, and another found that the adult and children's vests were all jammed together in the same locker. "None of the life jackets were labeled by size. What was complicating matters was that our friends were not familiar with how the life jackets worked. You have to remember that things were crazy. When we finally did make it home, I was wearing a child's life jacket. I weigh 270 pounds."

Warren Mueller was sailing single-handed when he was caught in a storm in August on Lake Ponchartrain. Instead of a storm blowing for the usual 20 or 30 minutes, it blew for well over an hour so that the boat, with the sails down, was 6 miles farther out on the lake. He managed to drop the sails, close the hatches, and secure the cockpit locker, but he forgot to don his life vest, an inflatable model. However, he says the even bigger oversight was forgetting to slip on his safety harness, "a sin for a single-handed sailor."

Dan Arsenault noted that in April, no one would have survived very long in Lake Michigan if they had gone overboard. "We were in hurricane conditions and we learned you'd pay any price to keep everyone aboard. We practice using safety harnesses in less trying conditions so they're second nature to us." (Good advice for life vests also.)

Vision, or a lack of vision, was mentioned by practically everyone. If you don't wear glasses, the rain pelts you in the eyes. If you do wear glasses, like Jeff Burcham, a member from Oklahoma, you have to take them off constantly because the lenses are wet. Unfortunately, there aren't many solutions to the problem. Dan Arsenault recommended goggles, and said a friend keeps a motorcycle helmet aboard for such occasions. Dan says he might do that also. In either case, you'll need to keep a rag handy to wipe the lenses off. And any sunscreen on your forehead, if it isn't wiped off, will likely wind up stinging your eyes.

Finally, Stephen Ragone notes that even on the Chesapeake Bay in summer, you can get very cold from the rain and wind chill. His advice: "Dress warmly and don't forget boots; they provide traction and keep your feet warm and your toes safe from any big hail."

Stow or Secure Lines Walter Kruppa was having plenty of trouble working his way down South River near Annapolis, Maryland, because the 50 mph wind and driving rain had reduced visibility to 30 feet. An initial wind gust had blown his bimini apart and, unbeknownst to him, knocked a line into the water, which soon became tangled in his prop. Walter managed to get an anchor out, which prevented his boat from being blown ashore.

All lines, Walter said, should be stowed *securely*. The line that went overboard had been stowed on the cockpit bulkhead, but somehow managed to find its way to the water—and the prop.

Secure Hatches and Cockpit Lockers Securing hatches and cockpit lockers is critical, especially on smaller boats. Several years ago, a woman who was down below on a 22-foot sailboat drowned when the boat was knocked onto its beam ends during a thunderstorm on Chesapeake Bay. The cockpit locker popped open—the boat filled with water and sank before she could climb out of the cabin.

Six skippers reported that their sailboats were knocked down so far that their boats' masts touched the water. In each case, water flooded the cockpit, but fortunately the hatches had been secured. Powerboat owners had similar difficulties. When his 23-foot cruiser was caught offshore in a thunderstorm, Al Rodriguez said, "The vessel slid sideways down the crest of the wave and water filled the cockpit and very nearly put us under."

Take Command! When his boat was first hit by a severe thunderstorm, Tom Buell thought about his responsibility to the crew: "It's amazing that at a time like that the first thing I thought about was my basic boating class. I am the captain of the boat and all of the passengers are my responsibility."

Before the storm, John Fasulo of Beacon, New York, said his crew complained that wearing life jackets seemed "a little extreme," but he insisted and was glad he did. The wind speed reached 70 mph, and the rain was intense; "It was no ordinary summer squall." With the crew in life jackets, John said he had one less thing to worry about.

No matter what tactic you plan to employ, communicate it to the crew. L. J. Wallace Jr. was about to beach his catamaran when one of the crew "panicked" and let go of the main halyard, so the boat stopped too soon. Instead of spending the storm tucked safely up on the beach, the boat was blasted downwind when the storm hit a few seconds later and eventually wound up in a marsh.

Maintain Fuel Systems Properly Keep fuel tanks clean and have spare fuel filters aboard. After his sails were torn to shreds by a storm's initial blast, Buddy Trexler of Clearwater, Florida, started his engine: "The engine turned over, but as I turned to starboard the waves hit on the beam and the engine died. I ran down into the engine room and found the filters had clogged with sludge. Since I had no spare [filters], the engine was useless."

Boats get bounced around more than usual in a storm, and any sludge or water in the tanks will soon find its way to the filters. The engine dies when it's needed most.

Avoid Alcohol   Craig Dilsdorf admitted that he and his wife had been drinking before getting caught in an especially severe storm. He made a few muddled decisions, including ignoring weather forecasts. That was thirteen years ago, and the storm obviously made quite an impression. "Drinking while operating a boat" Craig says, "is a thing of the past."

Drop Sails Completely   If you're on a sailboat, drop your sails completely at the first sign of bad weather; don't reduce sail in stages as you might in other situations. There were several accounts of sailboats that, for various reasons, got caught with their sails up. Even though severe thunderstorms had been predicted for the St. Petersburg, Florida, area, Buddy Trexler, for example, said that the storm caught him by surprise. He only managed to bring the sail part of the way down before the wind tore it to shreds.

One of the most dramatic accounts came from Dan Erlich, who recalled sailing in the 1978 Lake Ontario International Race aboard a 53-foot oceangoing sailboat. As is sometimes the case in a race, competitiveness clouded good judgment. When the boat's skipper saw a line of thunderstorms approaching, he decided to raise the heavy-air spinnaker and drop the light-air spinnaker. Most of the crew who came on deck to help were not wearing life jackets or safety harnesses. The storm hit right after the second spinnaker was raised and before the first one could be brought down. With two spinnakers flying, the boat was knocked down and both sails were blown apart. Two men went overboard but managed to pull themselves back aboard. Dan's assessment: "We were all luckier than we had any right to be."

One other tactic that *doesn't* work is to leave a few feet of a furling jib exposed to take advantage of a freshening breeze (a temptation after a hot, windless day) with the idea that you can bring it in later if you have to. George Hatfield was caught in a storm on the Chesapeake Bay with only a few feet of the furling jib exposed. (The main was secured before the storm with extra sail ties.) After the storm hit with a vengeance, one of the crew took the furling line off its cleat to furl the rest of the jib; instantly the wind yanked it from his hand. The jib went shooting out, and the boat was knocked down.

And once you drop your sails, make sure they are well secured. Donald Launer, of Forked River, New Jersey, was anchored in Little Egg Harbor, New Jersey, with his sails furled. Suddenly his boat was blasted by 75 mph winds. Don says in his sixty years on the water he had never seen a more intense storm. For a moment, the boat seemed to be doing well, then he heard a loud snap as the roller-furling genoa came shooting out. Just a tiny section of the sail had remained exposed, but it was enough to pull out the rest of the sail and send the boat rocking over onto its beam ends, with the spreaders touching the water. A friend was thrown into the water but managed to hold onto a Sunfish

Communicating with Our Friends from the Deep

OVER THE YEARS, Hollywood has made movies like *Jaws*, *20,000 Leagues Under the Sea*, and *Moby Dick* about gigantic sea creatures that chewed, squeezed, or bashed boats to bits, then devoured the crew. These were wildly popular movies, and the bad guys—the sea creatures—were every bit as scary as the aliens in space movies.

Sea creatures in the real world are somewhat more benign. Every year there is an encounter or two between a member's boat and a sea creature, typically a whale. Unlike whales in Hollywood, though, real whales are much more likely to be the ones who are hurt in encounters with humans.

Frank Graves was off the coast of Massachusetts on the way to Maine when his son Peter took this picture of a giant humpback whale breaching near another boat. Several other humpbacks in the area were also breaching. Graves' first reaction was that the whales were playing, but according to Diane Hustad with the American Cetacean Society, no one is sure why whales breach. The two most likely theories, she says, are for communication or as an aggressive display to warn an intruder away.

Graves said there were several calves in the area, and if the whales were trying to warn the boats to keep away, it worked. The sailboat in the photo, with the man standing on the spreader, had just taken a sharp turn to port when the whale suddenly shot high out of the water on the starboard side. Both boats quickly took the hint, and headed away to do their whale watching at a safer distance.

sailboat they had been trailing astern. (This incident is a good argument for safety harnesses, not to mention life jackets—and Sunfish.)

Greg Gilsdorf of Michigan left his unsecured jib and staysail on the foredeck. When the storm hit, the sails were blown back up the stays, and his boat was knocked down. The knockdown was so sudden that Greg's infant son wound up buried under a pile of bunk cushions—his wife could hear the baby crying but couldn't find him at first. Out on deck, meanwhile, Greg somersaulted into the cockpit and was lucky he didn't go overboard.

And like a lot of skippers who have been through an intense thunderstorm, when the sun finally came out he was a wiser man.

15

Hurricane Warning

BOATOWNERS FROM MAINE TO TEXAS have reason to become edgy in the late summer and fall: Each year, on average, two hurricanes will come ashore somewhere along the Gulf or Atlantic coasts, destroying homes, sinking boats, and turning people's lives topsy turvy for weeks, or even months. Where will they come ashore next? Florida is struck most often—in 2004 the state was pounded by four hurricanes—but in any given year every coastal state on the Atlantic and Gulf coasts is a potential target.

Planning ahead is essential. Where should you keep your boat so it has the best chance of surviving a storm? Is your marina well protected? Should you have the boat hauled ashore? Will there be time? What extra gear will you need? The BoatU.S. Marine Insurance claim files show that you can considerably reduce the probability of damage by choosing the most storm-proof location possible, then doing everything possible to prepare your boat. The time to ask yourself the tough questions and to begin preparing your boat for a hurricane is before a hurricane hits.

In a hurricane, where to leave your boat is the single most important decision you'll have to make to protect your boat. Almost every boat at this South Miami marina was damaged or destroyed in Hurricane Andrew by a combination of waves and surge that tore the docks apart.

Where to Keep Your Boat in a Hurricane
Storage Ashore: Evaluating Your Marina and Yacht Club

There is considerable evidence that boats stored ashore are less likely to sustain severe damage in a hurricane than boats left in the water. That was the conclusion of a study by MIT after Hurricane Gloria, and it has also been borne out by the BoatU.S. Marine Insurance claim files. The boats ashore that suffered the least damage were above the storm surge on high ground. According to the Saffir-Simpson Hurricane Scale, the expected storm surge is as follows:

Saffir-Simpson Expected Storm Surge

Hurricane Category	Expected Surge (feet)
1	4–5
2	6–8
3	9–12
4	13–18
5	18+

If your plan is to have your boat hauled, you'll need to talk to your marina manager to see what plans, if any, have been made for getting boats out of the water quickly before a hurricane. This is a big issue for marina managers, and it can be resolved, at least partially, by careful planning. One of the first things Philip Hale did after Hurricane Bob battered his marina (Martha's Vineyard Ship-yard on Martha's Vineyard, Massachusetts) was to put together a list of emergency employees, including many former employees and some local boatowners, who were familiar with the marina's boats and grounds. He organized this emergency staff into teams, giving each team a specific assignment and a team leader, who could be called upon to join the regular staff whenever a large storm was approaching. Some teams secure the buildings and grounds, but Hale's largest team, the one with the marina's most experienced professional staff, hauls the boats and blocks them ashore.

Aside from being on high ground, a boat stored ashore must have a sufficient number of jack stands (at least three per side), and the jack stands must be chained together. Because so many boats are hauled at once, jack stands are often in short supply during a hurricane. (Marinas in hurricane areas would be well advised to keep a reserve.) A lot of boats in the Port Charlotte, Florida, area, especially sailboats with deep keels, were blown off their jack stands in Hurricane Charley. In some cases, it was because too few stands had been used. In others, stands failed because they were placed on loose gravel, which has a tendency to roll, and the stands hadn't been chained together. The latter is standard practice at most marinas and must be done if a boat is to have any chance of surviving a hurricane.

One technique that worked beautifully, and holds considerable promise for marinas in future hurricanes, was used successfully at the Sebastian River Marina in Florida during Hurricanes Frances and Jeanne. The technique involves blocking the boats ashore and strapping them with 1-inch nylon line to eyes embedded in the concrete. It should be noted that the only thing protecting Sebastian River Marina's docks in a hurricane is a 2-foot high seawall. Beyond the seawall there is a daunting 3-mile fetch of open water across Sebastian River. Of the boats that were strapped to the concrete storage lot (there were fifty-six in Jeanne with an average length of 40 feet and about half that number in Frances), *none* were damaged. The boats that were left in the water didn't fare so well; most were either sunk or washed ashore.

A similar haulout/strap-down system was used at the Hinckley Yacht Services in Stuart, Florida. All of the 178 boats at Hinckley were stored ashore, and most were held in place by 2-inch nylon straps that had been secured to eyes embedded in long concrete runners. Most boats had at least two straps, although some had only one, and a few that weren't near runners couldn't be strapped down at all. According to Gary Rolfe, Hinckley's yard manager, only three were blown over in Hurricane Frances and two in Jeanne. That was far less damage than other nearby marinas, many of which were devastated.

The Hurricane Club Another innovation at Sebastian River Marina is a voluntary Hurricane Club for slip holders. For $1,000, a Hurricane Club member is entitled to having his or her boat hauled out and blocked ashore for two hurricanes. This amounts to $500 per hurricane, and the price includes having the boat strapped down to the embedded anchors.

The only thing Doug Hillman, Sebastian River's owner, will change in the future is that membership in the Hurricane Club will no longer be optional. Before Frances, some boatowners hadn't bothered to join the club, so only about 60% of the marina's boats were hauled out of the water. Hillman called it a function of experience; Frances made them believers. With future slip holders, he won't wait for boatowners to experience a hurricane to be convinced; anyone who wants a slip at the marina will have to join the club.

The Houston Yacht Club Probably the best-known and most comprehensive hurricane plan for a facility was devised by the Houston Yacht Club after Hurricane Alicia wrecked the club's docks and 141 of its members' boats in 1983 (see bottom photo page 197). The Houston Yacht Club plan has been used as a model by many other yacht clubs and marinas.

The plan is anchored by the individual efforts of all its members, each of whom is required to submit a hurricane plan with their harbor rental agreement. Each plan must include details on where the boat will be kept, what equipment is available, and the name of a "boat buddy" who will take care of the boat if the member is sick or out of town. The plan must be approved by the club's Hurricane Committee.

Individual plans must conform to the overall guidelines set by the club. In the event of a storm, boatowners report to one of the fourteen dock captains who coordinate the preparation efforts at each of the club's docks. There are other captains and teams to haul and secure boats in the club's one-design fleets and strip them of masts and sails. Each captain has a backup.

In addition to the dock and fleet captains, there are also crew chiefs who are responsible for the crane operations, harbor operations, and securing the clubhouse and grounds. The crew chief for the grounds, for example, is responsible for seeing that volunteers board windows, store outdoor furniture, shut off the electricity (but provide alternate sources of electrical power), and store emergency water.

The captains and chiefs report to the hurricane operations group at the clubhouse, and the entire effort is coordinated by the club's commodore and vice commodore. Preparations are implemented in carefully planned phases, beginning 72 hours before a hurricane's estimated arrival.

Perhaps the most notable accomplishment of the Houston Yacht Club is that their plan wasn't written, then left on a shelf to gather dust. Although it has been over two decades since Alicia, the overall plan continues to be examined and revised. Members must still submit individual plans whenever they bring a boat into the facility. And every year at the start of hurricane season, the entire membership gathers together to rehearse the plan.

Covered Dry Storage There have been precious few major hurricanes that didn't see at least one dry storage "boatel" blown over, damaging hundreds of boats in the span of a few seconds. Many more boats were damaged when roofs or walls of boatels were blown off. If possible, a boat in a boatel should be put on a trailer and taken inland.

High-rise storage racks can be toppled by a storm's high winds. If possible, put your boat on a trailer and take it farther inland.

Note, however, that some steel buildings are sturdier than others. Storage facilities built in the past few years are likely to have been constructed to a higher standard, with thicker steel, more and larger bolts, and more and larger bracing. Many counties in Florida, for example, have adopted the 2003 International Building Code standard for steel buildings that is significantly stricter than the standard it replaced. Older steel buildings near salt water have another disadvantage, which is the tendency to suffer from corrosion at bolt holes. Corrosion makes it more likely that the structural components of a building will begin working back and forth and eventually collapse in a hurricane.

Securing a Boat in the Water

If you plan to leave your boat in the water during a hurricane, secure it in a harbor that is sheltered and well protected from breaking waves. A storm surge of 10 feet or more is common in a hurricane, so a seawall or sandy spit that normally protects a harbor may not offer any protection. Entire marinas have been devastated because they weren't well protected, and docks were overcome by a tremendous surge and large, breaking waves. Note also that there may be another large hurdle to leaving your boat at a dock—the dock contract. To be safe, review your dock contract for language that may require you to take certain steps or to leave the marina when a hurricane threatens.

Besides docks in exposed locations, other types of docks to avoid in a hurricane include concrete pilings and floating docks. Concrete pilings have proven to be vulnerable; the pilings crack at stressed areas and are prone to breaking. At one marina in Pensacola, Florida, almost every piling was broken by Hurricane Ivan.

Floating docks may or may not be a good place to secure a boat in a hurricane. Because they rise with the surge, floating docks allow boats to be secured more readily than boats at fixed docks. There's no need to run lines to distant pilings

In Hurricane Isabel, the seawall that protected the boats at Herrington Harbor North in Deal, Maryland, was overcome by the storm surge, exposing the boats at the marina's A, B, C, and D docks to breaking waves. Large sections of the docks were destroyed, and some of the boats—a total of eight—were sunk. Many more were damaged.

An effort is underway to replace the older seawall with one that is taller. A second seawall is also proposed. The combination will offer much better protection to boats in the harbor.

The left photo shows the damage at Jordan Point Yacht Haven on the James River from Hurricane Isabel. The wind blew across the long, unprotected fetch of the James River, destroying the docks and sheds.

However, the marina had made the decision to haul all the boats and block them before the storm. So even though the boats sustained some damage from the 8-foot surge that came over the seawall, most survived (below), although with considerable damage. Dan Rutherford, a marine surveyor on the BoatU.S. Catastrophe Team, estimated that 75% of the boats in the parking lot were repairable. Had those same boats remained in the water, all would likely have been bashed against pilings and sunk. Blocking the boats ashore averted another costly problem: pollution from leaking fuel.

because the boat and dock rise in tandem with the surge. However, floating docks offer protection from the surge if—a HUGE "if"—the pilings are sufficiently tall. In almost every major hurricane, there has been considerable damage from floating docks that floated up and over pilings. The docks and boats, still tied together, then washed ashore in battered clumps. A good example is the floating docks at Masonboro Boatyard in North Carolina, all of which were devastated in Hurricane Fran. The boatyard was rebuilt with pilings that tower 18 feet above the water, which means that Masonboro is now much more "storm-proof."

Perhaps the most (in)famous story of marina destruction occurred at the Houston Yacht Club from Hurricane Alicia in 1983. The storm surge, pushed by 135 mph winds, combined with normal high tides to overcome the low-lying outer seawall. The protected harbor then became an open bay and all of the boats in the harbor—a total of 141—either sank or were carried ashore.

As a result of the storm, the Houston Yacht Club put together a remarkably detailed (75-page) hurricane preparedness plan that must be adhered to by all members. The plan calls for every boat in the outer harbor to be moved or hauled ashore.

The deadly 12-foot storm surge from Hurricane Fran lifted all Masonboro Boatyard's floating piers off their pilings and carried away most of the boats. When the marina was rebuilt, taller pilings were used that tower 18 feet above the water. The result is that Masonboro is now much more "storm-proof."

Here is another example of what can happen when boats are kept at floating docks during a hurricane. In this case, during Hurricane Hugo, hundreds of boats at a large Charleston marina suddenly came adrift when the surge lifted the docks off the pilings. Most of the boats and docks wound up in a massive clump in a nearby marsh.

If you do decide to leave your boat at a fixed dock, you'll need a docking plan that is liable to be far different than your normal docking arrangement. Members of the BoatU.S. Catastrophe Team (CAT Team) have consistently estimated that as many as 50% of the boats damaged during hurricanes could have been saved by better docking arrangements: lines that were longer, larger, arranged better, and/or better protected against chafing. By the time preparations are completed, a boat should resemble a spider suspended in the center of a large web. And you must use this web arrangement if your boat is to have any chance of remaining in position after

In heavy weather, use as many lines as possible to keep the boat in the center of the slip. This boat, in the aftermath of Hugo, looks like it would have survived with very little damage, but it ended up on top of the dock as the surge receded.

rising with the surge and being bounced around by the storm. Conversely, leading four lines to the nearest piling, which is the typical docking arrangement for everyday conditions—is almost guaranteed to doom the boat in a hurricane.

Take a look at your boat slip and its relation to the rest of the harbor. For some boats, you'll want to arrange the bow toward open water, or lacking that, toward the *least* protected direction. This reduces windage. An exception is boats that have swim platforms, which must be kept away from the dock. During Hurricane Frances in Florida, for example, many boats sank because their swim platforms bashed against docks and were shoved through the hulls, which left a gaping hole right at the waterline.

Next, look for pilings, dock cleats, even trees—anything sturdy that you could use for securing docklines. With the typical boat slip, lines will have to be fairly taut if the boat is going to be kept away from pilings. The key to your docking arrangement is to use long lines, the longer the better, to accommodate the surge. (A good rule of thumb: storm docklines should be *at least* as long as the boat itself.) You will probably want to use other boatowners' pilings (and vice versa), which calls for planning and cooperation with slip neighbors and marina management.

Lines should also be a larger diameter than those you normally use to secure your boat. Larger lines resist excessive stretching and chafe. In general, you should use at least ½-inch line for boats up to 25 feet, ⅝-inch line for boats 25 to 34 feet, and ¾- to 1-inch line for longer boats. You must have chafe protectors (see the Critical Points section beginning on page 205) on any portion of the line that could be abraded by chocks, pulpits, pilings, etc.

Given that most boats these days are so beamy that they're barely able to squeeze into their slips, docklines are liable to be stretched sufficiently to allow the boat to bang into pilings. If you're "lucky," the boat will only be scraped and

Chafe protection and multiple lines are essential when a boat is kept at a dock in a hurricane. Slips tend to be tight, however, and even with the best docking arrangement, it's likely that lines will be stretched, and the boat will come in contact with the dock or a piling. If you can't have the boat hauled out of the water, moving it to the largest (well-protected) slip that's available is one option. Using a fender board with several big, fat fenders is also advised. It may or may not prevent the sort of damage seen here, but it is certainly better than nothing. Single fenders are easily displaced and do little, if anything, to protect the boat in a violent storm.

gouged. If you're unlucky, the hull will be bashed in, and the boat sunk. If possible, move your boat to a larger—wider and longer—slip. Using more and larger lines offers additional protection. Using fender boards and fenders may also help. You should vertically hang *several* large fenders—the larger the better—behind each board. Single fenders hung horizontally will do little if anything to protect the hull at a piling; they will be quickly shoved aside by the boat's erratic motion.

To secure lines to hard-to-reach outer pilings, put the eye on the piling so that lines can be adjusted from the boat. For other lines, put the eye on the boat to allow for final adjustment from the dock.

Hurricane Holes: Canals, Rivers, and Waterways If you decide that your marina's docks are too vulnerable, plan on moving your boat to a more secure location. Wherever canals, rivers, or waterways are available, they serve as shelters—hurricane holes—and offer attractive alternatives to crowded harbors and marinas. Your mooring arrangement will depend on the nature of the hurricane hole.

In a narrow residential canal, secure your boat in the center of the canal with several large lines ashore (a "spiderweb") to both sides of the canal. This technique has been common to most of the boats in canals that survived with the least damage. Conversely, boats that are left at docks in canals and without the benefit of lines to both sides of a canal don't fare much better during hurricanes than boats at marina docks. Secure lines to pilings, large trees (preferably indigenous trees, which tend to be sturdier than nonnative "exotic" species), and even earth augers. Face the boat to the canal's entrance, locating the boat as far back from open water as possible. Besides sheltering the boat, securing the boat away

Canals are wonderful hurricane holes if boats are properly prepared. This sailboat was stripped and tied off in a canal in Gulf Breeze, Florida, using three large anchors and thirteen lines to shore. Despite considerable damage to other nearby boats and homes, the sailboat survived Hurricane Ivan without so much as a scratch.

A canal offers excellent protection only if a boat is centered in it with many long lines secured ashore. As this photo shows, a boat left at a dock in a canal receives little or no advantage.

from the entrance should help with the need to maintain a navigable waterway.

Securing boats in canals with private homes is possible only if you make arrangements with the homeowners whose trees and pilings you will be using to secure your boat. This can be difficult if your boat isn't normally moored in the canal. If your boat is already in the canal, getting other homeowners involved in planning for a hurricane increases the chances that everybody's boat will survive. This is critical. All it takes to wreak havoc in the confines of a narrow canal is for one or two neglected boats to come loose. A beamy 33-foot cruiser that was tied with four ⅝-inch docklines in the middle of a canal in Punta Gorda, for example, came loose in Hurricane Charley and sank three other boats. The concept was good, but the lines were too small and too few. As one CAT Team member said, "It has to be a neighborhood effort. You are depending on everyone else."

In wider canals, bayous, and waterways, secure boats using a combination of anchors and lines tied to trees ashore, preferably on the side that's likely to offer the best protection from wind and waves. The more lines and anchors you can use, the better. This technique was used frequently—and often successfully—to prepare boats in Florida and Alabama for Hurricane Ivan. Tall banks, sturdy trees, and the absence of homes are all a plus, although finding all three together may be difficult in most areas. In any case, moor your boat away from the main channel.

Besides securing your boat, here are some other considerations to keep in mind: A hurricane hole that ordinarily takes an hour to reach may take 2 hours when winds and seas are building; bridges may not open as frequently once a hurricane warning has been posted; or bridges may be locked down to evacuate

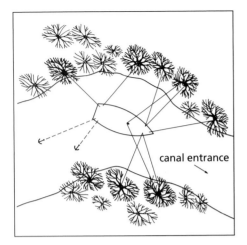

There are an almost infinite number of ways to secure a boat in a sheltered waterway. The arrangement above was used by a BoatU.S. member to secure her boat during Hurricane Andrew. The boat escaped without damage. The key is to use as many lines ashore and anchors as possible. The larger the anchors and lines, the better.

cars. (This was the case on the Miami River before Hurricane Andrew.) Plan on moving your boat early.

At a Mooring, at Anchor, or Both Mooring in a sheltered location can also be a good alternative to exposed and/or crowded marinas. A boat on a mooring can swing to face the wind, which reduces windage, and it won't be slammed into a dock unless the anchor or mooring drags.

The first question, then, is will your mooring hold? As a result of numerous moorings being dragged during hurricanes and northeasters, a search was launched to find a more secure mooring anchor. Using a large tug and several types of moorings, BoatU.S. and *Cruising World* magazine conducted a test and found that the moorings least likely to be dragged were the "embedment" type anchors—a helical or an expanding fluke anchor—which are deliberately screwed or driven into the harbor bottom (see photo on page 136). Traditional moorings—mushroom anchor and dead-weight blocks—were far more likely to be dragged. A mushroom anchor that isn't sufficiently buried has very little holding power. Although the holding power of a mushroom or dead-weight anchor can be increased significantly by extending the pendant's scope, you then have to consider the proximity of other boats. Embedment anchors do not rely as much on scope to maintain their holding power, but scope is always beneficial and must be sufficient to allow for tidal surge.

Every cloud has a silver lining. The widespread destruction of boats in New England during Hurricane Bob led to a series of meetings hosted by FEMA (Federal Emergency Management Agency) to develop better moorings. These meetings prompted interest in helix moorings, which began replacing traditional dead-weight and mushroom anchors.

If you have doubts about your mooring, you can significantly reduce the chances of its dragging by using one or two additional storm anchors to increase its holding power and decrease the room your boat will need to swing.

An arrangement that uses two anchors (or a mooring and an anchor) set 45° apart has often been used success-

Hurricane Ivan's 130 mph winds drove a 16-foot surge into parts of the Florida Panhandle. When you set anchors for a hurricane remember that boats anchored in shallow water with a scope of 10:1 could have significantly less scope and holding power at the height of the surge.

fully to moor boats in storms, although it may not swing in tandem with other boats that are on a single anchor. Three anchors, if they are set correctly, are even better. Three anchors should be set 120° apart and joined at a swivel. While effective, this arrangement takes considerable time (and practice) to be done correctly. With any arrangement, the size of the anchor or anchors is critical. The BoatU.S. CAT Team has consistently found that boats with everyday working anchors are far more likely to be dragged than boats secured with much larger storm anchors.

Whatever mooring/anchoring arrangement you decide on, it is important to have plenty of scope—at least 10:1, if that's possible—and a lot of heavy oversize chain. Probably 50-50 is the optimum chain-to-line ratio. An all-chain rode, while fine for moderate conditions, is not desirable in a hurricane. A boat that was anchored in Stuart, Florida, during Hurricane Frances with a combination nylon-chain rode survived without any problems. The same boat was anchored in the same spot with an all-chain rode in Jeanne and was dragged ashore. In moderate wind and sea conditions, chain relies on its weight to absorb shock. This is called the catenary effect. During a hurricane, the chain will be taut with no catenary effect. Without the nylon line to absorb shock, the surging waves and wind gusts are much more likely to dislodge the anchor. To absorb shock then, an all-chain rode must have a snubber (usually nylon line) that is at least 10% of the rode's length. (The ultimate source for anchor sizes and techniques is *The Complete Book of Anchoring and Mooring* by Earl Hinz.)

Trailer Boats

A trailer is, or should be, a ticket to take your boat inland to a more sheltered location and away from the tidal surge. But your boat won't get far on a neglected trailer that has two flat tires and rusted wheel bearings. Inspect your trailer before hurricane season to make sure it will be operable if it's needed.

If you take your boat home, you may want to leave it, and not your car, in the garage. A boat is lighter and more vulnerable to high winds than a car. If this isn't

Sailboats with deep keels on trailers have proven to be extremely vulnerable whenever the wind is on the beam. Jack stands should always be used to provide additional support.

practical, put the boat and trailer where they will get the best protection from wind, falling trees and branches, roof tiles, etc.

If the boat and trailer will be outside, let some air out of the tires and block the wheels. You can increase the weight of lighter outboard boats by leaving the drain plug in and using a garden hose to add water. (Rain will add a lot more weight later.) This has the added advantage of giving you emergency water (not for drinking) if the main water supply gets knocked out by the hurricane. Place wood blocks between the trailer's frame and springs to support the added weight. On a boat with a sterndrive, remove the drain plug so that the engine won't be damaged by accumulated water.

You can further secure the trailer with anchors or earth augers, or by tying it to a tree. Strip all loose gear, bimini tops, canvas covers, electronics, etc., then lash the boat to the trailer.

Boats on Davits and Lifts

After handling hundreds of claims that were filed for the four hurricanes that hammered Florida in 2004, BoatU.S. CAT Team members were asked, "Where *wouldn't* you want your boat to be in a hurricane?" Most team members quickly answered that they wouldn't want their boat to be on a hoist or davits. Damage to boats on lifts was extraordinarily high and included boats being blown off cradles; bunk boards that broke and spilled the boats; boats grinding against lift motors and pilings; boats being overcome by the storm surge; and boats filling with rainwater and collapsing lifts. Did any boats on lifts survive? In areas that were hard-hit, the answer was not many. The few that did typically were subjected to only a slight surge, and the lift had been secured so that the boat and its cradle couldn't be tossed around by the wind.

Whenever possible, boats on lifts or davits should be taken off and stored ashore or moved to a more storm-worthy location—a trailer, the center of a canal, a hurricane hole, or a dock.

A boat that sits out of the water on davits is especially vulnerable to high winds and storm surge. Securing the boat ashore or in the water, preferably tied across a canal, is a much better option.

Critical Points

Chafe Gear!

It is becoming increasingly more evident with each passing hurricane and north-easter that chafe prevention at a dock and chafe prevention at an anchorage or mooring must be considered separately when preparing a boat for a storm. The chafe protection that you use successfully at a dock likely won't be as effective on mooring or anchor lines. At a dock, rope is usually in a direct line between the boat and piling, and chafe occurs wherever the rope makes contact with another piling, a dock, or a chock. The rope fails externally as it is chafed through. If your chocks are large enough, fit a long—2-foot—section of garden hose around the line that fits snugly. Drill holes in the hose, and use cord to tie it securely to the line. There are also several varieties of ready-made chafe protection available at marine chandleries.

If you need chafe protection quickly, use duct tape—a lot of duct tape—to secure several layers of heavy canvas or denim to the lines. This won't be as rugged as hose, but it is certainly better than leaving a line unprotected.

When a boat is anchored, the nylon rope will be constantly working back and forth over the chock at a steep angle down to the anchor. This constant movement produces a tremendous amount of heat. (The farther the cleat is from the chock, the more the line stretches, and the more heat that will be generated; much less heat builds up when cleats are installed directly at a boat's rail.) At anchor or at a mooring, a rope will often fail *internally*—it melts.

There have been many examples of this type of failure, most recently during Hurricane Frances in Florida. Ed Carter, who owns Diamond 99 Marina in Melbourne, Florida, has always been careful to use chafe protection on lines when his boat was at a dock. In anchoring his 38-foot Downeaster for Hurricane Frances, he used a long section of fire hose as chafe protection on the boat's nylon anchor line. Ed's son anchored his own 37-foot sailboat nearby wrapping only denim around the line for chafe protection. The line on Ed's boat failed—it had melted in big plastic clumps under the fire hose—because, he said, water wasn't able to get to the line to cool the nylon fibers. His son's anchor line, with its wet denim for chafe protection, came through the storm intact.

Tests at MIT after Hurricane Bob showed that under heavy cycling loads, wet nylon yarn is more abrasion-resistant than dry nylon. (Under light cycling loads, the reverse is true—dry nylon yarn outlasts wet nylon.) Heat builds up because of friction between the fibers and internal molecular friction. Wet nylon is more likely to hold up in a hurricane when the storm's heavy rains provide additional lubricity. (Good marine nylon line, when it's new, has a finish on the fibers that helps reduce yarn-on-yarn friction.) Water also carries off heat, which cools the stressed fibers. Long lengths of nylon line that are protected with PVC tubing or fire hose, which don't let water reach the fibers, have a history of failing in storms. The MIT tests also found that polyester line is far more abrasion resistant than nylon line under heavy cycling loads. When the polyester and nylon lines are wet, the study found that the difference in abrasion resistance is even greater.

The obvious question then is, what is the best way to protect an anchor or mooring line? Norm Doelling, the assistant director of MIT's Sea Grant program, reasoned that a simple way to provide durability to an anchor line in a storm

Northeasters aren't usually the equal of a full-blown hurricane, but they can still pack an impressive wallop. The storm that demolished this boat in New Jersey had 50 mph winds and stirred up some unhealthy 6-foot seas in the harbor. Unlike a typical hurricane, which concentrates its fury over the span of a few hours, a northeaster can blow for several days, grinding away at lines and moorings.

Take a cue from some of the better marina owners and harbormasters— check your moorings and add extra chafe protection in late summer at the start of the storm season. And don't leave your boat in the water at an exposed location over the winter.

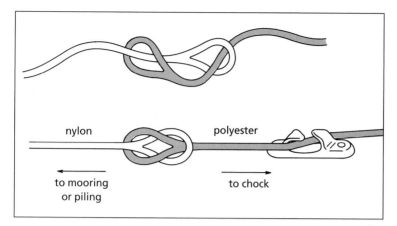

Use polyester line from a cleat through the chock and then use nylon line down to the mooring ball or anchor. Join the nylon and polyester lines with eye splices.

nylon   polyester

to mooring   to chock
or piling

would be to use polyester line from the cleat through the chock and then use nylon line down to the mooring ball or anchor. Instead of joining the nylon and polyester lines with a knot, which creates a weak spot in the rode, the two should be joined using eye splices. The polyester line can be passed through the existing nylon line in an eye-to-eye fashion, giving the anchor or mooring line the best features of both types of rope—polyester's abrasion resistance and nylon's stretching ability to absorb shock.

Cleats and Chocks

Many boats have cleats and chocks that are woefully inadequate. The problem becomes critical when more and larger-diameter storm lines are used during a storm. If necessary, add more and larger cleats and chocks now; they'll make securing the boat easier all year. *Chocks should be nicely rounded and smooth to reduce chafe!*

Assess the ability of cleats to carry heavy loads. This means making sure all are backed properly with stainless steel or aluminum plates. Since plates are usually hidden by the boat's interior liner, you may have to contact the builder. Marine plywood is OK if it's healthy—free of rot and delamination. On sailboats, winches (assuming they're backed properly) can also be used to secure lines at a dock.

Don't put too many eggs in one basket by leading numerous lines to a single cleat, even if it is backed properly. Two lines per cleat is probably the maximum. Also, a cleat is not as reliable when lines are led perpendicular to the base—the cleat can be wrenched out by the tremendous loads.

Reduce Windage!

Strip all loose gear that creates windage: canvas covers, tops, outriggers, antennas, anchors, running rigging, booms, life rings, dinghies, portable davits, etc. Remove cowling ventilators and seal the openings. Securely lash anything on deck that you can't remove.

If time permits, unstepping a sailboat's mast to reduce windage is strongly advised. If unstepping isn't possible (and it probably won't be, at least on larger boats), you *must* remove the roller-furling headsails. Roller-furling headsails create a lot of windage, especially when they come unfurled, which is almost guaranteed to happen no matter how carefully you secure them. Run all halyards to the masthead, and secure them with a single line led to the rail. Aside from reducing windage, the single line minimizes flogging damage to the mast, and later you can use the line to retrieve the halyards.

One mistake that is made in every hurricane is to "protect" electronics by leaving biminis and dodgers in place. Biminis and dodgers create a tremendous amount of windage until they're blown to smithereens, which is inevitable. Take them off and store them below. Also remove any electronics on brackets and store them below (or better yet, take them home). Protect flush-mounted instruments on dashboards by covering them with a large, plastic baggie secured with duct tape.

Preventing Theft
Take valuables home for safekeeping and also any personal belongings and other loose gear that could become potential missiles. Secure cabinets and cabin doors. Remove all ship's documents from the boat.

Preventing Water Damage
Use duct tape around hatches, ports, lockers, etc., that are prone to leaking. Close all seacocks except the ones for the cockpit drain and shove a plug into the engine's exhaust ports. If the boat takes on water, it will sit lower, and seawater could back up into the cylinders. (When the storm has passed, remember to remove the plug before starting the engine.)

Hurricane Preparation Worksheet
Don't wait until a hurricane is coming to prepare your boat. Use a worksheet like the sample provided and adapt it to your own circumstances, then distribute a copy to your alternate (someone who can prepare your boat in your absence). You may also want to give one to your marina manager.

Boat Owner's Hurricane Worksheet

Use this worksheet, after reading the material in this guide, to adapt it to your own circumstances. Then be sure to distribute copies to your alternates as well as your marina owner/manager.

Boat's Name: _____ Length: ____ Model: ____

Your Name: _____

Address: _____

City: _____ State: _____ Zip: _____

Phone Day: _____ Night: _____

Alternates/Caretakers (if you are not available):

Name: _____

Address: _____

City: _____ State: _____ Zip: _____

Phone Day: _____ Night: _____

Has Boat Keys? _____ Access to Hurricane Equipment? _____

Name: _____

Address: _____

City: _____ State: _____ Zip: _____

Phone Day: _____ Night: _____

Has Boat Keys? _____ Access to Hurricane Equipment? _____

Boat's Current Location: _____

Slip #: _____

Marina Name/Address: _____

_____

List All Equipment Needed Aboard to Prepare Boat:

Equipment	Current Location
1. Extra Lines	_____
2. Chafe Protectors	_____
3. Fenders	_____
4. Anchors	_____
5. Swivels	_____
6. Shackles	_____
7. Duct Tape	_____
8. Plugs (Exhaust Ports)	_____
9. _____	_____
10. _____	_____

List Equipment To Be Stripped from Boat:

Equipment	Storage Location
1. Electronics	_____
2. Dinghy	_____
3. Outboard/Fuel	_____
4. Sails	_____
5. Bimini	_____
6. Galley Fuel	_____
7. Ship's Papers	_____
8. Personal Effects	_____
9. _____	_____
10. _____	_____

Planned Location During Hurricane: _____

_____

If at a Dock: Slip #: _____

Marina Name/Address: _____

_____

Additional Lines #: _____ Length: _____ Size: _____

Chafe Gear: _____ Fenders: _____

If at a Hurricane Hole:

Travel Time by Water from Present Location: _____

Are There Any Bridges? _____

If Yes, Will They Open Prior to Hurricane? _____

Has Owner of Surrounding Land Been Contacted? _____

How Will the Skipper Get Ashore? _____

Type of Bottom: _____ Depth: _____

Additional Anchor Needed: #: _____ Size(s): _____

Type(s): _____

Additional Lines: #: _____ Length: _____ Size: _____

Additional Chain: #: _____ Length: _____ Size: _____

Chafe Gear: _____ Swivel: _____ Shackle(s): _____

If at a Mooring/Anchorage:

Has Mooring Been Inspected Within the Last Six Months? _____

How Will the Skipper Get Ashore? _____

Type of Bottom: _____ Depth: _____

Mooring Line Should Be Extended _____ to Increase Scope

Additional Anchors Needed: #: _____ Size: _____

Type(s): _____

Additional Lines: #: _____ Length: _____ Size: _____

Additional Chain: #: _____ Length: _____ Size: _____

Chafe Gear: _____ Swivel: _____ Shackle(s): _____

Diagram of Proposed Hurricane Docking/Mooring Arrangement:

If Stored Ashore:

Windage Reduced by Stripping Sails, Furling Gear, Bimini, Antennas? _____

Blocking Adequate for Storm Conditions? _____

What Arrangements Have Been Made for Hauling? _____

Storage Location: _____

Contact Name (Marina/Property Owner): _____

Phone #: _____

]6[Be Careful Out There

EXPERIENCE IS LIKE A TEACHER who gives the test first and the lesson later. Some lessons on a boat are obvious, like slowing down at night or when visibility is poor. Anyone who drives a car should know that. Other lessons, like the ones in this chapter, aren't quite so obvious. Anyone who can swim in a pool shouldn't have any trouble swimming from a boat, right? Well, no, there are some significant differences there too. And a thunderstorm can transform a sleepy, summer afternoon into a maelstrom. How do you keep your boat safe from lightning strikes? At home, you can duck into your house and shut the door. On a boat, the experience—the test—is liable to be far more intense. And you can't see or smell carbon monoxide, but it's more likely to be found in lethal concentrations on gasoline-powered boats than in a house or even an automobile. As with the other chapters in this book, it's best to spend time studying the lessons from the claim files before you are tested.

Boats and Swimming

Swimming from a boat—a thoroughly enjoyable pastime on a steamy, summer afternoon—is far, far different than swimming in a pool or even at the beach. A boat can be anchored in deep water, then seconds later—due to a puff of wind or increase in current—the terrain beneath the boat is different. There may be rocks (hard!) lurking just below the surface. The boat probably has a propeller (sharp!), and maybe a swim platform (slippery!). If you happen to include alcohol (uh-oh), a pleasant summer afternoon can suddenly turn deadly.

Given the hot summer temperatures in most parts of the country, nobody wants to throw cold water on a favorite summer activity. Instead, here are a few suggestions—let's call them "Pool Rules" for boats—to follow whenever the swim ladder is down. Swimming from a boat is far too enjoyable to be anything other than, well, enjoyable.

Seven "Pool Rules" for Boats

1. *Enter the water gradually.* Maybe a drought has lowered water levels, or

What's wrong with this picture? (Hint: Wwwhhhhheeeeeeeee . . . Splat!) Some boats have flying bridges and some boats have swimming slides. This boat has a slide with a big surprise at the end: the propeller. Oh sure, you could probably slide into the water safely, unless you have something protruding from your torso like, hmm, arms, legs, or a head. But why take the risk? Even if the engine is shut off whenever the slide is used, and it obviously should be, the chances of someone eventually being hurt are good.

This juxtaposition of a swim platform (slick) and a cleat (sharp) has led to several serious injuries. The cleat should either be moved, modified, or cushioned.

maybe the heat made the water look especially inviting, but for whatever reason, from time to time, there have been a rash of serious accidents from people diving or jumping off boats into shallow water. It is worth noting that several of the people who have been injured reported that they had been swimming in the "same spot" many times before. With an anchored boat, however, that's not likely.

The terrain beneath the hull changes constantly as the boat swings with the wind and current. A boat that was in 10 feet of water can, in the span of a few seconds, suddenly have only a foot or two of water beneath its keel. To be safe, *always* enter the water gradually, using a swim ladder or platform.

2. *Be especially careful on fiberglass swim platforms.* Every summer there are several injuries from swimmers falling on swim platforms. The platforms are almost always made of molded fiberglass (or sometimes teak), and the swimmers may have been injured when they landed on cleats. The nonskid (or antiskid as it is called by skeptics) on the molded platforms usually has a diamond pattern (the same as on the rest of the boat's deck), and it provides dicey footing when it's wet.

Beyond warning guests, you can do several things to make swimming from a platform—fiberglass or teak—safer. First, improve the nonskid surface by applying nonskid tape, which is inexpensive and much safer than molded-in patterns. You should also take a critical look at the positioning of deck hardware. A vertical cleat is especially dangerous. Consider moving it (or having a professional do the job) so the cleat is out of harm's way. It might also be possible to install a pop-up cleat that folds out of the way when it's not being used. As an alternative, you can improvise a cover, using something like a sailboat spreader boot or old tennis balls—anything that might soften the edges of the cleat should a swimmer fall on it.

3. *Don't swim from an anchored boat when there is a strong current or tide running.* Swimmers can be swept away from an anchored boat in the span of a few seconds. A couple in Virginia Beach spent the night clinging to a channel buoy after they went swimming from a boat anchored near the mouth of the Chesapeake Bay and got caught in an outgoing (ebbing) tide. In a similar incident, a scuba diver in Florida spent 6 hours drifting with the current (luckily he was wearing an inflatable vest) before being rescued by the Coast Guard.

   Reading the tide and current tables can provide guidance on local conditions, but as an added precaution, always check for telltale swirls coming off the stern of the anchored boat, which indicates moving water. As a further precaution, tie a life ring to a long line and float it behind the boat.

4. *NEVER put the engine in gear while someone is in the water.* Accidents involving swimmers and props occur with frightening regularity. In one case, a 44-year old man was injured when a boat's gears jammed in reverse, and the spinning prop badly gashed one of his legs. Shut off engines when swimmers are nearby.

5. *Don't swim near boats that are plugged into AC shore power.* The thought of someone illegally pumping a boat's head is usually all it takes to keep most people out of the water when a boat is at a dock. There are certainly more pleasant places to swim. But aside from being unpleasant, swimming next to a boat at a dock can also be dangerous. Electricity can sometimes leak into the water, either from the boat or from the marina's electrical systems, putting swimmers at considerable risk.

   Even a few milliamps of electricity in the water can be fatal. A man in Wisconsin had been swimming toward his boat. Just before he sank underwater, he told his wife that he felt an electrical "tingle"—he didn't come back up. According to the coroner's report the man drowned. This isn't unusual; some experts believe that authorities will typically attribute the cause of death to drowning without suspecting that electricity was involved. In this case, the widow thought otherwise and refused to accept the report. After a great deal of prompting by the widow, investigators discovered a short in the battery charger as well as problems with the boat's electrical system that had allowed electricity to escape into the water.

   It may be worthwhile to have an electrical expert examine your boat if you suspect a problem (the marina's electrical system could also be at fault). The man who died in Wisconsin had been shocked on at least one occasion when he touched a stanchion, but unfortunately, he failed to heed the warning. The only surefire way to be safe, however, is to stay out of the water while a boat is at a dock. If you must go into the water, to retrieve something lost overboard or clean the boat's bottom, first unplug the boat from the 110-volt, dockside electrical system. If the boat is in fresh or brackish water, nearby boats should also be unplugged. Better yet, ask someone to shut off the marina's master switch.

6. *Don't swim when the boat's (gasoline) generator or propulsion engine is running.* There have been several, well-documented cases of swimmers being affected by carbon monoxide (for more on this, see the end of the chapter) from generators while swimming behind the boat. *Turn off* gasoline generators (and propulsion engines) whenever swimmers are in the water. Diesel generators produce far less carbon monoxide (CO) and are not considered a hazard. Teak surfing, the practice of pulling "surfers" behind the swim platform in a boat's wake (they hold onto the swim platform), is an extremely dangerous practice that has resulted in the deaths of several children from CO poisoning. *Do not, under any circumstances, allow anyone to be pulled directly behind the boat without a towrope that keeps them well away from the exhaust and props.*

7. *Use common sense.*

   • Kids and adults who aren't strong swimmers should wear life jackets while they are in the water.

   • Always have a life ring or cushions nearby in case they are needed.

   • Stay near the boat. A head sticking out of the water is difficult for a passing boat to see.

   • Get out of the water if a storm is approaching. Several years ago, a boat-owner in New England was struck by lightning and killed while trying to swim out to his boat during a thunderstorm.

   • Don't forget that when swimmers enter the water they'll also have to get back out. Use a swim ladder that will allow even the least-athletic members of your crew to climb back aboard easily.

Drinking and Drowning

As should be clear by now, alcohol and boating don't mix. That goes for swimming too. In one case, after a few drinks at a popular Florida resort, a group of friends climbed aboard a boat for a moonlight ride in the harbor. About midnight, despite a 20-knot wind and choppy seas, the group decided to go swimming. They shut down the engine and allowed the boat to drift in a channel about 200 yards from a deserted island. As soon as they entered the water, the wind began

GREAT TASTE, GREAT SPRAY...COMBINED.

sweeping the boat away from the swimmers. The engine was restarted, and the boat was backed up in the direction of the swimmers. One by one, the swimmers were picked up, except for a 40-year-old woman who was missing.

Since the woman had not alerted any of the other swimmers that she was having trouble (see the Drowning Victims: Their Silent Pleas for Help section below) most of the group thought she would be found. But despite a thorough search, her body was never recovered.

Experienced skippers should quickly recognize the obvious risks that were taken that night: the decision to go boating in the dark after drinking; the decision to go in the water under those sea conditions; and the foolish practice of backing up the boat toward the swimmers.

What many people don't realize, however, is the extraordinary number of drownings that involve alcohol. Almost 90% of all boating deaths are the result of drowning, according to the Coast Guard. And while estimates vary, studies have shown that alcohol may have been a factor in about 50% of *all* adult drowning deaths. Some studies put the figure as high as 70%. Drowning is the second leading cause of unintentional death among adults 20 to 44 years old.

Obviously, anyone who is very drunk will have trouble swimming. But many of the people who drown were not legally drunk, and researchers have discovered several reasons why even moderate amounts of alcohol may affect a person's ability in the water.

In the claim above, the victim was a good swimmer in good health. She probably had considerably less to drink than some of the others on the boat. Her dinner, according to police interviews with her companions, was a salad and two glasses of white wine. This combination of alcohol, too few carbohydrates, and exercise—swimming—meant that she ran the risk of developing hypoglycemia, which is a drastic reduction of a person's blood glucose levels. Hypoglycemia causes sudden weakness and confusion and affects the body's normal temperature-regulating mechanisms. Medical researchers warn that alcohol and aquatic exercise, without ingesting sufficient carbohydrates, represents a "foolish confrontation with death."

Not all drowning victims enter the water voluntarily; at least 25% of all drownings are caused by falls overboard, according to Coast Guard statistics. Boats are inherently unstable anyway, and when someone has been drinking, the tendency to fall overboard is increased.

The Coast Guard conducted tests to document the effects of environmental stressors—sun, wind, wave motion, glare, and vibration—on a boat operator's reaction time and error rate. They found that these stressors produced a kind of boater's hypnosis, a fatigue that reduced an operator's performance much as alcohol does. But when operators were both intoxicated and exposed to these environmental stressors, they missed *ten times* as many cues as operators who were merely exposed to the environmental stressors.

Environmental stressors and alcohol combine to cause many boating accidents, including falls overboard. Both the stressors and alcohol were probably factors in a claim involving a young skipper and the accidental drowning of his friend. After spending most of the day sunning, sailing, and drinking beer on the young skipper's small powerboat, the friend stumbled and fell into the chilly New England waters. He was unable to climb back aboard and tried to swim ashore. The skipper dove overboard and tried unsuccessfully to reach his friend with a life vest. The skipper survived, but his friend's body was recovered two weeks later.

Hypothermia may well have been a factor in this case. Hypothermia causes swimmers to become sluggish and can occur in water as warm as 80°. Alcohol inhibits the body's signaling system so that swimmers don't realize how cold they are. Although it is rarely listed as the cause of death, researchers believe hypothermia is a contributing factor in as many as half of all drowning deaths.

Understanding Hypothermia In some parts of the country, it isn't unusual for the water to be frigid in early spring, even while the air feels as warm as summer. Water temperatures change more slowly than air temperatures. While most people know to be cautious aboard a boat in the winter, the warm spring air can easily lull a person into taking chances in a small boat.

A life vest is especially important on a boat when the water is cold. Not only will it keep your head above water if you fall overboard, a snug-fitting life vest will also act as insulation to reduce heat loss. Should you ever find yourself in cold water, remain still, if possible. Swimming burns up body heat and increases your body's cooling rate. Rapid heat loss occurs in the groin region, so tuck your knees up to your chest. Another zone of rapid heat loss is the area below your armpits. Keep your arms tightly against your body.

If you rescue someone who has been overboard in cold water, it is important to remember that hypothermia does not stop when someone is removed from the water. Use your VHF to arrange for the victim to get medical attention as soon as possible. In the meantime, to prevent *afterdrop* (a continued lowering of the body's core temperature), take off the victim's wet clothes and dry and warm the body's core areas (the chest, groin, head, and neck). Arms and legs should be warmed more slowly (heating the limbs causes cooler blood to flow from them to the torso, further cooling the core areas).

Ideally, the victim should be taken down below to a warm cabin and bath, but body-to body contact under a heavy blanket (such as when out of the wind in an open boat) will suffice. Warm, sweet drinks like hot chocolate, which don't contain caffeine, are also beneficial. Caffeine causes vaso-constriction, which causes the blood vessels to constrict and limits blood flow. Alcohol and exercise will encourage afterdrop and must also be avoided, even if the victim seems OK.

Disoriented Swimmers   Besides hypoglycemia and hypothermia, there are other ways that alcohol affects someone in the water. Sudden cooling of the skin can cause *caloric labyrinthitis* (an inner ear disturbance associated with a sudden drop in temperature) and/or hyperventilation, which may have contributed to the drowning death of a swimmer on a balmy spring day on the Potomac River. The victim (an experienced swimmer) had been talking and drinking beer aboard an anchored boat in a quiet cove, when, perhaps to cool off, he suddenly jumped into the water. He was never seen again.

Caloric labyrinthitis causes disorientation and explains why swimmers may sometimes swim down instead of up. Researchers believe that alcohol may increase the chances of caloric labyrinthitis as well as hyperventilation. Hyperventilation can cause someone to gasp and "breathe in" water.

Many drowning victims are strong swimmers. A professional diver hired to retrieve a fishing rod drowned after only a few minutes in the water. An autopsy disclosed a high blood-alcohol content. While it can never be known exactly why he drowned, investigators had little doubt that alcohol was a major factor.

There is still a great deal that is not known about alcohol and drowning. Dr. Gordon Smith, of the Johns Hopkins Center for Injury Research and Policy, has done considerable research on drowning deaths. He hears a lot of stories of people who are swimming, then suddenly disappear. He believes that drinking is a "major, major factor" in over half these deaths. Smith is concerned because alcohol is still promoted around water sports. People who have been drinking should stay out of the water.

Drowning Victims: Their Silent Pleas For Help

Many people drown within easy reach of other swimmers. Children have drowned within a few feet of their parents. "She was splashing and playing and then suddenly she was gone" was the way one parent described the last few seconds of his daughter's life. "She never called for help."

Recognizing drowning behavior is especially important because researchers have discovered that someone who is drowning lacks the lung capacity to call for help. Drowning victims act instinctively, moving their arms as though climbing a ladder, taking quick gulps of air, and then slipping back underwater. With an adult, this reflexive behavior lasts about 60 seconds before the victim sinks underwater for good. A child will last only for about 20 seconds before succumbing. The struggle is quiet and often looks "playful." Be aware of others in the water around you and be ready to respond at the first signs of distress.

Waterskiing Safety

Perhaps this won't come as a surprise, but an examination of the BoatU.S. Marine Insurance claim files found that of all the injury claims in one summer from waterskiing, novice water-skiers experienced the most injuries. These injuries were often caused by simple mistakes. A South Carolina woman, for example, looked down at her skis and almost immediately lost her balance and pulled a groin muscle as she was falling. Another claim involved a man who separated his shoulder because he continued holding onto the ski rope as he was falling and only let go when he smacked into the water.

Three Rules for Novice Water-Skiers

Waterskiing need not be dangerous, but it is a demanding sport that requires a certain level of expertise to make even basic maneuvers. The three rules below won't help anyone learn to water-ski, but they could make the learning experience less painful.

1. *Listen and watch.* Experts recommend that novice skiers get some professional instruction and spend time as a spotter watching other people ski before trying it themselves. The alternative—learning by trial and error—can lead to many spills and even injuries that may dampen your enthusiasm for waterskiing.

Working as a spotter allows you to learn and practice hand signals, which are used to communicate between skier and boat.

2. *Use proper form.* Once you're in the water and ready to give the driver the "go" signal (make sure the rope is taut), remember to keep your knees bent, your back straight, and *both* hands on the towrope handle. (If you try to hold on with only one hand as you're taking off, you'll be pulled sideways with predictable results.) As the boat pulls you up and out of the water, keep your skis together with the tips up and make adjustments slowly. Keep your arms straight. Pulling back on the rope seems to be a natural tendency of many people, but this will force the skis forward, and you will fall backward. If you do fall, and sooner or later you will (probably sooner), *let go of the rope immediately!* Avoid falling forward, as this is more likely to cause injury.

   Whenever you cross a wake, keep your knees bent to absorb the bumps and to help maintain balance. Always look up. Looking down tends to make you lose your balance, not to mention making it impossible for you to see oncoming obstructions. One of the more serious injury claims involved a woman who was skiing outside the boat's wake and didn't notice an oncoming piling. The result of her lapsed attention was a serious head injury.

3. *Remember rules 1 and 2.* When you've been skiing for a few minutes, don't be tempted, as many people are, to begin signaling for more and more speed. Experts recommend going no more than 25 mph the first few times, until you become comfortably proficient. Be forewarned: as you work your way up from novice to expert, there is always the risk of an accident, especially if you become overconfident and forget to practice the basics. One injured skier was skiing barefoot at over 40 mph, when, according to the claim file, he lost his balance and failed to let go of the rope. He fell forward and injured his neck.

Nine Rules for Pulling Water-Skiers Safely

In addition to skiers knowing how to ski safely, it's vital for boat operators to know how to pull water-skiers in a safe manner. Following are nine rules to adhere to:

1. *Parents should exercise good judgment whenever children will be waterskiing or operating boats.* Over one-third of the claims for waterskiing accidents involve children aged 15 years or younger. Not only are kids likely to have less experience as skiers, they typically are less cautious and more willing to take (unsafe) risks than adults.

2. *Where you ski is as important as how you ski.* Avoid taking skiers, even expert skiers, through crowded channels. In some active boating communities, areas may be specified only for waterskiing. If not, find a section of water away from

passing boat traffic. Remember in crossing situations, your "boat" will include the towrope and the water-skier, and thus will be much longer.

3. *Always use a spotter.* Nothing beats an extra pair of eyes trained only on the skier. Spotters can pass along signals and will let you know when the skier has fallen. In some states, spotters are required by law.

4. *If there's a problem, get back to the skier immediately.* Several serious accidents have involved skiers who were run down by other boats while they were waiting to be picked up. Life jackets (required by law) as well as skis, kneeboards, wetsuits, and T-shirts should be brightly colored so that the skier will be easily visible to you and other boat traffic. Skiers in the water who are waiting to be picked up should hold a ski up out of the water so that they will be more visible to you as well as to other boat operators. The color of the equipment is important. One skier who was run down had a kneeboard and life vest that were both black, which is far less visible against dark water.

5. *Avoid obstacles in the water.* When a skier is being dropped off near a dock or beach, come in slowly and run parallel to the shore.

6. *NEVER put the engine in reverse and back the boat toward a skier (or anyone else) in the water.* When you pick up a skier, make a gradual circle back, then put the engine in neutral (or better yet, shut it off) *before* you come alongside. When the wind is blowing, always approach from the lee.

7. *Don't put the motor in gear until you see that everyone is safely seated in the boat.* Just because you hear a voice nearby, don't assume that person is aboard. In one claim involving a serious injury, a skier who was seated on the swim platform *sounded* like he was inside the boat, and the skipper gunned the motor without looking back to check. The unsecured skier fell off the platform and was injured when he was struck by the propeller.

8. *Bring ski ropes aboard before putting the motor in gear.* In one case, a ski rope that was being brought back aboard got caught in the prop, severely injuring the 15-year-old boy (not a BoatU.S. claim) who had been winding it between his elbow and thumb. Props generate a lot of suction; the accident occurred even though the rope was floating on the surface of the water.

9. *Check the equipment.* Be sure attachments on the boat for ski ropes are well secured. The rope itself should be free of chafe with no knots or broken strands.

Even if you aren't waterskiing, use common sense and common courtesy when you're around water-skiers. The most common complaint you'll hear from water-skiers regards the tendency for other boaters to "tailgate" someone who is waterskiing. This thoughtless practice is dangerous. If you own a boat, never follow directly behind or beside a water-skier. Even though the spotter may be aware of your boat, the skier may not know you're there. And a moment of lapsed attention on your part could be disastrous if the skier falls.

Wear Your Personal Flotation Device (PFD)!

The skipper of a 43-foot trawler in Florida was scrubbing the bow of his boat with a mop—a routine job he'd done hundreds of times before—when he leaned a little too far over the lifelines and tumbled into the water. His female friend, the only other person aboard, threw a cushion over the side, but the man couldn't reach it because he couldn't swim. She then raced aft to get a boathook, but in the few short seconds she was gone, the skipper had disappeared. Divers recovered his body later that afternoon.

In another claim, a small sailboat with three people aboard was capsized by a strong gust of wind during a race. Although a chase boat was on scene in minutes, a 77-year old man was found floating unconscious, barely breathing. A few minutes later, as he was being transported ashore, he had a heart attack and died. The victim had been wearing an inflatable PFD, one of the models that has to be inflated manually. He apparently was too stunned to inflate the vest and was struggling to stay afloat when help arrived.

Most people are good swimmers and don't want to be told when or where they should wear a PFD. A few years ago, a poll of BoatU.S. members found that 98% of the 10,000 respondents were opposed to a federal law requiring adults to wear PFDs on recreational boats. (Thirty-eight states have laws that require children to wear PFDs.) But at night, in rough conditions, or if you don't swim, a PFD makes a heck of a lot of sense.

Boats and Lightning

Peter Stoops was sailing his 36-foot sailboat, *Freedom*, back from Bermuda after the Marion–Bermuda race when he got caught in a persistent thunderstorm off Cape Cod. The wind blew hard, and lightning seemed to be everywhere. Then, with three people down below and three in the cockpit, lightning hit the top of *Freedom*'s mast.

As the mast was struck, the startled crew on deck watched fuzzy bolts of light travel down the shrouds and disappear into the chainplates. A split second later, *Freedom* was again sailing quietly along in the darkness as if nothing had happened. Nobody was hurt. Even the electronics were still working. Peter attributed the lack of damage to the boat's grounding system and maybe a little good luck.

A thunderstorm can contain the same raw power as an atomic bomb, which is one of those daunting facts you don't like to think about when dark clouds start building on a warm afternoon. Unlike *Freedom*, most boats aren't well grounded, and it isn't unusual for a boat to be damaged or even destroyed by millions of volts of electricity ricocheting around as it seeks a path to ground.

What can happen when a boat is struck, and it provides no effective path to ground? For starters, a lightning strike can cause one heck of a power surge if it finds its way into the boat's electrical system, which it usually does. A 39-foot sailboat in North Carolina, to cite a typical example, was underway when lightning hit its VHF antenna, wrecking all of the electronics, the boat's refrigerator, and much of the boat's AC and DC electrical systems.

Less typical, but no less menacing, is the damage that can occur from heat, which is a by-product of the massive current flow. When the electricity passes through something that is not a good conductor of electricity—a bulkhead, for example—a tremendous amount of heat is generated. The result may be a blackened, squiggly line of scorched wood or, in rare cases, a fire. A BoatU.S. member in Florida returned from dinner ashore one night and was greeted by the unpleasant smell of melted wires and burned wood when he opened the hatch of his boat. Lightning had struck the boat, starting a fire that was only extinguished by a lack of oxygen in the cabin.

After the electricity passes through a boat on its way to ground, it invariably makes its exit somewhere down in the hull. *Freedom* was saved in part because the electrical charge exited through the boat's nonencapsulated 7,000-pound lead keel—an almost perfect ground. Without an effective ground, however, like a lead keel or a strip of copper, lightning is likely to be squeezed through underwater fittings, which, in rare instances, can sink a boat. A 24-foot powerboat in Georgia sank when lightning struck its VHF antenna and blew out a plastic transducer.

It should be noted that even though there are well over 2,000 claims for lightning damage in the BoatU.S. Marine Insurance program over the past decade, only one involved a fatality aboard a boat: A man in Maryland was killed as he stepped onto the dock. Apparently he was touching either a shroud or metal stanchion when the bolt hit. (Another lightning fatality claim occurred while a man was swimming back to his boat.)

Lightning Protection

When lightning strikes a boat, the electricity flows like water through pipes of various sizes on its way to ground beneath the boat. A lightning protection system provides large "pipes"—the straighter the better—so the electricity can flow easily, with less chance of a "spill." Without a lightning protection system, the flow is much more likely to encounter an electrical "dam" that will block the flow and "spill" the electricity (or burst a pipe) just about anywhere, arcing to other nearby objects. The latter are known as side flashes.

A lightning protection system consists of a lightning rod (air terminal), a downlead, which bonds to other major metal components, and the ground. On sailboats, the mast acts as the lightning rod, which is probably why sailboats have a greater chance of being struck. Some powerboats have masts that can function as lightning rods, but others would require a portable rod to be carried aboard and deployed in an emergency.

The *downlead*—a heavy copper cable—connects the mast (lightning rod) to the ground. ABYC standards recommend bonding major metal components— fishing tower, shrouds, engine, railings, davits, etc.—to the downlead. Bonding is recommended to prevent dangerous side flashes of current.

The charge exits the system via a *ground*, which consists of at least 1 square foot of metal—typically Monel, copper, or bronze—on the bottom of the hull. Larger is better.

Finally, some boats have a *lightning dissipator* at the top of the mast, which theoretically bleeds off some of the charge, helping prevent a lightning strike or at least lessen its impact. The operative word here is "theoretically." For more on dissipators, see below.

Here are a few things that boatowners should know about lightning protection systems:

- The vast majority of boats don't have a lightning protection system, at least not one that's built to ABYC standards.

What Are the Chances of Lightning Striking Your Boat?

THE FOLLOWING STATISTICS are based on all of the BoatU.S. Marine Insurance claims for lightning damage over a five-year period. The percentages suggest the chances of various types of boats being struck in any given year.

Lightning Strike Probability

Boat Type	Percentage
auxiliary sail	0.60%
multihull sail	0.50%
trawlers	0.30%
sail only	0.20%
cruisers	0.10%
runabouts	0.02%

The following probabilities of lightning strikes by state were taken from the BoatU.S. claim files and are based on the number of boats insured in each state compared to the numbers that were struck by lightning in a given year. One obvious question is: Why are the chances of being struck in Rhode Island and Maryland greater than in Florida? The answer is that Rhode Island and Maryland have a much higher percentage of sailboats.

Lightning Strike Probability by State

State	Percentage
Rhode Island	0.355%
Maryland	0.336%
Florida	0.276%
North Carolina	0.265%
Wisconsin	0.253%
Mississippi	0.252%
Kansas	0.175%
Alabama	0.171%
Maine	0.164%
South Carolina	0.163%
Iowa	0.149%
Virginia	0.145%
Washington, D.C.	0.136%
Louisiana	0.117%
Delaware	0.114%
Connecticut	0.110%
Michigan	0.097%
Tennessee	0.097%
Oklahoma	0.092%
Texas	0.092%
Indiana	0.083%
New York	0.082%
Massachusetts	0.081%
West Virginia	0.077%
Illinois	0.073%
Ohio	0.073%
Kentucky	0.065%
New Jersey	0.061%
Vermont	0.058%
Georgia	0.054%
Pennsylvania	0.031%
New Hampshire	0.029%
Minnesota	0.015%
Washington	0.005%
California	0.003%
Average (all boats)	**0.131%**

- Even when a boat does have one, it must be kept free of corrosion, which tends to develop at connections, to be effective.

- Lightning is unpredictable; even the best system is no guarantee that electricity won't behave erratically.

- All things considered, however, *a properly installed and maintained lightning protection system is your best guarantee that you and your boat won't be injured or damaged in a lightning strike.*

Learning how to install a system, one with a good chance of containing the charge, takes considerably more expertise than the usual kibitzing with other boatowners at the marina. The ABYC (www.abycinc.org) publishes a detailed standard (E-4) for lightning protection systems that you can download for $40.

Can Dissipators Prevent Lightning Strikes? When Bill George's 42-foot sailboat was struck by lightning, he had almost the same reaction as Peter Stoops: he almost jumped out of his skin, paused briefly to regain his composure, then started searching for damage. The boat itself seemed OK, but the electronics had all been knocked dead by the jolt, or so he thought. After about 30 seconds, one by one, they started blinking back on. A miracle? George didn't think so; he attributed the lack of permanent damage to a No-Strike lightning dissipator system he'd recently installed at the top of the mast.

George, a mechanical and aerospace engineer at the University of Buffalo, studied the idea of dissipators before deciding the theory behind their operation is firmly grounded in physics. Not all experts, however, share his enthusiasm for dissipators, at least not when they're used on boats.

When thunderstorm clouds begin to form, the upper portions of the clouds develop a positive electrical charge, and the lower portions develop a negative charge. Most lightning strikes, about two-thirds, occur between the positive and negative portions of the clouds and never reach the ground. But as the cloud passes over land or water, it also creates a "shadow" of positive charges on objects below. These positive charges tend to accumulate on the highest objects, which on boats typically means masts, radio antennas, or tuna towers.

A strike from cloud to ground begins with "stepped leaders" that branch out from the cloud. When the stepped leaders are within about 500 feet of the ground, the electric field intensity of the ground becomes so strong that streamers shoot from the tallest objects—tuna towers or masts, etc.—up toward the stepped leaders. When a streamer connects with a stepped leader, the ionized path becomes the channel for the main lightning discharge.

Lightning dissipators are placed at the highest point on a boat to allow a

Lightning Protection and Open Boats

A LIGHTNING PROTECTION SYSTEM starts at the top of the mast and goes all the way to the bottom of the boat. According to the ABYC's E-4 standard, the mast should be tall enough so that a 45° line drawn from the top does not intersect any part of the boat. This provides a zone (cone) of protection for the boat and crew. On sailboats and some power-boats, mast height is not a problem. But on smaller open boats, a portable pole would have to be carried aboard for use during a thunderstorm.

A BoatU.S. member in Alabama noted that to implement the cone on his 24-foot Stamas, he would need a 20-foot pole to protect the boat from the bow pulpit to the swim plat-form. The pole would support a heavy copper wire that would be attached to a copper plate under the boat. He wondered if there was an alternative lightning protection system for small boats. Unfortunately there isn't. Paul Fleury, who is a member of the ABYC E-4 com-mittee, says that if you want a system on your boat, the pole, cumbersome though it may be, is the only solution.

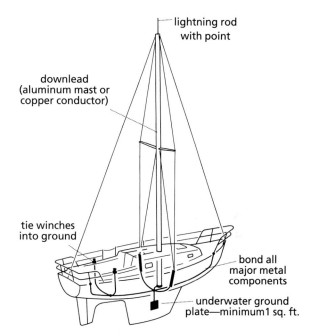

A proper lightning protection system.

Should someone ever be caught out in a thunderstorm in an open boat that lacks a lightning protection system, the best defense is to sit low in the boat and remove any metal jewelry.

small amount of the charge to bleed off—enough, according to proponents, to retard the formation of streamers. This bleeding off is typically done via dozens of tiny points on the dissipator. The technology has been used successfully for many years to protect radio antennas ashore.

One of the concerns of skeptics, however, is a boat's grounding system, or lack thereof. Unlike radio towers, which have long, straight runs of heavy cables to earth, boats typically have much lighter cables that twist and turn down to a relatively small grounding plate below the waterline. One company's literature discounts the difference and even discourages the use of a grounding system with its dissipator: "Gone is the need to rely on 'grounding' techniques that are inadequate and even dangerous."

Bob Loeser, former senior marine engineer at Underwriters Laboratories, strongly disagrees and thinks that a boatowner who installs a lightning dissipator instead of a grounding system would be at serious risk if lightning were to strike the boat. Not only is proper grounding necessary for safety reasons, Loeser thinks a good ground is responsible for whatever success lightning dissipators may have had ashore. With the less effective ground on a boat, he wonders if a dissipator would be effective at all: "If you consider the cloud and the earth as plates of a very large capacitor covering many acres, the 1-foot ground plate offered by the boat is very small. If the boat happens to be near the lower end of the stepped leader path, then the boat is likely to send up a streamer and be hit. Because the boat ground is small, it does not seem reasonable to believe that a dissipator could alter the condition set up by the large capacitor."

The way to protect a boat, Loeser says, is to install the best lightning ground possible. Bruce Kaiser, who is president of Lightning Master, the company that makes the "fuzzy ball" dissipator marketed by Forespar, agrees that a boat must be grounded, if for no other reason than to get rid of the charge if it is hit. (He says he knows of several boats with Lightning Master systems installed that were struck.) In the event of a strike, Kaiser says, the dissipator will act like a lightning rod, and it is important that there be a good ground and bonding system to prevent damage. But in most situations, he says, it bleeds off enough charge to sufficiently reduce the streamer and prevent a strike.

Since a boat needs a lightning rod anyway, and since a dissipator might help prevent a lightning strike or at least reduce its impact, it would seem like a worthwhile piece of equipment to place at the top of a mast. As a marine surveyor in New England said, "What harm can they do?"

Dr. Ewen Thomson, formerly an associate professor and lightning researcher at the University of Florida, emphasizes that he doesn't know if dissipators work or not but worries that if lightning dissipators work at anything less than 100%, they might only protect the top of the mast. In that case, lightning might strike somewhere else on the boat, perhaps injuring someone who would otherwise have been protected.

Kaiser agrees that anything is possible with lightning, but he thinks it is highly unlikely that the streamer could get through the *Faraday cage* (zone of protection) provided by a sailboat's standing rigging. Another lightning expert, however, wonders what would happen on powerboats, which lack the protection of a Faraday cage.

Do lightning dissipators work? The ongoing debate is not even close to resolution. Mitchell Guthrie, an electrical engineer who is chairman of the NFPA's 780 Lightning Protection Committee, says that when it comes to electrical safety, the scientific community tends to be conservative. He notes that it is cer-

Lightning Dissipators—A Good Idea Gone Bad?

BOATS WITH LIGHTNING DISSIPATORS have been struck by lightning, which critics say proves dissipators don't work. Supporters, however, contend that when dissipators don't prevent a strike, they will at least reduce the severity of the strike. There's no body of scientific knowledge to support either view, but a recent lightning strike may have dealt a setback to the dissipator camp.

In this case, lightning struck a radio antenna at the top of the mast on this sailing catamaran. The antenna was only inches away from a dissipator. The blast blew the radio antenna and anchor light to smithereens (below) and then traveled down the stays and exited at a plastic through-hull. The latter was cracked open, and the boat sank a few hours later.

There are two points to note here: (1) A

lightning strike can be devastating to a boat, even if it has a dissipator. (2) A dissipator clearly isn't a substitute for a proper lightning protection system, i.e., one that is grounded to metal, not plastic.

tainly within the interest of the scientific community to gather more information and data on dissipators.

In the meantime, boatowners should keep in mind that there is always a considerable risk with lightning, and whether lightning dissipators can reduce that risk remains to be seen.

If You're Caught in a Lightning Storm:

- *Stay inside the cabin.* The fewer people on deck the better. A man in North Carolina (not a BoatU.S. member) was killed when lightning jumped from the backstay to his head and then to the metal wheel he was holding. If you are on deck, stay well away from the mast, stays, outriggers, metal railings, etc. Down below, avoid chainplates and large metal appliances like refrigerators. Don't use your VHF in a thunderstorm, unless there's an emergency.

- *In an open boat, stay low in the center of the boat.* Don't become a human lightning rod! Remove all metal jewelry. The Coast Guard reported a case a few years ago of a man who was struck while standing up in the boat wearing a large metal medallion.

- *Stay out of the water.* Don't swim or even dangle your toes overboard. And don't fish during a thunderstorm.

- *Disconnect power leads and antenna leads on electronics.* In many lightning strikes, damage to the boat is confined to the electronics. Disconnecting the power and antenna leads goes a long way toward minimizing damage. Disconnecting leads is also recommended whenever the boat is not being used. (*Note:* This should be done *before* the storm arrives. Don't disconnect leads if there is already lightning in the area.)

- *Lower the antennas,* unless one of them is serving as the lightning rod in your boat's lightning protection system. (The same note about doing this early or not at all applies here also.)

If Your Boat Is Hit:

- *With any serious injury, contact the Coast Guard immediately.* If someone has been injured and is not breathing, he or she may be saved with CPR.

- *Check the bilge for water.* Although rare, lightning can rupture a through-hull fitting or punch a hole in the bottom of the boat. Some insurance companies will pay the complete cost for a short haul and bottom inspection after a strike to protect you from future flooding problems.

- *Check electronics.* If they are not working, try checking fuses and circuit breakers. Also check your compass. Lightning magnetizes iron objects on a boat, which can wreak havoc with a magnetic compass.

- *Report the strike to your insurance company as soon as possible.* Make a report even if you were not able to find any damage.

Boats and Carbon Monoxide

As mentioned at the beginning of this chapter, carbon monoxide (CO) is a silent killer: you can't see or smell it, and small concentrations can have fatal consequences. In one case, a couple in Michigan arrived at their boat late in the fall, started the gas generator, turned on the boat's electric heater, and set to work on a few end-of-season projects. While they were working, CO from the gas generator began creeping silently into the main saloon from somewhere down in the bilge. Without a CO alarm, the couple had no idea—not even the tiniest hint—that the deadly gas was mixing with the air in the boat's cabin. Since its initial symptoms—drowsiness, headaches, nausea, and dizziness—aren't especially alarming, victims often don't realize they're being overcome until it's too late.

The unsuspecting couple soon "fell asleep" and would have died had it not been for the early arrival—almost 2 hours early—of their son. He quickly shut off the generator, opened ports, and phoned the rescue squad. They were extremely lucky; most CO claims have a much sadder outcome.

An investigation afterward concluded that the CO had come from a drain plug in the generator's muffler that had worked loose and lay in the bilge. The report also noted the lack of a CO detector aboard, which wasn't a surprise. The lack of a CO detector is the one thing all the claims for CO fatalities or near fatalities in a boat's cabin have in common. According to the claim files, CO can enter a cabin from many different sources: a hot-water heater; a galley stove; the boat's exhaust (i.e., the station wagon effect where exhaust is sucked aboard from astern); a generator; and other nearby boats. There have also been

CO quickly overcame all four people without warning aboard this boat on Lake Powell, Arizona. One person was killed, and three others were unconscious for 14 hours. The boat was moving slowly with the front end closed, and fumes entered the open stern via the station wagon effect. One of the survivors emphasized that there was no warning, which probably indicates there were very high levels of CO aboard—and no CO detector.

The owners of this boat, a husband and wife, died when CO leaked into the cabin from a rotted hose in the boat's generator exhaust. The husband had recently finished doing a considerable amount of work on the old boat, including installing a new CO detector. According to the surveyor who investigated the accident, most of the work had been done correctly. The one exception, however, was that the CO detector had been wired through the boat's ignition switch. The couple anchored for the night and shut off the engine, which also shut off the CO detector, and then started the generator.

If you install a CO detector yourself, it is critical that you follow the manufacturer's recommendations—no shortcuts. For most people, that shouldn't be too hard. But if you're unfamiliar with marine wiring, hire a competent marine electrician to do the installation. Considering what is at stake, it is a wise investment.

fatalities and injuries from people swimming under swim platforms when an engine or generator was being operated.

Certainly it is important to recognize the symptoms of CO poisoning: headaches, drowsiness, and nausea (see table below). In most of the BoatU.S. claims, one or more of these symptoms were present. It is also advisable to inspect the engine and generator for leaks in the exhaust system and to avoid, or try to avoid, the many situations that could bring CO into a boat's cabin. That isn't easy. Besides the station wagon effect, accidents have been traced to wind direction, proximity to a dock or seawall, boats rafted together, an open hatch or port, a canvas cover, or a combination of several causes. It isn't unusual after an accident for an inspector to spend many hours, or even days, trying to ascertain how CO got into a boat's cabin.

Carbon Monoxide Poisoning Symptoms

CO Amount (ppm)	Symptoms
200	Slight headache within 2 to 3 hours.
400	Frontal (migraine-type) headache within 1 to 2 hours.
800	Dizziness, nausea, and convulsions within 45 minutes. Insensible within 2 hours.
1,600	Headache, dizziness, and nausea within 20 minutes. Death within 60 minutes.
3,200	Headache, dizziness, and nausea in 5 to 10 minutes. Death within 30 minutes.
6,400	Headache and dizziness in 1 to 2 minutes. Death in less than 15 minutes.
12,800	Death in less than 3 minutes.

While guarding against the many possible sources of CO is certainly advisable, the most reliable safeguard is a CO detector. As of August 1, 1998, the ABYC began recommending that all boats with enclosed accommodation areas and a gasoline generator or a gasoline inboard propulsion engine have a CO detector installed. (Diesel engines are not included because they are much less likely to

Swim Platforms and the Danger of CO: A Personal Account

FOLLOWING IS A LETTER the BoatU.S. office received:

On Sunday, July 18, my family and I were boating on Table Rock Lake in Branson, Missouri, which is a usual weekend event. My daughter (age 12) and my son (age 3) were swimming off the back platform of my 31-foot Thompson Cruiser, and I had the gasoline generator on to keep the cabin cool. My son was attempting to climb on to the boat when he was overcome by carbon monoxide fumes. He went into a coma-like state and fell back into the water with his eyes rolled back in his head. When I pulled him out of the water, he was not conscious or breathing. My wife managed to revive him with mouth-to-mouth resuscitation. We called 911 while heading back to the marina in a sheer panic, not knowing what had happened. We did not know at that time that it was carbon monoxide poisoning. It took over an hour for the ambulance to get to the marina after my boat had arrived. By that time, my son was coming around, crying and startled from the experience. He was taken to Skaggs Hospital in Branson where blood tests showed that he had a high level of carbon monoxide in his system, as did my daughter (who had started to feel ill with headaches and nausea). My son and daughter recovered fully from this event.

The reason that I am writing you this letter is to let people know the danger of carbon monoxide gas coming from the exhaust under swimming platforms. There was no manufacturer warning anywhere on the back of this boat. We purchased the boat in order to have safe family boating fun. My wife and I feel that the boat manufacturers should be responsible for letting people know that there is a possibility of carbon monoxide poisoning from these exhaust configurations.

—Richard Huebner
Branson, Missouri

Editor's note: Far from being an isolated case, there have been several well-documented cases of swimmers being affected by CO that accumulated under swim platforms. The concentration levels are so high that even a brief exposure can be deadly.

produce deadly levels of CO. Gasoline engines produce 10,000 to 100,000 parts per million [ppm] of carbon monoxide, while diesel engines produce only about 1,000 ppm.) The recommendation that CO detectors be installed on new boats is great news for anyone who will be buying a new boat . . . but what about boats built before August 1998?

Installing a CO Detector

One reason the ABYC may have been slow to recommend the use of CO detectors may be their reputation in the past for emitting unnerving false alarms periodically. Sue Snavely, who works for Fireboy-Xintex, admits that prior to

1992, the older "single point" alarms sounded whenever they detected even the slightest trace of CO. Since a whiff or two of CO is likely to drift into a cabin several times a day, the frequent alarms were an ongoing nuisance, and people frequently responded by turning off the alarms. After 1992, however, manufacturers began making more technically advanced units that use time-weighted averaging to greatly reduce the number of alarms. By averaging readings over a period of a few minutes, these newer alarms will not sound unless they repeatedly detect CO above a certain level. Some of the newer units can even do things like disengage the generator if CO is detected. A proper marine CO detector, incidentally, will be stamped "UL 1524," which means it was tested by Underwriters Laboratories standard 1524.

The ABYC does not say where on the boat to locate a CO detector. The gas, which is about the same weight as oxygen, tends to dissipate evenly in an area and isn't any more likely to be found up near the ceiling or down by the cabin

Another Reason to Install a CO Detector

THREE MEN were spending the night aboard this newly refurbished sportfisherman at the dock. The weather earlier in the day had been a steamy 103°, and the gasoline generator was running to power the air conditioner.

One man had trouble sleeping and left to spend the night in his camper. The next morning he returned to the boat to find one of his friends was dead and the other was near death. Miraculously, the second man,

the boat's owner, eventually recovered.

It took investigators many hours to piece together what had happened. There were no leaking hoses or loose fittings, as there often are in CO cases. Instead, a combination of still air surrounding the boat and a blower that was left operating to cool the engine room had combined to bring the CO aboard through various vents, gaps in doors, etc.

There are many, many ways that CO can find its way into a boat's cabin, but only one way to know for certain that it is there: a CO detector. Because of changes in the ABYC standards, most boats with enclosed accommodation spaces and gasoline propulsion engines or generators built after August 1, 1998, probably have a CO detector. Skippers of boats built before the standard was enacted are strongly advised to have one installed.

What's Wrong with This Picture?

Terri Parrow's boat.

SHORTLY AFTER SHE BOUGHT her 33-foot Egg Harbor, Terri Parrow, vice president of Internet Operations at BoatU.S., took an action photograph of the boat as it went zooming by on the Patuxent River near Solomons Island, Maryland. The photo turned out well, with a blue sky, puffy clouds, and lots of exciting spray. The more she studied the photograph, though, the more it seemed that something was wrong. Then it dawned on her that the ship's ensign—the flag on the stern—was flapping *forward*, toward the two people on the flying bridge. Aren't flags supposed to point aft?

The canvas on the flybridge had just been added, and when the flaps were closed, exhaust from the boat's twin 340 hp gasoline engines was being sucked back into the cabin and onto the flybridge (an example of the station wagon effect). After seeing the photo, Terri made some changes. First, she cruises with the forward canvas flaps and hatch on the foredeck opened slightly to keep fresh air flowing throughout the flybridge and cabin. And she also replaced one of the boat's two CO detectors, which wasn't working. These two simple changes have saved her a lot of potential headaches, or worse, whenever the boat is underway.

sole. As a practical matter, placing an alarm at eye level allows you to easily monitor any meters or warning lights on the unit. Sleeping areas, main saloons, enclosed flybridges, and anywhere else people spend time are candidates for a CO detector. However, do not place an alarm in areas where fresh air might distort the readings, such as near hatches or doors, or in dead-air spaces such as corners.

Take CO Detectors Seriously

While the older alarms were often a nuisance, the improved technology means that when a newer alarm sounds it should be investigated. CO that drifts in and out of a cabin can be dangerous, since the effects of CO are cumulative and can build up gradually in a person's bloodstream over hours or even days before it reaches critical levels. This is true even when the person breathes fresh air periodically; the CO remains in the bloodstream. How quickly the CO builds up is a factor of the concentration of the gas being inhaled (measured in ppm) and the duration of the exposure. The half-life of CO is approximately 5 hours, which means that it takes 5 hours for the level of CO in the blood to drop to half its level after the exposure.

Mirna Lynch, a boatowner in Texas, wrote about a frightening encounter her family had with CO while they were rafted with other boats on a lake in Texas. The first day Mirna had a slight headache, which got worse, until the following day, it became almost unbearable. "With me, [carbon monoxide] was building up, building up, and building up, even though for an hour or two I may have been swimming or in a place where we were breathing fresh air." Other people in the group also began to get severe headaches, and when a baby who had only been aboard for a few hours got listless and nauseated, Mirna realized that something was wrong. (Children and small adults are affected by CO much sooner than larger adults.) Only later, after they had gone to the hospital, did she find out that the headaches and nausea were being caused by CO from the boats' gasoline generators.

There is also some recent research that challenges the traditional thinking that the effects of CO poisoning are transitory. Researchers who studied ninety-six victims for a year after their CO exposure found that over 25% showed evidence of brain damage twelve months after exposure. These long-term CO effects included apathy, memory loss, inattention, and depression.

Winterizing and Spring Fitting Out

IF YOU'RE GOING TO BE SAFE ON THE WATER, there is no better place to start than the boat. Many boats get used hard and, as the saying goes, put away wet. The BoatU.S. claim files have consistently shown that boats that receive minimal attention in the fall and spring are much more likely to give their owners problems out on the water in the summer.

Winterizing

Winterizing a boat isn't much fun. While you're liable to have a lot of volunteers for the spring fitting out, winterizing a boat in the fall is like cleaning up after a party; there are few volunteers and even less effort.

Here's a true story: A man in Minnesota was planning to spend the weekend hunting. As he was heading out the door with his buddies, his wife asked when he was going to winterize his boat. The man put his arm around her and said, "Honey, I think of it as our boat. You do it."

The price of forgetting to close the seacocks over the winter can be high: a sunk boat.

So she drove to the boat, poured kerosene in the bilge, and tossed in a match.

Two points: The wife's winterizing "shortcut" created more problems than it solved; and the couple are no longer married. (For the record, BoatU.S. didn't insure the boat.)

The Minnesota mishap wasn't the first time a boat was damaged by a hasty winterizing effort. Many boats are damaged or even destroyed every year because their systems weren't prepared for cold weather. This isn't something that only happens in deep-freeze states like Minnesota and Maine. Quite the contrary. Of all fifty states, the one that has the most freeze-related claims is balmy California. While winters may be much colder in deep-freeze states, the bitter temperatures are a fact of life and preparations for winter are taken very seriously. But in the more temperate states, like California, Florida, Texas, Louisiana, Alabama, and Georgia, winter tends to be relatively comfortable in most areas with only an occasional cold spell. And if forecasts haven't been taken seriously, the cold weather can do a lot of damage.

Storage Ashore

In some parts of the country, where winter means several months of bitterly cold weather, storing boats ashore is the norm. In warmer climates, however, ice and snow occur less frequently, and the choice between storage ashore and storage in the water is open to discussion.

Storage in the water means you might get a jump on the boating season next spring. On the other hand, boats stored ashore won't sink. If you have a choice, storage ashore is a safer bet. Storage ashore may also be less expensive over the life of a boat, since a hull surrounded by air for several months each winter is probably less likely to develop blisters.

One note of caution: The vast majority of the claims in temperate states involved boats that were being stored ashore. Since water retains heat longer than air, boats surrounded by air are more vulnerable to a sudden freeze than boats surrounded by water. Even a brief cold spell that lasts only a night or two can do considerable damage. *In temperate states, boatowners must winterize engines and freshwater systems, especially when boats are stored ashore.* In deep-freeze states, boats stored ashore must be winterized sooner than boats stored in the water.

Supporting Hulls To say that a boat is better off stored on land is to assume it will be resting on something that provides adequate support. According to one industry expert, three times as many boat hulls are damaged by mishandling ashore than are damaged in the water. Some of the boats onshore are damaged suddenly when they are blown over by windstorms. Many others, however, are damaged slowly because hulls were distorted in storage, creating problems ranging from poor engine alignment to broken stringers and bulkheads.

The most reliable support is provided by custom-made cradles, which are designed specifically to support critical areas of a boat—its engines, bulkheads, and keel. (Don't store your boat on a cradle that was built for a different model boat.) Steel cradles are best, but wood cradles will also do the job if they have been inspected for deteriorated wood and corroded fastenings. Shipping cradles are probably OK, but most require some modification to improve lateral support before they can be used for winter storage.

Despite the advantages, storing cradles in the off-season is often a problem at many crowded boatyards, which instead rely on a combination of screw-type jack stands, blocks, and timbers to support hulls. Most boatyards do a competent job of positioning the supports, but it never hurts to discuss technique with the yard manager before your boat is hauled.

You could also take a cue from commercial vessels, which have their own blocking plans indicating where blocks and jack stands should be placed to provide the best support. Manufacturers may be able to supply you with a plan, or you can work with the yard manager to devise one yourself using a diagram of your boat. Save the plan and give a copy to anyone who hauls your boat in the future.

Jack stands should be perpendicular to the hull so that the boat's weight is directed toward the ground. Misalignment of the stand will force it out as the load is applied. Even if the stand is aligned perfectly, safety chains must be used to prevent stands from slipping out from under the hull.

Jack stands should be placed as far out from the boat as practical to support the boat in high winds, with at least three stands per side for boats over 26 feet and additional supports at overhangs. Plywood must be placed under each base to prevent its sinking into mud, sand, or asphalt. Even when stands rest on clay that seems brick-hard, they can be loosened by heavy spring rains, shift, and spill the boat.

While jack stands must be placed properly to prevent the boat from falling over, most of the boat's weight usually rests on its keel. Some boats have specific requirements for support of the keel, but at least one manufacturer warns *against* putting weight on the keel. If the marina manager isn't familiar with your boat, check your manual or contact the manufacturer.

Keels must be supported by wide timbers or blocks—the wider the better to distribute the load. On powerboats, additional support is usually recommended for inboard engines, fuel tanks, and heavy machinery.

With outboard and outdrive boats, weight should be taken off the transom by lowering the drive units onto a block.

After the boat is blocked, sight along the hull and keel to make sure the jack stands aren't depressing the hull. (You should also check again in about two weeks, after it has settled.) The boat must also be level, or water could pool and cause stains, mildew, and/or gelcoat crazing. Finally, the boat's winter cover should *never* be secured to the jack stands or support blocks. There are several accounts in the claim files of boats that fell over after stiff winds filled the covers and yanked supports from under the boats.

What's Wrong with These Pictures?

1. Here the jack stands are too close to the center of the boat, are not positioned to direct the load down, and are not resting on plywood. The photo was taken after the boat had fallen and been reblocked. According to the surveyor's report, the jack stands were not chained together prior to the fall.

2. Cinder blocks are stacked up, up, up, with pieces of wood between the last block and the boat to prevent scratching. Ask any kid what happens when blocks are stacked too high.

3. This configuration has stacked blocks, too few jack stands, no chains, and no plywood.

4. The boat's cover filled with water, and the added weight drove the keel-support block into the ground. The block is being supported with a tiny piece of plywood

Storage on Racks and Trailers An increasing number of boats are being stored ashore on dry storage racks. These racks are designed to support "typical" boat hulls, but can't always be adjusted to support unusual or atypical designs.

If you have doubts about the support provided by a rack, consult a marine

that is barely as large as the block. And there are too few supports along the chine.

5. No chains, no plywood, no jack stands —no good support. (Anyone missing a telephone pole?)

surveyor or consider storing the boat on a trailer, which has adjustable rollers and pads to support the keel, chine, and engine. The exception is deep-draft sailboats. Trailers are designed to support these boats when the wind is on the bow, and they are rarely wide enough to provide adequate protection for certain boats (typically, racing sailboats) when strong winds are on the beam. To provide additional lateral support, extra jack stands should be used along the hull and the mast unstepped to reduce windage. Centerboard boats will probably be OK on a trailer, especially if they are secured to the trailer's frame and the mast is unstepped.

Storage in the Water

> *They bored a hole below her line*
> *To let the water out,*
> *But more and more with awful roar*
> *The water in did spout.*
> —"A Sailor's Yarn," J. J. Roche

If the boat will be left in the water, protect the through-hulls by closing all seacocks and, if the boat has them, gate valves. Leaving a through-hull unprotected over the winter is like going on an extended vacation and leaving your home's front door wide open. Failure to close through-hulls is a major cause of loss in the BoatU.S. insurance program. In a recent study of forty winter-related claims, seacocks or gate valves left open caused or contributed to the sinking of *seven* of the boats in the sample group. It should be noted that raising and refurbishing a boat that sinks, even at a dock, is an arduous job that can keep the boat in the repair yard for many weeks over the spring and summer.

Whenever a boat is stored in the water over the winter, all through-hulls, with the exception of the ones for cockpit drains, must be closed, or the boat could be on the bottom next spring. And all through-hulls, especially the ones for the cockpit drains, should be double-clamped with stainless steel hose clamps at each end. While not required by ABYC standards, double-clamping is nonetheless critical for cockpit drains in colder climates (and it's a good idea on all other through-hulls, regardless of climate.) The reason being that as water freezes, it expands

Want to have a miserable spring? Pull your boat in the fall, park it on its trailer under a tree in your backyard, and leave it uncovered over the winter. Soon it will fill with leaves, which will block the scuppers so that rainwater won't drain. Water will find its way into places that it shouldn't. The leaves will steep, forming a brownish goo that stains the fiberglass and upholstery. Mildew will soon be everywhere. No matter how hard you scrub next spring, the boat will never look the same.

Spring fitting out will be far less onerous if you store the boat somewhere far away from blowing leaves or, better yet, invest in a winter cover (but make sure it has adequate ventilation).

and consequently will lift a poorly secured hose off a fitting. The hose itself is also important. Lightweight hose and PVC tubing can rupture or crack. Use only a heavily reinforced hose, especially at cockpit drains.

If your boat has through-hulls below the waterline that can't be closed, either because they are mechanically frozen open or broken (typical with gate valves, which is why they are not recommended), store your boat ashore for the winter.

Close seacocks by moving the handle *down* so it is parallel to the hull. Close gate valves by turning the wheel *clockwise*. After closing the seacock or gate valve, remove the hose so that it drains and use an absorbent cloth or turkey baster to eliminate any residual water, which can freeze and crack the nipple. (Taking off the hose also assures you that the valve has closed properly.) Reinstall the hose immediately and secure the two clamps.

It should be noted that through-hulls above the waterline are not required to have seacocks and most don't. That doesn't mean that these through-hulls aren't vulnerable. Ordinary plastic through-hulls deteriorate in sunlight and have been broken when they were shoved underwater by the weight of snow and ice in the cockpit, which then sinks the boat. Plastic through-hulls near the waterline are especially vulnerable; replace them with bronze or Marelon (the latter is the only type of plastic approved for marine use by UL).

Other Through-Hulls Remove any removable knotmeter impellers and depth-sounder transducers on your boat and replace them with locking dummy plugs. If your stuffing box (where the propeller shaft exits the hull) is dripping, tighten the nut until the dripping stops. (Remember to loosen the nut in the spring, so that you don't burn up the packing material.) And while you're crawling around back there, check the rudder stuffing box (or boxes) if your boat has one.

Exhaust Ports It is advisable to plug exhaust ports when a boat is stored in the water because snow piles up on the stern, and exhaust ports get pushed below the surface. Water then gets into the exhaust system and maybe the cylinders. If this happens, the pistons rust, and the engine is ruined. Plugging exhaust ports is certainly less critical when a boat is stored on land, but some skippers feel that even corrosive air can harm cylinders. (Don't forget to remove the plugs next spring.)

Docks and Docklines Nylon lines stretch and absorb shock, which is good, but this stretching works—chafes—the line against chocks and other contact points. Always use chafe guards on lines when you leave your boat unprotected for long periods.

A dockline is usually the culprit when a boat sinks after being caught under

Use chafe protection, and never confuse winter winds with summer breezes. All it takes is one good winter storm to abrade an unprotected dockline—and bash a hole in the hull. This sailboat in North Carolina was badly damaged when a spring line failed in a late-winter storm.

If you leave your boat in the water over the winter, double up on lines and use chafe protection wherever lines could be abraded.

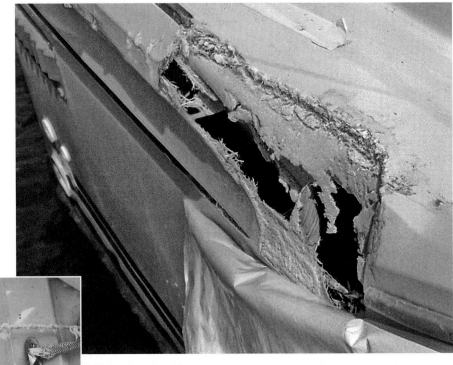

a dock. This can occur anytime, but seems to happen more frequently in the winter, probably because of higher winds and exaggerated tides. Use docklines and springlines to keep the boat well away from the dock.

Batteries You may want to leave a battery aboard to operate a burglar alarm or an automatic bilge pump. These are both useful in the winter, but *don't* expect an automatic pump to overcome bad deck, cabin, or hull leaks—not in the summer or winter. The pump, battery, or float switch can fail, leaving the boat unprotected. A boat with chronic leaking problems should be dry-stored and repaired ASAP.

If you do leave a battery aboard, make sure the cells (wet-cell batteries) are filled with distilled water and fully charged so they don't freeze. Frozen cells will ruin a battery. Clean the terminals with baking soda and rinse with cold water. Coat terminals and cables with petroleum jelly to prevent rust. If you don't need a battery aboard, take it home and do all of the above anyway, preferably sooner rather than later. Store it in a cool dry room.

Winterizing Engines

You might think that winter layup—those interminable months of downtime for your boat each year—would be the mechanical equivalent of a well-deserved "nap" for the boat's engine. After all, its many parts aren't exploding up and down thousands of times a minute. But the reality is somewhat different. An engine is designed to be used, with oil distributed routinely to internal parts, and fresh fuel pumped through the fuel system. Stop the engine, and oil will no longer be coating the metal parts. Fuel gets old and gummy. So any prolonged period of inactivity, especially in a damp environment, has the potential to greatly reduce an engine's useful life. Here's a scary thought: the long, dreary months of winter, which play havoc with your own delicate psyche, could also be wrecking your boat's engine.

Here's a better thought: when an engine (and your psyche) is winterized properly, the annual winter hiatus should have little or no effect.

Winterizing Chores

The following list of winterizing chores includes more than just what needs to be done to get your engine through the freezing weather next year; it's a guide to minimizing the debilitating effects of prolonged inactivity.

Oil and Fuel Systems

Gasoline and Diesel *Step 1: Change the oil.* With any four-cycle inboard engine, gasoline or diesel, the more often you change the oil the better. But changing the oil and oil filter is especially critical when the boat will be laid up for the winter. Any residual acids and moisture left in the crankcase over the winter will pit bearings and other vital engine parts, so it is especially important to change the oil just before laying up the boat. For best results, run the engine for a few minutes, which lowers the oil's viscosity and suspends any grit lying in the pan.

Next, shut off the engine, change the oil, and replace the filter. Rubbing oil on the filter's gasket will help it seat better. (One note of caution: *To assure a tight seal, make certain that the old filter gasket isn't stuck to the engine!*) Restart the engine and run it for about a minute to circulate the fresh oil to internal parts. While it's running, check to make sure the oil filter isn't leaking.

Step 2: Replace the fuel filters. Like the oil filter, a fuel filter should be checked for leaks while the engine is still running.

Gasoline Engines *Step 3: Fog the carburetor* (if your engine has one). Mechanics warn that this is one job that is often overlooked by skippers. With a gasoline engine, spraying light oil (Marvel, CRC, etc.) into the air intake inhibits the formation of rust on internal surfaces as well as the throttle and choke plates.

While the engine is idling (at a fast idle), shut off the gasoline supply and continue spraying oil into the air intake until the engine sputters and quits. What you *don't* want to do is simply dump oil into the intake, as this can create a hydrostatic lock on a piston and buckle the rods.

Note: If you plan on winterizing the cooling system by drawing antifreeze

Heat lamps are hardly a bright idea. In many parts of the country, some skippers try to extend the boating season using various shortcuts to "winterize" their boats. A skipper in Chesapeake Bay, for example, used a heat lamp to protect the engine from freezing and keep the boat cozy for weekend visits. A visit in April seemed routine until the hatch was opened, releasing the stench of a fire-blackened cabin.

The lamp had fallen and ignited flammables that eventually snuffed themselves out, probably for lack of oxygen. The smoke and soot damage was extensive—$50,000! Most of the summer boating season was devoted to repairs and replacing many ruined personal items, instead of fun on the water. Heat lamps should not be left unattended, and light-bulbs of any kind are no substitute for winterizing your boat properly.

through the raw-water intake, you'll have to wait until the antifreeze is circulating before you fog the carburetor.

Step 4: Cover the carburetor. Put a baggie or duct tape over the air intake to keep damp air away from the manifold and valves. This is especially critical when the engine is directly below a hatch. There have been instances in the claim files where scuppers were blocked, and water found its way into the cylinders and exhaust manifold via an unprotected carburetor.

Step 5: Other chores. Clean the flame arrester with kerosene and reinstall. Spray the linkage to the carburetor with coating oil to inhibit rust. Take out the spark plugs, and spray a light coating of oil into the cylinders. Clean the plugs, and replace any that look worn. Remove the coil, then "bump" the engine a few times to spread the oil. Loosening the alternator and water pump belts prolongs their useful lives.

As mentioned above, unused fuel can go "stale," creating a sludge that jams injectors and fuel lines. How long the gasoline resists oxidation depends on temperature stability (wide temperature swings are not good) and the quality of the gasoline. Emptying the tank prior to laying up the boat solves the stale gas problem, but since an empty tank attracts condensation, it increases the chances you'll have water in the tank next spring. Fumes also make an empty tank more vulnerable to explosion in a fire. Filling the tank is a better alternative, but it should be topped off to only 95% full, since gasoline needs room to expand. A half-empty tank invites both moisture and stale gas problems.

Adding a stabilizer puts antioxidants in the gasoline to help prevent degeneration. (The sooner it's added the better.) And using a premium grade (higher octane) gasoline, which has a higher detergent level, also helps increase the gasoline's stability.

Note: If possible, avoid filling the tank with ethanol. This is a gasoline-alcohol mixture, which is prone to separation in the presence of water (and there's some water in just about any boat's tank). When separation occurs, the alcohol will then attract even more water.

Diesel Engines *Step 3: Coat the cylinders.* On small (sailboat) diesels equipped with a hand crank, fogging is done by slowly pouring about 2 ounces of oil into the intake pipe or manifold while *hand-cranking* the engine. DO NOT use the starter to turn the engine while pouring in the oil, or you can cause serious damage.

For larger diesels, it is not critical to coat cylinders; in fact, you should not attempt it unless the manufacturer specifically recommends it. Cylinder walls in a diesel are not as prone to rust as they are in a gasoline engine, and fogging can damage the delicate injectors.

Step 4: Other chores. Tape the openings of the intake and exhaust manifolds to

Winter and absentee owners are a bad mix. There are many, many reasons to visit your boat regularly over the winter. Besides averting potential problems like clogged scuppers or chafed docklines, you can open ports and hatches for awhile to circulate fresh air down below. You can inspect docklines and check the bilge. You might want to arrange with friends to check on each other's boats whenever one of you visits the marina. Remember, more visits mean fewer potential hassles next spring.

keep moisture out of cylinders. Drain and clean all fuel filters. Replace fuel elements and gaskets. Bleed air from the fuel system.

Diesel fuel is even more vulnerable than gasoline when the boat is laid up for several months; the most common headache is the formation of microbes ("bugs"). Idleness encourages condensation, which is what microbes need for spawning. In the spring, the engine may run OK for awhile, but the first time the boat and the fuel tank get bounced around, the microbes will be stirred up, resulting in clogged fuel filters and no fuel to the engine. In a few cases, this scenario has led to damaged injectors. Add a microbiocide to the fuel to inhibit the formation of microbes, preferably each time you fill the tank.

In addition, diesel fuel can break down over the winter; therefore, also add a diesel fuel stabilizer to the fuel when you lay up the boat in the fall. (The two treatments should be poured into the tank separately.) There are also various water absorbing products that you should pour into the tank periodically—follow the manufacturer's instructions.

Transmissions Check the dipstick. If the oil looks milky (indicating water) or dirty, drain and add fresh lubricant.

Outboards *Cooling system.* Start the engine and flush the cooling system with fresh water until it reaches normal operating temperatures. (Various devices are available to adapt a garden hose to the engine intake.) Make sure all gear housing drain holes are open. An alternative to draining the system is to add antifreeze using a gadget that connects the engine intake to a jug of antifreeze.

Fuel system and powerhead. Disconnect the fuel line from the tank, start the motor, and inject fogging fluid (a light lubricating oil) into the carburetor just before the motor stops. This procedure prevents corrosion of the powerhead parts. (Fogging fluid has rust inhibitors that are lacking in regular two-cycle motor oil.) Next, remove the spark plugs; clean and replace any that look worn. Clean the fuel pump filter. Lubricate the carburetor and choke linkage, cam follower, starter spindle, throttle shaft bearings, and gears. Consult the manufacturer's lubricating chart for specifics.

Lower unit. This is a job best done on land. With the bow of the boat slightly up, lower the outdrive unit as far as possible. Drain the gear case and add fresh lubricant (from the lower drain hole to eliminate air pockets). When you loosen the drain plug, watch to see if water or oil comes out first; water or metallic shavings indicate a broken seal. If you're not sure, have a mechanic pressure-test the unit.

Outdrives are expensive and have become a frequent target for thieves. Even if you keep your boat in your driveway, consider taking the outdrive off and storing it in your garage or basement for the winter.

Props Winter is the best time to have dinged and/or pitted props refurbished. A difference in pitch of only ½ to ¾ inch can affect performance, cause vibration, and eventually lead to engine problems.

Cooling Systems

Gasoline and Diesel Ensuring the longevity of the cooling system (and, hence, the engine) involves more than just making sure the water doesn't freeze, although this is obviously critical. Winterizing chores are predicated on the type of cooling system. Some engines only have raw-water cooling systems, whereas others have both raw-water and freshwater systems. With the latter, the manifolds and risers are raw-water cooled, while the block and head are fresh-water cooled.

Step 1: Winterizing the freshwater cooling system. If your engine has a freshwater cooling system, check the antifreeze with a hydrometer. (Follow any manufacturer's recommendations for a specific type of antifreeze.) If you top off the system (you shouldn't have to do this very often), use a premixed solution of water and antifreeze. Many skippers simply add antifreeze, and over time this increases the percentage of antifreeze in the system. Using a solution that is more than 70% antifreeze can leave a residue that will damage your engine. A 50-50 solution works best.

Antifreeze has rust inhibitors, which lose effectiveness over time. Even though the antifreeze itself will still prevent freezing, it's a good idea to change the antifreeze-water solution every two years to help prevent rust buildup. Any system will also benefit from a periodic squirt of rust inhibitor.

Step 2: Winterizing the raw-water system. Open the petcocks and drain the system to make sure the flow of water is not being restricted. According to the BoatU.S. claim files, one of the most common ways engines are damaged over the winter is from muck—salt, silt, rust, seaweed, soap etc.—hardening and clogging the raw-water cooling system. If the system fails to drain when the petcocks are opened (a weak dribble is *not* sufficient), you can use a garden hose, under pressure, to blast the muck out. If that fails, try using a coat hanger. Either way, muck must be loosened and flushed out or the engine will be ruined, if not during a hard freeze over the winter then in summer when the flow of cooling water is severely restricted. Don't forget to drain the seacock body and the water-lift muffler (if installed). This is also a good time to replace zinc anodes, if any, that are more than 50% wasted away (check your manual for locations).

And don't forget to drain the sea strainer! This is located in the engine's raw-water intake line, where it filters out debris before it gets to the engine. Like the engine, the sea strainer must be drained or residual water could freeze and rupture the watertight seal.

A 40-foot sailboat that sank in Rhode Island is a typical example. The bronze sea strainer wasn't drained, and it bent in a freeze. The owner had not only failed to drain the strainer when he winterized the boat, but he had also left the seacock open. The boat sank as soon as the ice in the strainer thawed. The BoatU.S. insurance files have other claims of boats that sank after seacocks were opened in the spring.

For both gasoline and diesel engines, adding antifreeze to inhibit rust can protect the cooling system further. Before flushing a system with antifreeze, close the petcocks and run the engine at fast idle until it reaches its normal operating temperature, which will open the thermostat so that antifreeze can reach the manifold.

The next step, especially if a boat is used in salt water, is to flush the system with fresh water to get rid of salt and other deposits. With the engine still running, close the seacock at the raw-water intake and place the intake hose in a 5-gallon bucket filled with fresh water. As the bucket is emptied, pour in the nontoxic antifreeze and keep the engine running until the solution flows freely from the exhaust.

Note: Cold water or antifreeze may prevent the engine from reaching its normal operating temperature, which may prevent the thermostat from opening. If this happens, you'll have to remove the thermostat (check your manual for its location) to be sure that antifreeze reaches all areas of the cooling system.

Water Pumps A healthy impeller is critical to the flow of water through the cooling system. Without the flow of cooling water, the engine can suddenly burn up underway. The failure may initially be attributed to a mysterious plastic bag in the intake strainer, but the culprit is typically a worn out, crumbled impeller.

At the very least, remove the impeller to prevent its taking a set over the winter (store it on the key ring with your boat's ignition key so you won't forget to install it in the spring). Don't take chances; if the impeller looks worn, replace it. Manufacturers typically recommend impellers be replaced every two years. To be safe, some mechanics suggest installing a new impeller every year, regardless of the apparent condition of the old impeller.

Air Conditioners There are two ways to winterize an air conditioner. With the first, you drain the system, including the raw-water pump and strainer. Or you can also close the intake seacock, place the intake hose in a bucket of nontoxic antifreeze, and run the motor until the antifreeze is running from the exhaust. When the system has been winterized, seal the motor air inlets with plastic and tape to protect the unit from moist air.

Other Boat Systems Down Below

Valuables and Perishables Most marinas are like floating ghost towns over the winter, with little to deter prowlers. Electronics and other valuables that can be dismounted should be taken home for safekeeping. If you have an EPIRB, make sure it won't be activated accidentally.

Besides electronics, remove all flammables—spare cooking fuels, paints, thinners, and varnish—and store them ashore, preferably in a toolshed away from the house. These are all fire hazards. Never store portable propane canisters below on a boat, even during the season, as the canisters can rust and leak. Leave at least one fully charged fire extinguisher in clear sight.

Take home all foodstuffs, including canned and bottled goods. Prop up bunk cushions, or better yet, take them home. Open various locker doors, hatches, icebox lids, etc., to circulate air and inhibit mildew.

Potable Freshwater Systems Winterize any freshwater system, automatic or manual, by using nontoxic antifreeze in the tank and throughout the system. Merely draining the system can leave residual water that can burst pipes and possibly destroy the pump.

Nontoxic antifreeze is available at marine chandleries, or—the old salt's trick—you can use cheap vodka as a readily available substitute. Although the latter works well and is safe, the alcohol may deteriorate hoses. NEVER use engine antifreeze (ethylene glycol) in a freshwater system—it is very toxic and cannot be reliably purged from the system in the spring.

To winterize the freshwater system, shut off the dockside freshwater hookup (if you have one) onshore and drain and stow the hose. Next, go below and open all water outlet spigots to drain the onboard freshwater tank(s). When water sputters from the outlets, close them and pour 2 or 3 gallons of nontoxic antifreeze (more if you have a hot-water heater) into the tank. Next, open the outlets farthest from the tank and run until the antifreeze flows out. (Do this with both the hot- and cold-water outlets.) Close the outlets and work backward toward the tank, repeating the procedure at each outlet. Finally, pour antifreeze into the sink drains and close the seacocks.

Hot-Water Heaters Water heaters are usually emptied as the water system is drained. See manufacturer's literature for specific instructions.

Heads *Heads without holding tanks:* Pour disinfectant into the bowl, and pump throughout the system. Close the intake seacock, disconnect the hose, and put it in a bucket of nontoxic antifreeze. Pump the antifreeze through the head, reconnect the hose, and close the remaining seacock.

Note: Manufacturers of some heads, such as the Raritan PH II, advise against using nontoxic antifreeze, at it may soften gaskets. If you use toxic antifreeze, do not pump it overboard.

Heads with holding tanks: Empty the holding tank, and then pump first disinfectant and then antifreeze through the bowl and into the tank (and through the Y-valve if you have one). Close all seacocks.

Marine sanitation devices: Consult manufacturer's instructions.

Portable Electric Heaters A boat that has been properly winterized doesn't need a portable electric heater to keep it warm and snug over the winter. Boats aren't puppies. Closing seacocks and winterizing the various systems guarantee the boat's security far better than a portable electric heater, which, to the contrary, is a bona-fide fire hazard on a boat.

Another consideration is that any heater, no matter how "safe," will only function when it's supplied with electricity. A skipper in Maryland used a heater in the engine room to keep it warm during a predicted cold spell until he got more time to winterize the boat properly. During the night the electricity went off long enough for the water to freeze and bend the engine's bronze sea strainer. The boat sank.

Other Boat Systems Above Deck

Boat Covers If your boat could talk, it would ask—perhaps plead—for a winter storage cover. Winter covers, typically canvas or synthetic, are a terrific benefit to your boat's gelcoat and general well-being. Canvas covers tend to last longer but are also more expensive than their synthetic counterparts.

With any cover, use a frame, either wood or aluminum, so air can circulate and thus prevent pooling on the cover. Merely draping an old tarp over a cabin may do more harm than good.

Some boatyards use shrink-wrapping, a technique borrowed from grocery and department store packagers, to keep boats dry over the winter. With shrink-wrapping, heat is applied to a thin plastic so it fits snugly over a plastic frame. At the end of the season the entire cover, including the frame, is disposed of. While shrink-wrapping is very effective at keeping moisture out, it also traps any moisture inside and creates horrendous mildew problems if vents aren't used. Another problem with unvented covers is that two-part polyurethane paints on cabins and decks can peel or bubble. (This has also happened with blue polyethylene tarps when they were resting directly against a painted surface.) Use vents along the entire length of the cover. Inserting a series of foam pads between the hull and cover also allows condensation to escape.

Finally, some skippers mistakenly believe that biminis, which shield the crew from glaring sun, will also protect the boat from freezing rain and snow. Quite the contrary; expensive biminis tend to rip apart or degrade prematurely

Whether a boat is stored ashore or in the water, mildew is always a potential headache whenever a boat is left unattended for long periods. A cover can help, but only if it's supported properly to allow air to circulate beneath. Aside from mildew, however, there is another potential problem with covers that are not well ventilated, one that can be much more expensive to remedy: a beautiful, two-part paint job can be marred with tiny, peeling bubbles. The bubbles usually occur on boats that are shrink-wrapped, but it has also happened on boats that had poorly supported plastic covers. The bubbles occurred wherever the sagging cover rested against the damp, painted deck.

The technical service manager at Awlgrip, a manufacturer of two-part polyurethane paints, acknowledged the problem and recommended that only well-ventilated covers be used when a boat has been painted with one of Awlgrip's products.

when used as a winter cover while also doing absolutely nothing to protect the boat. Stow biminis below, or better yet, take them home to be cleaned and stored over the winter.

To clean a bimini, soak it for approximately 20 minutes in a gallon of lukewarm (not hot) water with a solution of ½ cup of *nonchlorine* bleach and ¼ cup mild laundry soap. After it has soaked, rinse it thoroughly in cold water to remove all of the soap. Residual soap can cause leaks. Note, however, that even with proper rinsing the fabric could lose some of its ability to repel water. Should this happen, you can make it waterproof again by using one of the commercially available air-dry water repellents.

Clear vinyl windows on spray dodgers also require some attention. The vinyl is protected by a plasticizer, which leaches out over time and causes the window to become hazy and brittle. Ultraviolet rays, flexing, cold, and salt spray all hasten the aging process. To prolong the window's life, rinse it frequently with fresh water and occasionally wash it with a mild laundry soap. If possible, keep it shaded in the summer and always store it indoors over the winter. If you do any restitching, use only polyester thread, which is stronger and more resistant to UV deterioration.

Masts, Rigging, and Sails In a perfect world, a sailboat's mast would be unstepped and stored in a shed over the winter with plenty of support along its entire length. Unstepping the mast reduces windage, which is especially helpful when a boat is stored on land. Unstepping also eliminates rig vibration, which is one source of cracked fittings, especially lower fittings, as vibration tends to travel downward. Cracked fittings are often the culprit when boats are dismasted. If you unstep the mast, be sure to check the fittings for tiny cracks and signs of corrosion that could spell trouble next season.

If the mast is to be left up, there is no need to slacken the standing rigging, since the aluminum mast will contract more in cold weather than the steel stays and shrouds. (Wood masts, on the other hand, won't contract, and you will have to relax the rig.) Be sure to tie off the halyards. Besides driving liveaboards crazy, slapping halyards scar the mast.

Stow sails below or take them home. Fold or roll them neatly so they'll last longer. You can also add to a sail's longevity by taking them to a sailmaker for a bath. You can clean smaller sails in your bathtub using one of the commercially available sail cleaners.

Finally, even if your boat is stored ashore, secure the wheel or tiller to keep the rudder from swinging all winter.

Outriggers If your boat has outriggers, they should be taken off and stored inside. If that isn't possible, leave them on the boat but vertical, to reduce the chances they will be bent by ice and wind.

BoatU.S. has received several insurance claims over the years for outriggers that were bent by a combination of ice and wind. They typically had been stored at a 45° angle and were facing the wind. If your boat has outriggers, the best defense against damage from winter ice and wind is to disassemble them for storage ashore until spring. However, some models are easier to disassemble than others, so if disassembly isn't practical, leave poles vertical. A vertical pole does a better job of shedding ice, which reduces weight on the ends and makes it less likely that it will be bent.

A Few Last Details

If you store your boat on a trailer, don't forget that trailers, like boats, need some attention in the fall so they'll still be rolling in the spring. Hubs that have been immersed in water during the season must be cleaned thoroughly with kerosene and then butyl alcohol before being repacked with grease. Sand, prime, and repaint rusted areas on the frame. Inspect the tires, especially the sidewalls, which tend to crack and wear out before the treads. Finally, remove the wheels and add support at the blocks under the frame rails, which will prolong the life of the tires, minimize sagging on the springs, and discourage theft.

Before heading home, make sure the marina manager has an extra companionway key (no need to leave an ignition key) labeled with your boat's name, your address, and your phone number so he or she can contact you in an emergency. Before leaving, double-check all of the locks and give the boat a reassuring pat on the gunwale.

Don't plan on staying away too long. Visit your boat every few weeks to make sure lines are secure, drains haven't become clogged, bilges are dry, etc. Checking the boat is especially important after heavy storms or extended cold spells. If you have friends with boats at the marina, arrange to check each other's boats whenever possible.

Winterizing Worksheet

Winterizing your boat requires planning and some effort on your part. Plan ahead. The worksheet below has two purposes: to jog your memory when you're gathering everything together—fogging fluid, antifreeze, etc.—before winterizing; and to reassure yourself (if after the job is completed, doubts arise) that you

Winterizing Contracts: When in Doubt, Spell It Out

A WORD OR TWO ABOUT HIRING SOMEONE else to do the work is in order here. A casual agreement to take care of the boat, or worse, an assumption that a marina or boatyard automatically protects boats from an unexpected freeze can have chilling results.

Here's one example. A skipper in Minnesota was seriously ill, so he called his boatyard and casually asked if they could winterize his houseboat. No problem! The boat was hauled and blocked. The engine's cooling system was drained and nontoxic antifreeze was flushed throughout the freshwater system. Unfortunately, an expensive winter cover that had been stored below was left untouched in a locker and the boat was left to endure the harsh Minnesota winter au naturel.

By the following spring the boat was a mess. Snowfall after snowfall had piled on its decks, and water had trickled into the cabin at the corners, causing serious structural damage. The engine hatches were sagging. The cabin's wood paneling was covered with mildew, and the cabin sides were cracked.

Every fall, the term "winterize" is tossed about loosely by owners who think it has some universal meaning that is instantly comprehended by marina operators. Winterize what? Maritime attorneys make a good living helping boatowners and marinas resolve disputes over what work was or wasn't supposed to have been done on boats and engines. Usually these legal disputes involve the cost of repairs, but when the details of winterizing aren't spelled out, the disputes typically involve much bigger costs, like raising the boat or replacing the engines.

If you're not going to winterize your boat yourself, select a repair facility that is competent to do the job, and spell out in writing exactly what they are supposed to do. It would be helpful if all marinas insisted on written contracts, but some don't; therefore, it may be up to you to take the initiative. Don't assume anything. Telling someone to winterize the engines and freshwater system doesn't mean they'll also close the seacocks and winterize the head. And whenever you will be unable to attend to the boat for a long period of time, a separate arrangement must be made (in writing!) with a marina or service contractor to look after things.

Another mistake boatowners make is to assume that the marina will routinely inspect your docklines and bilge over the winter. If you won't be able to visit your boat regularly, look at your marina contract to see if routine inspections are included. (They probably aren't.) Marinas may offer these inspections at an extra cost.

Whatever you want done, spell it out in writing. The purpose is not to give yourself clout in court later but to make sure that you and your marina are on the same wavelength; it's one area where a misunderstanding could spell disaster.

did everything that should have been done. *Tip: Give yourself enough time to do the job properly.*

Included here is a sample winterizing worksheet. Following that are some other items and chores you should keep on your list.

Winterizing Worksheet

Winterizing your boat requires planning and some effort on your part. Plan ahead. The page below has two purposes: It will jog your memory when you're gathering everything together—fogging fluid, antifreeze, etc.—before winterizing. And it can also be used long after the job is completed, should doubts arise, to reassure yourself that everything that should have been done was done. *Tip: Give yourself enough time to do the job properly.*

Boat's Name: _____

Your Name: _____

Marina Telephone: _____

List All Equipment Needed to Lay-up Boat

Product	Quantity
Non-toxic Antifreeze	_____
Engine Antifreeze	_____
Crankcase Oil	_____
Fogging Fluid	_____
Plugs for Exhaust Ports	_____
Fuel Additives	_____
Extra Lines	_____
Chafe Guards	_____
Storage Cover/Supports	_____
Tools (Including an Oil Drain Pump and a Container)	_____

Have Fuel Tanks Been Topped Off? ☐

****

Boats Stored Ashore

Is boat level to prevent damage from pooling water? ☐

Is the boat adequately supported at bulkheads, engines, and keel? ☐

If boat is on jack stands, are the stands chained together beneath with plywood beneath the base? ☐

Equipment Stored Ashore

Equipment	Storage Location		Equipment	Storage Location
Electronics	_____		Bimini	_____
Dinghy	_____		Battery	_____
Outboard/Fuel	_____		Other	_____
Sails	_____		Other	_____
Galley Fuel	_____		Other	_____
Ship's Papers	_____		Other	_____

Boats Stored in the Water

Indicate Location and Whether Thru-Hull Is Closed and Double-Clamped

Thru-Hull _____ Location
Closed ☐
Double-Clamped ☐

Thru-Hull _____ Location
Closed ☐
Double-Clamped ☐

Thru-Hull _____ Location
Closed ☐
Double-Clamped ☐

Thru-Hull _____ Location
Closed ☐
Double-Clamped ☐

Thru-Hull _____ Location
Closed ☐
Double-Clamped ☐

Thru-Hull _____ Location
Closed ☐
Double-Clamped ☐

Thru-Hull _____ Location
Closed ☐
Double-Clamped ☐

Knotmeter Impeller
Dummy Plug Inserted ☐

Thru-Hull _____ Location
Closed ☐
Double-Clamped ☐

Rudder and Stuffing Box Tightened ☐

Equipment needed to winterize boat   Quantity

[ ] oil filter   [   ]
[ ] engine replacement parts (fuel elements
     and gaskets)   [   ]
[ ] spark plugs   [   ]
[ ] fuel filter   [   ]
[ ] baggie and duct tape (carburetor)   [   ]
[ ] transmission lubricant   [   ]
[ ] distilled water, baking soda, and petroleum
     jelly (battery)   [   ]
[ ] knotmeter impeller, and depth-sounder
     transducer   [   ]
[ ] fuel additives
[ ] premium grade gasoline (have fuel tanks
     been topped off?)   [   ]
[ ] zinc anodes   [   ]
[ ] 5-gallon bucket   [   ]
[ ] garden hose   [   ]
[ ] disinfectants   [   ]

Equipment stored ashore   Location

[ ] valuables   [   ]
[ ] flammables (galley fuel, paints, thinners)   [   ]
[ ] foodstuffs   [   ]
[ ] bunk cushions   [   ]

For boats stored in the water:

[ ] Is the cockpit drain open?
[ ] Are plastic through-hulls broken or deteriorated?
[ ] Depth-sounder transducer: dummy plug inserted?
[ ] Exhaust ports: dummy plug inserted?
[ ] Chafe guards in place?
[ ] Battery, if left aboard:
     [ ] Cells filled with distilled water?
     [ ] Fully charged?
     [ ] Terminals cleaned and coated?
[ ] Gasoline engines:
     [ ] Change oil
     [ ] Replace fuel filters
     [ ] Fog the carburetor
     [ ] Cover the carburetor

For boats stored in the water (cont.):

[ ] Check flame arrestor
[ ] Coat carburetor linkage
[ ] Check spark plugs; clean or replace
[ ] Coat cylinders
[ ] Loosen alternator and water pump belts
[ ] Top off fuel tank; add stabilizer

[ ] Diesel engines:

[ ] Change oil
[ ] Replace fuel filters
[ ] Coat the cylinders (optional)
[ ] Tape openings intake and exhaust manifolds
[ ] Replace fuel elements and gaskets
[ ] Bleed air from fuel system
[ ] Add microbiocide and diesel fuel stabilizer

[ ] Transmission: check oil

[ ] Outboards:

[ ] Cooling system
[ ] Fuel system and powerhead
[ ] Lower unit

[ ] Cooling systems

[ ] Freshwater cooling system tasks
[ ] Raw-water cooling system tasks

[ ] Water pumps: remove impeller; place on ignition key chain

[ ] Air conditioner

[ ] Boat systems below:

[ ] Valuables/perishables
[ ] Potable freshwater systems
[ ] Hot-water heater
[ ] Heads
[ ] Portable electric heaters

[ ] Boat systems above deck:

[ ] Boat cover in place
[ ] Bimini removed

[ ] Masts, rigging, and sails

[ ] Mast
[ ] Sails stowed or removed
[ ] Wheel or tiller secured

For boats stored ashore:

[ ] Blocking plan needed?

[　] For boats on jack stands:
    [　] Are jack stands placed to provide the best support for your boat?
    [　] Do you have the correct number of jack stands for the size of your boat?
    [　] Are jack stands perpendicular to the hull?
[　] For powerboats: Are the inboard engines, fuel tanks, and heavy machinery supported properly?
[　] For outboard and outdrive boats: Is the transom positioned correctly?
[　] Trailers:
    [　] Clean and grease hubs
    [　] Sand, prime, and repaint frame
    [　] Inspect tires
    [　] Remove wheels and support frame with blocks

Spring Fitting-Out Checklist

If your boat was tended to properly in the fall, you should have a minimal amount of work to do in the spring (especially if your boat was covered). Aside from the usual sprucing up chores, however, there are the somewhat more mundane inspections that must be looked after every spring to minimize hassles and ensure the boat will be safe during the upcoming season. Hope springs eternal in the spring; take care of the details now so the boat won't spring any unpleasant surprises later in the summer.

Out of the Water

- Inspect and, if it wasn't done last winter, lubricate seacocks. Inspect and replace as necessary the hoses and hose clamps (preferably two) at each fitting below or near the waterline. This is also the best time to replace gate valves, if any, with seacocks. Gate valves are prone to failure and are not as reliable as seacocks. You also can't just glance at a gate valve to see if it has been closed.

- Replace deteriorated anodes (zinc, aluminum, or magnesium) if not done in the fall. They disintegrate and give a good indication of what would happen to vital underwater machinery if the anodes were not there. Use zinc or aluminum anodes in salt and brackish water. (Aluminum protects as well as zinc but lasts longer than zinc.) Magnesium works best in fresh water.

  Note: If an anode has vanished or has been reduced to powder, check the other metal surfaces, especially underwater, to make sure they did not also suffer from electrolysis. Anodes that

A corroded hose clamp.

disappear after less than one season indicate a problem with the boat's bonding and/or electrical system. (Look first for chafed wires or battery cables, which also have the potential to cause a fire.)

- Inspect prop(s) for dings, pitting, and distortion (out of pitch) that can create excessive vibration and can loosen everything from screws and bulkheads to dental fillings. Make sure cotter pins are secure. Grip the prop and try moving the shaft. Looseness usually indicates the cutlass bearing needs to be replaced. Incidentally, "tired" props, which are dinged, pitted, and/or out of pitch, can be rejuvenated by a machine shop.

- Check the rudderstock to make sure it hasn't been bent. Also try moving the rudder. Any rudder looseness must be corrected (the remedy depends on the type of installation you have).

- Inspect the hull for blisters, distortion, and stress cracks. Dry, sand, and fill any small "pinhead" blisters you find. Large blisters may require professional attention. Distortion and/or stress cracks are two other hull problems that should be addressed by a marine surveyor or repairer.

- Make sure the engine intake sea strainer is free of corrosion and properly

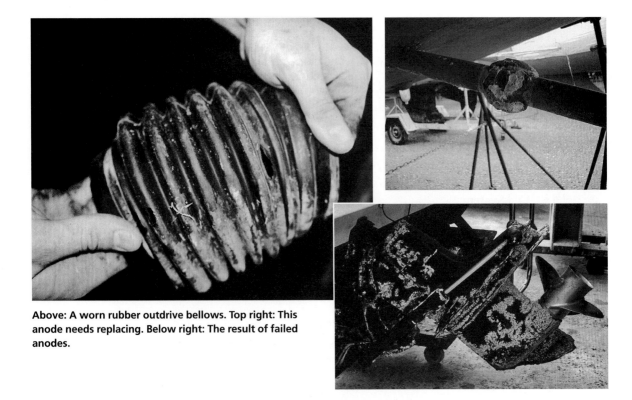

Above: A worn rubber outdrive bellows. Top right: This anode needs replacing. Below right: The result of failed anodes.

secured. Strainers that were not drained properly in the fall could have been bent by ice over the winter. Replace any questionable parts.

Outdrives and Outboards

- Inspect rubber outdrive bellows for cracked, dried, and/or deteriorated spots (look especially in the folds). Replace any bellows that is suspect.

- Replace deteriorated outdrive anodes.

- Check power steering and power trim oil levels. Follow manufacturer's maintenance schedule or use factory-authorized mechanic.

Control Cables

- Inspect outer jacket. Cracks or swelling indicate corrosion and mean that the cable must be replaced. (*Note:* Don't try to remedy the problem by squirting lubricant into the cracks or wrapping duct tape around the outer jacket; most lubricants are incompatible and will only make things worse.) To check the condition of the cable itself, hold the outer jacket in your hands and move it back and forth. A brittle, "crunchy" sound indicates rust. Don't even think about trying to get one more season out of the cable; sudden failures have caused serious accidents.

In the Water

- Check the engine shaft and rudder stuffing boxes for steady leaks and looseness. Some weeping or even an occasional drip should be evident at the engine shaft stuffing box (not the rudder). If you cannot stop the leaking by tightening the nut, repack the gland. (Caution: Overtightening the nut prevents leaking underway, which will burn out the packing material.)

- Use a hose to check for deck leaks at ports and hatches. Renew caulk or gaskets as necessary. Don't rely on a bilge pump to overcome multiple deck leaks.

Engines and Fuel Systems

- Inspect fuel lines, including fill and vent hoses, for indications of softness, brittleness, or cracking. Replace any that are suspect using Coast Guard–approved J1527 hose. Check all joints for leaks (or use your finger and look for stains under or around the fitting) and make sure all lines are well supported with smooth (no rough edges), noncombustible clips or straps.

- Inspect all of the other components in the fuel system—fuel tanks, fuel pumps, filters—for leaks. You can use a dry rag at connections or trust your nose. Check that clamps are snug and free of heavy rust.

- Replace fuel filters.

For want of a pin, a boat was lost (well, almost). This 19-foot runabout was passing under a bridge on Alafia River in Florida when it suddenly spun out of control and smacked into a wood abutment. Fortunately, the boat had slowed to pass under the bridge and nobody was hurt. The cause of the accident was soon traced to the steering cable, which had slipped off the out-drive because a cotter pin hadn't been properly secured.

Cotter pins (inset) need to be flared out, way out, so they'll stay in place. They also need to be free of rust. Every spring, your fitting-out chores should include an hour or so of poking around the boat looking for potential buga-boos—excessive wear and tear, rust, leaks, even missing or loose cotter pins. It's surprising how even the least mechanically inclined skippers can recognize—and avoid—potential problems if they take time to look.

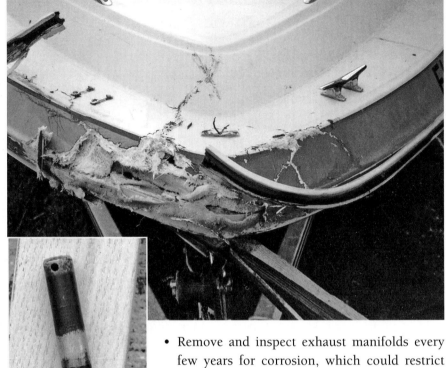

- Remove and inspect exhaust manifolds every few years for corrosion, which could restrict water flow.

- Clean and tighten electrical connections, especially both ends of the battery cables. Loose connections can arc, which will create an enormous amount of heat and is a fire hazard. Studs, nuts, and washers should be copper—not aluminum or steel. Dissimilar metals have the potential to cause galvanic corrosion. Problems ranging from a weak contact to arcing could be the result of a poor choice of washers. Use a wire brush to clean battery terminals; if you have wet-cell batteries, fill the cells with distilled water.

- Be sure that cooling hoses and fittings fit snugly and are double-clamped. Replace hoses that are showing signs of old age — rot, stiffness, bulges, leaks, and/or cracking.

A burst fuel hose.

A corroded (and leaking) fuel pan.

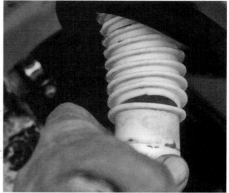

A rusted exhaust manifold.

- Inspect the muffler and exhaust system. Aside from carbon monoxide (and noise), a leaking muffler can sink the boat.

- Inspect bilge blower hose for leaks.

A cracked cooling hose.

Sailboat Rigging

- Inspect fittings, especially swage fittings, for cracks and rust. Also inspect wire halyards and running backstays for "fishhooks" and rust, which snag fingers and are an indication that the standing rigging is nearing the end of its useful life. Make sure spreaders bisect the shrouds at equal angles.

A cracked swage fitting.

A corroded muffler.

This spring you may find it necessary to add a new cleat or maybe replace a worn fitting. If you do your boating on salt water or even brackish water, here's a word of warning: don't use Zamac fittings.

Zamac, a zinc alloy, corrodes quickly around salt water, especially when the fitting is secured with a "more noble" fastener. Zinc is at the bottom of the galvanic scale, making it the least noble metal. Therefore, any fastener you use will be more noble than zinc, causing the zinc to corrode first. That's the reason zinc is used for sacrificial anodes on shafts, outdrives, heat exchangers, etc.

The fitting shown here had cracked and was replaced without incident. In years past, however, there have been claims for people who were seriously injured when a Zamac fitting on the railing broke and someone tumbled overboard. Zamac has also been used to make cleats and even fuel fills, with predictably grim results when the boat was in salt water.

- Remove tape on turnbuckles and lubricate threads (preferably with Teflon). Give the turnbuckle a twist or two to help prevent mechanical freezing. Replace with fresh tape.

- Recaulk chainplates mounted through the deck as necessary, preferably every two or three years. Leaks can cause problems, ranging from delaminated cores to rotted bulkheads. Be sure to remove ALL the old caulking.

- Aluminum is an "active" metal that is way down the galvanic scale. Since fittings on masts tend to be made of more cathodic metals like stainless steel, masts will occasionally develop galvanic corrosion problems. Look for bubbles around a fitting; they are an indication that the fitting needs to be rebedded. On an unpainted mast, look for white powder (oxidized aluminum) and pockmarks around fittings. Some powder is normal on an aluminum mast and as such is usually insignificant. But heavy concentrations of powder, bubbles, and/or pockmarks, especially deep pockmarks, indicate a serious problem. Be sure to check for corrosion at the mast step, which may be made of stainless steel and often sits in salt water.

A Few Other Chores

- Refill or replace fire extinguishers as necessary. Place extinguishers where they will be clearly visible.

- Examine stoves and remote tanks for loose fittings and leaking hoses.

- Clean the bilge. Inspect the bilge pump and float switch to make sure they are working properly.

- Replace outdated flares. Keep old flares aboard as spares.

Trailers

- Inspect tire treads and sidewalls. Cracks on sidewalls or a lack of tread indicates the tire needs replacing. Use a gauge to check pressure, and don't forget to check the trailer's spare tire.

- Sand and paint badly rusted areas.

A rotted bulkhead.

Oxidized aluminum.

A badly rusted trailer.

- Inspect bearings. Repack as necessary.

- Test tail and backup lights. Replace any burned-out bulbs and chafed wires. Clean corroded terminals. Make sure the white ground wire is securely attached to the trailer's frame.

- Test the winch, manual or electric, to make sure it is working properly.

- Don't forget the drain plug! This happens more often than you might think. One trick is to keep the plug attached to the ignition key or throttle.

At the risk of stating the obvious, don't launch into the boating season next spring without inserting your boat's drain plug. It happens more often than you might think. As a reminder, try attaching the plug to your boat keys or the throttle.

A Few Final Words

Well, that's it. Spring commissioning is complete and your boat is ready to go. The preceding chapters have included a lot of descriptions of what you can expect out on the water, some of which are downright scary. Boats have bashed into each other, caught fire, exploded, flipped over, sunk, and been swallowed by waves. If boating is supposed to be fun, then what should you take away from a book—let's be honest here—that instills fear?

The answer, I think, has to do with the role of fear in everything we do. The late Monk Farnham, a boating writer and former member of the BoatU.S. National Advisory council, once held the record as the oldest man to sail single-handed across the Atlantic. It would be easy to describe him as fearless, but he wasn't. Fear, Monk used to say, made him a better boatman. But while Monk may have been afraid or at least a little apprehensive around boats, he also enjoyed being on the water as much as anyone I've ever met. People tend to fear things—in this case, potential boating accidents—in proportion to their ignorance of them. That's why Monk got so much joy out of boating while still being careful to retain at least some "fear"; fear gives you the edge you need to remain alert, even in your home waters.

I hope this book has shed some light on why accidents happen on boats and how they can be avoided. I hope this book has made you a better boatman.

Resources [

Further Reading

Bruce, Peter. *Adlard Coles' Heavy Weather Sailing.* 30th anniv. ed. Camden, Maine: International Marine; London: Adlard Coles, 1999.

Burch, David. *Radar for Mariners.* Camden, Maine: International Marine, 2005.

Calder, Nigel. *Boatowner's Mechanical and Electrical Manual: How to Maintain, Repair, and Improve Your Boat's Essential Systems.* 3rd ed. Camden, Maine: International Marine, 2005.

Calder, Nigel. *How to Read a Nautical Chart: A Complete Guide to the Symbols, Abbreviations, and Data Displayed on Nautical Charts.* Camden, Maine: International Marine, 2003.

Eldridge Tide and Pilot Book. Boston: Robert White.

Gerr, Dave. *The Elements of Boat Strength: For Builders, Designers, and Owners.* Camden, Maine: International Marine, 2000.

———. *The Nature of Boats: Insights, and Esoterica for the Nautically Obsessed.* Camden, Maine: International Marine, 1992, 1995.

Hinz, Earl R. *The Complete Book of Anchoring and Mooring.* 2nd rev. ed. Centreville, Maryland: Cornell Maritime Press, 2001.

———. *Heavy Weather Tactics Using Sea Anchors and Drogues.* Arcata, California: Paradise Cay, 2000.

Kotsch, William J. *Weather for the Mariner.* 3rd ed. Annapolis, Maryland: Naval Institute Press, 1983.

Marchaj, C. A. *Seaworthiness: The Forgotten Factor.* Rev. ed. London: Adlard Coles, 1996; St. Michaels, Maryland: Tiller, 1996.

Maloney, Elbert S. *Chapman Piloting: Seamanship and Small Boat Handling.* 64th ed. New York: Hearst Books, 2003.

Mustin, Henry C. *Surveying Fiberglass Sailboats: A Step-by-Step Guide for Buyers and Owners.* Camden, Maine: International Marine, 1994.

Reed's Nautical Almanac. Boston: Thomas Reed Publications.

Rousmaniere, John. *The Annapolis Book of Seamanship.* 3rd rev. ed. New York: Simon & Schuster, 1999.

Sorensen, Eric. *Sorensen's Guide to Powerboats: How to Evaluate Design, Construction, and Performance.* Camden, Maine: International Marine, 2002.

Wing, Charlie. *Boating Magazine's One-Minute Guide to the Nautical Rules of the Road.* Camden, Maine: International Marine, 1998.

Associations

American Boat and Yacht Council (ABYC)
3069 Solomons Island Rd.
Edgewater MD 21037
410-956-1050
Fax: 410-956-2737
E-mail: info@abycinc.org
www.abycinc.org
The E-11 DC and AC electrical standard can be downloaded for $120.

Boat Owners Association of the United States (BoatU.S.)
880 South Pickett St.
Alexandria VA 22304
800-395-2628
Fax: 703-461-4674
www.BoatUS.com

International Association of Marine Investigators (IAMI)
711 Medford Center, #265
Medford OR 97504
866-844-4264
E-mail: iamimarine2@aol.com
www.iamimarine.org

National Association of Marine Surveyors (NAMS)
P.O. Box 9306
Chesapeake VA 23321-9306
800-822-6267
Fax: 757-638-9639
E-mail: nationaloffice@
    nams-cms.org
www.nams-cms.org

National Fire Protection Associations (NFPA)
1 Batterymarch Park
Quincy MA 02169
617-770-3000; 800-344-3555
Fax: 617-770-0700
E-mail: marine@nfpa.org
www.nfpa.org
NFPA-302 includes AC, DC, and fuel system standards. It costs $32.25 plus $7.95 for shipping and handling.

National Oceanic and Atmospheric Administration (NOAA)
14th St. and Constitution Ave., NW, Room 6217
Washington DC 20230
202-482-6090
Fax: 202-482-3154
E-mail: answers@noaa.gov
www.noaa.gov

Society of Accredited Marine Surveyors (SAMS)
4605 Cardinal Blvd.
Jacksonville FL 32210
800-344-9077
Fax: 904-388-3958
E-mail: samshq@aol.com
www.marinesurvey.org

U.S. Coast Guard (USCG)
Commandant (G-NAB)
2100 2nd St., SW
Washington DC 20593
www.uscg.mil
Boating Safety: www.uscgboating.org
Customer Information and Defect Reports: 800-368-5647
Navigation Center:
    www.navcen.uscg.gov;
    uscginfoline@gcrm.com

Acknowledgments

BACK IN 1985, Bill Oakerson and I would routinely drive to the gym during our lunch breaks to swim and work out. He was then in charge of our insurance department (we weren't large enough to call it a "division") and I was a catalog writer. One day after we had just gotten into the car, Bill handed me a copy of the first-ever issue of *Seaworthy*, a newsletter that had just been published by BoatU.S. Marine Insurance. It was a modest effort, only eight pages, but the concept was huge: Use actual insurance claims to help other boaters avoid making the same mistakes.

This sort of approach was typical of Bill: Take a negative (accident/claim) and make it a positive (prevent similar accidents/reduce claims). In the years since, there have been many people who have contributed to the success of *Seaworthy*, but none as much as Bill.

Richard Schwartz, the founder of BoatU.S., played a major part in the conceptualization and development of *Seaworthy*. When I began writing for *Seaworthy* (Vol. 4, No. 1), it was Richard who insisted that for every claim mentioned in *Seaworthy*, there should be a well-researched explanation on how it could have been prevented. There were to be no exceptions; he was adamant that the publication not scare readers and take the fun out of boating.

Someone once said that a writer should only write about what he knows. If I'd listened to that advice, this would be a very short book. My approach to boating has always been to raise the sails, grab the tiller, and hope nothing breaks. Ernie Braatz, the original editor of *Seaworthy*, had a strong technical background that made it a much more interesting publication. Ernie died suddenly in an automobile accident, and left a void at *Seaworthy* that has never been filled.

Since I lacked Ernie's technical expertise, I have had to rely on other people's input whenever I ventured into arcane topics like electrical and fuel systems. First and foremost, I relied on Chuck Fort and Doug Cowie, the current and former associate editors of *Seaworthy*, who have strong technical backgrounds as well as being excellent writers. This is their book too. And since BoatU.S. is only a few miles from the American Boat and Yacht Council offices in Annapolis, Maryland, I have had the considerable benefit of working with ABYC's technical directors, past and present: Tom Hale, Philippe Ras, and John Adey. These three are walking encyclopedias on every detail in the ABYC standards. So too is Dave Gerr, the naval architect and writer who heads ABYC's Westlawn School. In addition to lending his considerable expertise in boat design and construction, Dave contributed to this book by giving me a crash course in dealing with book publishers. With regard to the latter, my sincere thanks to Tony Gibbs for helping me make some tough decisions and for writing the Foreword.

Every claim file comes with the name of a marine surveyor who was the BoatU.S. adjuster's eyes and ears in the field. I've often thought that among all of the marine professions, surveying ranks at the very top for doing the most good for the most people. Surveyor reports have been invaluable in presenting the facts of a claim and suggesting how the accident could have been prevented. Most surveyors I know are genuinely dedicated to making boats and boating safer. To name but a few: Jack Hornor, Jonathan Klopman, Mike McCook, Dave Wiggin, Larry Montgomery, Charlie Corder, Jim Wood, Todd Schwede, Bolling Douglas, Greg Davis, Dan Rutherford, Tom Benton, Kim MacCartney, Brian McCauley, Paul Tobin, Henry Mustin, Dexter Holaday, Ken Weinbrecht, Bill Novak, Pat Kearns, Ronnie Lawson, Neil Haynes, Jim McCrory, Jim Merritt, and the late Fred Struben.

Other marine professionals who have put their stamp on *Seaworthy* include Bob Loeser, the former senior marine engineer at Underwriters Laboratories. Bob cares passionately about making boats safer and has devoted a considerable amount of his time to that end. The same is true of Paul Fleury, an expert on marine electrical systems. Dr. Gordon Smith, of the Johns Hopkins Center for Injury Research and Policy, is an authority on many personal injury topics but none more important than boating and swimming accidents that involve alcohol. He certainly opened my eyes to the magnitude of the problem. Ewen Thomson, formerly with Florida State University, is one of the few people on the planet who devotes all of his working energy to understanding lightning and lightning protection systems. His insights and ideas have been invaluable. For insight into another arcane topic, fiberglass boat construction, I received input from three of the best: Bruce Pfund at *Professional BoatBuilder* magazine, Rick Strand of Matrix Impact Systems, and naval architect Rob Schofield.

Two professors from MIT's Sea Grant program, Norm Doelling and the late Stanley Backer, have done a tremendous amount of research on why rope and moorings fail in hurricanes. No one has done more to mitigate the tremendous damage done by storms than these two. James Bartlett III in Baltimore and Jim Mercante in New York are two highly respected maritime attorneys who have the rare ability to clearly explain complex legal matters in a way that anyone can understand. Good things seem to be coming in pairs: meteorologists Dave Feit, chief of the Marine Forecast Branch at NOAA, and Dr. Bill Sprigg, the principal architect at the National Weather Service Climate Prediction Center, both are weathermen's weathermen, and Dave is also an avid sailor who happens to be insured by BoatU.S.

In addition to being technically correct, the other obstacle that had to be overcome before *Seaworthy* had any chance to be taken seriously was the writing. What good are accounts from claim files if they become hopelessly garbled in the telling? Richard Schwartz spent a great deal of time patiently teaching me the fine points of writing clearly. So too did Dick Ellison and David Breasted. Jon Eaton and Margaret Cook at International Marine edited this book with skill and extraordinary patience. The one who deserves the most credit, however, is Anthony Chapman, my high school English teacher. One day after class he took me aside and said that I should consider writing as a profession. Many years later, when I began to realize I couldn't do much else, I remembered those words and my life hasn't been the same since. Such is the power of a good teacher. Thank you, Mr. Chapman, wherever you are.

Finally, nothing ever gets done without the will to do it. In my case, that has always been supplied by my remarkable family, LaDuska, Oliver, Sarah, and Paul.

Index

Numbers in **bold** refer to pages with illustrations.

About BoatU.S.

THIS BOOK IS BASED ON MATERIAL originally published in *Seaworthy*, a publication that uses actual BoatU.S. marine insurance claims to learn why boating accidents happen and how they could have been avoided.

Marine Insurance, however central to the material in this book, is only one facet of BoatU.S.—the Boat Owners Association of the United States. BoatU.S., with over 600,000 members in 50 states, has represented millions of boatowners nationwide since 1966 and has been a strong voice for recreational boatowners, lobbying against unfair taxes, fees, and discriminatory regulations. People tend to think that ill-conceived legislation, like the wildly unpopular federal "user fee" tax or the luxury tax on boats, magically disappears when individuals complain and legislators come to their senses. That's not how the system works. The user fee tax would have cost boatowners $600 million per year, and it took the lobbyists in our Government Affairs office several years of hard work to get rid of it. More recently, BoatU.S. lobbied successfully to expand the Wallop/Breaux Act, which now returns well over $50 million that was collected in gas taxes from boatowners to the states for boating safety and clean water programs as well as improving boating access and sportfishing.

Aside from lobbying, one of the basic tenets of BoatU.S. has always been to help boatowners save money. Membership includes product, insurance, and marina discounts, on-the-water (TowBoatU.S. and Vessel Assist) and over-the-road towing, boat financing, and a subscription to *BoatU.S. Magazine*, America's most widely read boating publication. Our Consumer Protection Bureau's listing of reported problems with various makes and models of boats was recently made available to members online.

BoatU.S. also established the Foundation for Boating Safety and Clean Water to educate boaters about safe boating practices and help them become better stewards of our waterways. Among its many programs, the Foundation loaned children over 10,000 life vests nationwide and has distributed millions of safety and clean water brochures. The EPIRB Rental Program has saved over a dozen lives. Each year the Foundation provides $80,000 to local groups to work on safety and environmental education for boaters. And the innovative National Clean Fueling Program is linking marinas and boaters with the techniques and products they'll need to prevent accidental spills at the fuel dock.

For more information about BoatU.S, call 800-395-2628 or visit www. BoatUS.com.